Looking at *Medea*

Related titles from Bloomsbury

Looking at Lysistrata, edited by David Stuttard
9781853997365

Euripides: Medea (Companions to Greek and Roman Tragedy),
by William Allan
9780715631874

The Plays of Euripides (Classical World), by James Morwood
9781853996146

Costume in Greek Tragedy, by Rosie Wyles
9780715639450

Euripides Talks, edited by Alan Beale
9781853997129

Looking at *Medea*

Essays and a translation of Euripides' tragedy

Edited by David Stuttard

B L O O M S B U R Y

LONDON · NEW DELHI · NEW YORK · SYDNEY

Bloomsbury Academic

An imprint of Bloomsbury Publishing Plc

50 Bedford Square   1385 Broadway
London   New York
WC1B 3DP   NY 10018
UK   USA

www.bloomsbury.com

First published 2014

British Library Cataloguing-in-Publication Data
A catalogue record for this book is available from the British Library.

ISBN: PB: 978-1-47253-051-6
HB: 978-1-47252-772-1
ePub: 978-1-47253-016-5
ePDF: 978-1-47253-399-9

Library of Congress Cataloging-in-Publication Data
Looking at *Medea*: essays and a translation of Euripides' tragedy
edited by David Stuttard.
pages cm
Includes bibliographical references and index.
ISBN 978-1-4725-3051-6 (pbk) — ISBN 978-1-4725-2772-1 (hbk)
1. Euripides. Medea.   I. Stuttard, David.   II. Euripides. Medea. English. 2014.
PA3978.L65 2014
882'.01—dc23
2013046260

Typeset by RefineCatch, Bungay, Suffolk
Printed and bound in Great Britain

To Theo

Contents

List of Illustrations

Acknowledgements

I first translated and directed *Medea* in 1996 for a touring production by Actors of Dionysus (**aod**), which included a residency at London's Turtle Key Arts Centre. Many performances were introduced by talks given by eminent UK academics, a combination of scholarship and drama which was, in some respects, the inspiration for the present volume. My translation was thereafter recorded by **aod** for Penguin Audiobooks, and my subsequent adaptation has since been staged several times. I am grateful to the many actors involved in these productions for enhancing my understanding of the play.

At the heart of this volume are the essays, and my profound thanks go to all the contributors, who have given so generously of their time and expertise. I for one have greatly enjoyed reading and working through this collection, and have learned a great deal from it. Special thanks go to Charlotte Loveridge at Bloomsbury Press, who has been an enthusiastic champion of the project from the start, to the excellent copy editor, Jon Ingoldby, and to Ian Buck and Claire Turner, for designing the book and its cover. My greatest thanks go to my wife, Emily Jane, whose support is fundamental to everything I do, and without whom (like Jason on his *Argo*) I would truly be at sea.

List of Contributors

David Stuttard is a freelance writer, classical historian and dramatist who founded the theatre company, Actors of Dionysus

Jasper Griffin was Fellow of Balliol College, Oxford, Public Orator and Professor of Classical Literature at the University of Oxford until 2004

Carmel McCallum-Barry is Lecturer in Classics at University College, Cork

Ioanna Karamanou is Assistant Professor in Greek Drama at the University of the Peloponnese

Rosie Wyles is Lecturer in Greek Language and Literature at King's College, London

Ian Ruffell is Lecturer in Classics at the University of Glasgow

James Morwood is Emeritus Fellow of Wadham College, Oxford

Richard Rutherford is Tutor in Greek and Latin Literature at Christ Church, Oxford

Sophie Mills is Professor of Classics at the University of North Carolina at Asheville

Hanna M. Roisman is Professor of Classics, Arnold Bernhard Professor in Arts and Humanities at Colby College, Maine

Douglas Cairns is Professor of Classics at the University of Edinburgh

Edith Hall is Professor of Classics at King's College, London

Betine Van Zyl Smit is Associate Professor of Classics at the University of Nottingham

Foreword

Medea is one of the most frequently performed of all Greek tragedies. With its universal themes of love, betrayal and revenge, it resonates with modern audiences. However, although the 'script' has remained (for the most part) unaltered since Euripides wrote it two and a half millennia ago, the experience and expectations of audiences have changed significantly. Today's religious beliefs, political structures and social norms are very different from those of polytheistic, imperial, slave-owning, patriarchal fifth-century BC Athens. So, while the human emotions at the heart of the play may be immediately recognizable, their context cannot but be alien, and, as a result, Euripides' audience is likely to have experienced *Medea* very differently to a modern one. Certainly, Euripides cannot have imagined that *Medea* would have proved an inspiration to the early twentieth century suffragette movement, and it is debatable to what extent he conceived the play as the psychodrama as it is so often presented today.

To set *Medea* firmly in its fifth-century BC context and to trace something of its later history, this volume presents twelve new essays by some of the leading authorities on this play in particular and Greek tragedy in general, along with my introduction and a slightly revised version of my 1996 translation. The subject matter of the essays covers a wide range of issues from earlier versions of the Medea myth and the play's original performance context to twentieth-century interpretations. As was the case in *Looking at Lysistrata*, authors were given great freedom to choose which aspect of the play to write about, and each was relatively unaware of what the others intended to say. For this reason, there is occasionally a small degree of overlap between some of the essays, with which (to preserve the integrity of each piece) I have deliberately not interfered. Similarly, certain authors disagree with each other (and with me) about the extent to which Euripides used *Medea* as a vehicle for his own political comment. Again, I have deliberately not tried to impose a three line whip, believing that both this diversity of views and the occasional commonality of subject matter lend a special dynamic to the collection, underlining the fact that *Medea* remains as vibrant and controversial a play today as it was when it was first performed.

Revisiting the translation has been interesting. Since 1996, when I originally wrote it for a production (and subsequent Penguin Audiobook recording) by Actors of Dionysus (The *Independent* kindly declared that it 'gives Euripides' wisdom a classic turn of phrase'), my style has changed considerably. However, publication of this translation still (I hope) has something to recommend it, not least because it benefited greatly from having been closely read and rigorously commented upon by the late Sir Kenneth Dover. So, aside from a very few revisions, I have kept that original translation essentially as it was. This also means that anyone wishing to hear the words performed can listen to the Penguin Audiobook, a CD of which is now available directly from www.actorsofdionysus.com. Readers wishing to compare my 2001 adaptation of *Medea* can order it from www.davidstuttard. com, where applications for performance of both translation and adaptation should be made before the commencement of any rehearsals.

David Stuttard
Brighton, 2013

Introduction – *Medea* in Context

David Stuttard

'In peace time sons bury their fathers, but in war fathers bury their sons.' If the historian Herodotus was in Athens' Theatre of Dionysus on that brisk March morning in 431 BC, he may well have thought of these, his own words, as he watched *Medea* unfold to its bitter end, where Jason cannot even touch his dead sons, let alone bury them.

For, that spring, war was in the air – indeed, tradition suggests that it was to chronicle the coming conflict that Herodotus returned to Athens at around this time – and, although the democracy's 'first citizen', Pericles, was promising a relatively easy victory, many knew that, once conflict is unleashed (in the words of the late American political scientist, George Kennan), 'war has a momentum of its own and it carries you away from all thoughtful intentions when you get into it'. To judge by his later works, Euripides was probably cautious of Athens' escalating conflict with Corinth and her Peloponnesian allies, and it may be that he was hinting at these cautions in *Medea*.

So, to set *Medea* in its historical context and to provide something of a general background to the play and to this book, we should begin by outlining a little of the history of the times and (first) of some of what *Medea*'s original audience might have come to the theatre expecting to see.

Greek Drama – a brief history and some technicalities

Tragedy was only one of a number of performing art forms current in classical Athens. Music, song and literature pervaded private homes as well as village and state festivals, where audiences could hear soloists and small ensembles sing to the accompaniment of oboes (*auloi*) or lyres. In the Theatre of Dionysus itself, its wooden benches set on the southern slope of the Acropolis above the flat *orkhēstra* ('dancing ground'), where the chorus sang and danced in front of the *skēnē* (stage building), they could enjoy not only dramas but also performances of choral *dithyrambs* (hymns to Dionysus). Indeed, it was from these that tragedy was said to have been born, when at a village festival at Icaria one performer, Thespis, assumed the role of one of the songs' characters and interacted with the chorus to become the first recorded actor. Drama had been born, but it took until just before the middle of the fifth century BC for it to settle into the form we see in Euripides' *Medea*.

Performed by three actors and a chorus of fifteen (all masked, all male), plays were written entirely in verse: iambic trimeters for much of the dialogue and soliloquies, with other verse forms used for choral songs, or for passages of heightened emotion, sung by actors. All (surviving) tragedies began with a prologue given by one or two actors. The chorus then entered (*parodos*), usually to remain in view in the *orkhēstra* until they exited at the very end, generally to the accompaniment of a brief song.

The rest of the play consisted of scenes of monologue or dialogue between actors and chorus (*episodes*), linked by *stasima* (singular = *stasimon*), bridging passages of choral singing and dancing. These *stasima* were often used to add new layers of meaning, to provide moments of reflection, or to widen the focus out from the specific story being explored in the play, sometimes through references to parallel myths. The accompanying music (now sadly lost), as well as the chorus' physicality, would have added considerably to their emotional impact.

Most plays included at least one debate (*agon*) between two characters, in the form of a relatively lengthy speech from each (with concluding two-line comments from the chorus) followed by punchy dialogue, in which characters conversed in (often) one-line sentences (*stichomythia*). All extant plays also include a messenger speech, a relatively lengthy account of a usually violent incident, which has happened offstage, and which typically begins in the calm world of the everyday before reaching a crescendo of horror, and ending with a sometimes generalized aphorism.

So popular was the new genre of drama that, in 534 BC, just over a century before *Medea* was first performed, an annual state dramatic festival, the City Dionysia, was introduced into the Athenian calendar. Held in the month of Elaphebolion (mid-March to mid-April), this part-religious, part-artistic festival was attended not only by Athenians but by foreigners, too, and soon became a showcase for not just Athens' creative prowess but her political might as well. Spanning five days, by 431 BC the City Dionysia began with sacrifices, parades and propaganda – an elaborate procession to the theatre, a display of military hardware and of tribute from Athens' subject states, donations of armour to war orphans, and the slaughter of bulls – all before a contest between choruses performing *dithyrambs*.

Competition was at the heart of the City Dionysia: not just Athens' competitiveness to be recognized as the leading *polis* (or city state) in the Greek world, but a contest between performers striving to be judged the best in their class. Thus, while the final day of performances was (probably) devoted to a competition between the writers and producers of five comic plays, the other three days were given over to a contest between three tragedians.

Each day one author presented a *tetralogy*, three tragedies followed by a *satyr* play, a light-hearted romp based loosely on an episode from mythology, in which the chorus were costumed as Dionysus' anarchic snub-nosed, horse-tailed, rampant followers, the satyrs. The *satyr* play was in part an emotional safety-valve, designed to dissipate the undoubted pressures built up during the highly-charged *trilogy* of tragedies which preceded it and allow the audience some respite before leaving the theatre.

Earlier in the fifth century BC, some tragic *trilogies* (exemplified by Aeschylus' extant *Oresteia*) had explored different episodes from the same myth over several generations, but by 431 BC tastes had changed. Now the three tragedies (and probably the *satyr* play) were linked not narratively but thematically. Thus (as Ioanna Karamanou explores), *Medea* was linked to its 'sister' tragedies, *Philoctetes* and *Dictys*, and perhaps to the *satyr* play, *Reapers*, by themes of otherness and exile. Although these 'sister' plays survive only in fragments, it is important to recognize that, as it was in conjunction with them that Euripides intended his audience to enjoy and judge *Medea*, understanding them more fully can afford us greater insights into his original intentions. It should remind us, too, that, although Euripides' *tetralogy* of 431 BC did badly (it came last in the competition), the judgement was not based on *Medea* alone, and, lacking, as we are, not only *Medea*'s 'sister' plays but the two competing *tetralogies*, we are in no position to criticize the judges' decision.

In fact, the artistic merits of a script (the only element, which now survives) were only one of the criteria by which a production was judged – and probably a minor one at that. Of more immediate and popular impact were elements like choreography and music, actors' performances, costumes and stage effects (discussed by Rosie Wyles). Even a dislike of something as superficial as Philoctetes' ragged costume may have been enough to consign the *tetralogy* to third place.

Incidentally, we know that, even if Euripides very rarely came first at Athens' City Dionysia, many other Greeks *did* appreciate his dramas; in 413 BC, eighteen years after *Medea*, enemy Syracusans (presumably barred from recent City Dionysias and craving their 'fix' of Euripides) freed Athenian prisoners of war, who could sing his latest choruses, while when, in 404 BC, at the end of the Peloponnesian War, Athens was defeated, the recollection of a

Euripidean threnody (from *Electra*) is said to have spared the city from destruction and her people from slavery and death.

Foreigners may have appreciated Euripides more than his fellow citizens, but who *was Medea*'s first audience? In recent years, evidence has begun to emerge, suggesting that in 431 BC the Theatre of Dionysus was smaller than previously supposed, being able to hold not 15,000 spectators, as was once believed, but perhaps under half that number – roughly the same as that of the citizens who could be accommodated in the (exclusively male) democratic Assembly on Pnyx Hill. However, 7,500 is still a sizeable audience, around a quarter of Athens' citizenry (although some seats were reserved for foreign visitors), and the correspondence between Assembly and theatre has often been noted. Indeed (as personal experience reveals), because of the architecture and acoustics of Greek theatres, performers must direct their lines not to each other but 'up and out' towards the audience in the manner of an orator addressing a crowd. Even 'internal' monologues, such as Medea's soliloquy (1019–1080), in which she debates killing her children, must be delivered with no little volume to the audience, almost as if seeking their advice or approval – something which increases spectators' involvement in her decision-making. So, if the Church of England was once described as 'the establishment at prayer', the City Dionysia may in many ways be thought of as the Athenian Assembly at play.

This is one of several reasons why I personally believe that the audience at the City Dionysia was exclusively male. Another has to do with Athenians' shamefully misogynistic view of women, especially clever women. Literary sources for fifth-century BC Athens come exclusively from men and cannot conceal the vitriol (worthy of the worst modern tabloid journalism) with which the average Athenian male viewed talented, well-educated women. They smeared one, Elpinice, with rumours that she not only posed for a publically-exhibited painting (which was beyond the pale for a decent matron) but regularly committed incest with her brother, while they accused another, Aspasia (wife of Pericles), of prostituting free-born women. A decent woman's place was in the home. Her role was childbearing and housekeeping, not cleverness, and I find it unlikely that most Athenian males would have countenanced exposing their womenfolk to the kind of political and moral debate which raged in the Theatre of Dionysus, not to mention potentially destructive role models such as the much-too-clever Medea.

The presence of (albeit Greek-speaking) foreigners in the staunchly patriotic Athenian audience had certain implications. It encouraged high production values, as playwrights and producers vied ever more spectacularly to utilize the latest technology – such as the *mechanē*, or crane, which allowed actors and props to 'fly', or the *ekkuklema* (the 'rolling-out machine'), on which tableaux showing horrors committed 'inside' could be shown – or to dress their characters in sumptuous costumes (another reason why Philoctetes' rags may have provoked a hostile reaction among judges). However, the presence of foreigners had another, less positive effect. It tended to prevent playwrights from openly expressing views which could be construed as hostile to the Athenian political consensus. Just four years after *Medea*, the young Aristophanes was prosecuted for slandering Athens at the Great Dionysia in his comedy, *Babylonians*.

Indeed, Athenian audiences were notoriously volatile. At the beginning of the fifth century BC, they had imposed a heavy fine on the playwright, Phrynichus, for upsetting them with his tragedy, *The Capture of Miletus*. Later, they are said to have rioted when, thinking that some lines of Aeschylus revealed details of the sacred (and taboo) Eleusinian Mysteries, they invaded the stage – only by clinging to the altar of Dionysus did Aeschylus escape death. On another occasion, feelings between one faction, which supported Aeschylus, and another, which supported Sophocles, ran so high that, instead of the usual civilian judges, Athens' ten generals were co-opted onto the panel. However, this did not stop playwrights (comedians especially, but also – *pace* Jasper Griffin – tragedians) from imbuing their work with (albeit veiled) references to, and comments on, current affairs. So, it is to the politics of 431 BC that we must next turn.

Athens in 431 BC

In 431 BC, Athens was at her height. For more than a hundred years (since the time of Peisistratus, who had inaugurated the City Dionysia), despite some severe setbacks, Athens had enjoyed a seemingly unstoppable growth in power and influence. At the end of the sixth century BC, her citizens had embraced *isonomia* (equality under law), a prototype democracy, and, at the beginning of the fifth, they had recovered with remarkable resilience from temporary defeat at the hands of Persian invaders, quickly establishing their dominion over the *poleis* (city states) of the Aegean islands and the western coast of modern Turkey. In the late 460s BC, Pericles, a dangerously charismatic aristocrat, who knew how to bend the people's will to suit his own, began to imbue the Athenians with his own brand of nationalism, plunging them into occasionally disastrous but ultimately survivable wars (a campaign against the Persians in Egypt in the 450s BC was particularly catastrophic), while enhancing their city and the surrounding countryside with an ambitious building programme, at whose heart was the Parthenon.

By the time that temple was dedicated (in 438 BC) and its sculptures complete (a year before *Medea*, in 432 BC), Athens' economic dominance could be felt from Sicily in the west to the Black Sea in the east. A list of imports by the contemporary comedian, Hermippus, includes carpets from Carthage, ivory from Libya, salt fish from the Bosphorus and almonds from Paphlagonia on the Black Sea's southern shores. But not everyone was happy. Athens' economic rival, Corinth, just over forty miles away to the west, found the situation particularly irksome, especially when Athens (bent, thanks in part to Pericles' propaganda, on being recognized as the leading *polis* in the Greek world) became increasingly determined to impose her military dominance as well.

In 433 BC, the two cities clashed over Corinth's colony, Corcyra, on the island known today as Corfu, where a failure of delicate politicking led to Athens' victory in the sea-battle of Sybota. The next year, Athens and Corinth were fighting once again, this time in northern Greece over control of Potidea, a city whose status was ambiguous, being both a colony of Corinth and a tribute-paying member of Athens' imperial league. Meanwhile, to punish her for choosing the wrong side at Sybota, Athens imposed a trade embargo on Megara, a city halfway between her and Corinth, forbidding Megarian merchants access to any ports under Athenian control. In support of Megara, Corinth set about enlisting the help of fellow members of the Peloponnesian League and especially the militarily powerful Sparta. In 431 BC, as Athenians took their seats in the Theatre of Dionysus to watch Euripides' *tetralogy*, of which *Medea* was the first play, the international stage seemed set for a major war.

Indeed, as Thucydides (writing in the third person) explains at the beginning of his history:

> he believed that it would be a great war, more deserving of record than any which had gone before. There was good reason for his belief. Both sides were in a state of perfect readiness and he could see that all Greeks everywhere were taking sides ...

The air was thick with expectation.

Medea, a tragedy for its time

Only ten lines into *Medea*, Euripides reveals the scene of his tragedy: 'this land of Corinth'. In many respects, the drama is set firmly in the heroic world of Jason and his Argonauts – a world, moreover, ruled by kings (whereas fifth-century Corinth and Athens were respectively an oligarchy and democracy). But many of the audience must have been familiar with contemporary

Corinth, having visited the city either on business or while attending the nearby Isthmian Games or, like the orator Lysias a generation later, to enjoy the delights of its internationally renowned brothels. So, the almost throwaway yet homely detail, which Euripides gives to the tutor ('I was going to play back-gammon where the old men sit around the sacred waters of Peirene'), cannot but have conjured up personal memories. For modern visitors, the Fountain of Peirene is still an unforgettable site. Thus, as was usual in Greek tragedies, Euripides allows the mythical world to elide with the contemporary in such a way as to blur the boundaries between Corinth 'then' and Corinth 'now'. And Corinth 'now' was the enemy.

Whether the audience did gloat at Euripides' depiction of the murder of Corinth's leading family members we cannot tell. Possibly not. But the link between Medea and Athens, which Euripides takes care to emphasize, must surely have caused many in the theatre to stop and think. In a pivotal scene positioned exactly halfway through the play (there is nothing haphazard about Euripides' craftsmanship), Aegeus, king of Athens, ignorant of the horrors which Medea is about to unleash, is duped into offering her asylum. Despite what Aristotle may have thought, the episode is dramatically brilliant. Having arrived at Corinth with an innocent agenda – to ask Medea to interpret an oracle about his fathering children – Aegeus has become embroiled in something altogether more nasty, exposing Athens to the corrupting influence of an infanticide. The choral *stasimon*, which comes a little after Aegeus' departure, is surely crucial in giving us at least a flavour of the audience's expected response. Beginning with an achingly beautiful evocation of Athens and Attica, the Chorus imagine the impact of Medea's arrival:

Since time began, the citizens of Athens have been rich indeed, the children of the blessed gods, dwellers in a holy land that's whole and pure. And so they grew strong in the shining light of wisdom, stepping lightly in the clear pellucid air, where once they say that golden-headed Harmony gave birth to the nine sacred Muses – and the clear-flowing waters of Cephisus nurtures them.

And so they say that Aphrodite, goddess of Desire, drinks deep of the Cephisus, sailing in her barge to Athens, fanned by breezes scented in the honeyed air, and on her hair her retinue of Lusts, which bring sweet knowledge in their train, sweet loveliness, scatter flowers, seductive in the soothing scent of garlands twined with blushing damask rose.

And so I ask, how will the city welcome you, Medea? How will Cephisus with his sacred streams, how will the very soil of Athens learn to love

you, stained by the blood-guilt of your sacrilege, your own sons'
murderess.

All has been made more chilling by the oath which Medea forces a reluctant
Aegeus to swear (and after which she bundles him off without another
word), especially as the audience (familiar with myths, which described the
aftermath, and which are outlined in Richard Rutherford's essay) would
know what happened, once she reached Athens. For, in mythology, Medea
sets up house with Aegeus (the scene between them in this play may already
contain a *frisson* of eroticism), has sons by him, and then tries to murder
Aegeus' elder son, Theseus (whom he fathers in Trozden shortly after leaving
Medea in Corinth). As a result, Aegeus exiles Medea from Athens – according
to Herodotus, she flees east, giving her name to the Medes, synonymous in
Athenian thought with Greece's foes, the Persians – and so he breaks his oath,
which adds significance to the interchange between the two:

> **Medea**   But if you don't abide by what you've sworn, what would you
> suffer then?
>
> **Aegeus**   The punishment that waits for all who break the bonds of piety.

By breaking his oath, Aegeus will provoke the Erinyes, or Furies, against
Athens – and, lest we, the audience, somehow forget Medea's destination at
the end of the play, Euripides has her remind us. Snarling from her flying
snake-drawn chariot, the matricide gloats to Jason, 'I shall go to Aegeus in
Athens, and there shall live with him'. There can be no escaping her.

So, tricked, Aegeus, the representative of Athens, invites the plague, that is
Medea, to come from Corinth to take up residence in Athens. What seemed
straightforward at the time (poor Medea, so badly treated by her husband,
surely deserves compassion) will turn out to have quite ghastly, unforeseen
consequences. Is it too far-fetched to see Medea as an allegory for war? To
repeat George Kennan's words, 'war has a momentum of its own and it carries
you away from all thoughtful intentions when you get into it'. I suspect that
there were at least some in Euripides' first audience who saw this warning in
the play. Sadly, the reality of what happened next was even more hideous than
anyone could possibly have foreseen.

The historical aftermath of *Medea*

In spring 431 BC, a matter of weeks after the City Dionysia, the first fighting
in what would become known as the Peloponnesian War came, when Thebes

Figure 1   Medea in her chariot drawn by serpents, depicted on a Calyx-Krater attributed to Near the Policoro Painter c. 400 BC (© ArtPix/Alamy)

(not strictly a Peloponnesian *polis* but an old enemy of Athens) attacked the little town of Plataea, Athens' only ally at the Battle of Marathon fifty-nine years earlier. Soon most of mainland Greece was under arms. In time, the conflict would spread not only east throughout the Aegean to Ionia, the Bosphorus and Byzantium, but west to South Italy and Sicily, too. War's momentum would, indeed, carry its architects away from all thoughtful intentions.

   Nonetheless, in 430 BC at the end of the first year of the war, Pericles (whose war, in the main, it was) was chosen to make a speech in honour of Athens' fallen. After elaborating at length on his city's greatness and the heroism of its men, Pericles addressed the women, advising that for them (in Thucydides' account): 'glory lies in not showing greater weakness than is natural for the female sex, and not being spoken of by men, either for good or evil'.

Since Pericles himself had recently been attacked in the lawcourts through his association with the clever Aspasia, this may have been heartfelt advice, but, in its reinforcement of prejudices about the lower status of women compared to men, it reflects, too, the boast of the philosopher Thales (ascribed by some to Socrates), that he gave thanks to Good Fortune, 'first, that I was born a human being and not an animal; second, that I was born a man and not a woman; and third, that I was born a Greek and not a barbarian'. (No wonder that the barbarian Medea says with only a little exaggeration, 'of everything that lives, all creatures sentient, we women are most abject of them all'.)

But Pericles' policies had unforeseen consequences. To avoid fighting the Peloponnesians on land, where the Athenians were weaker, Pericles had ordered all the inhabitants of Attica (the land of which Athens was the chief city) to leave their homes and villages and take refuge within the city walls. The city, Pericles assured them, could easily survive on imports from abroad, shipped in to their port at Piraeus. As a result, Athens' population was swollen to bursting point. Conditions were bad enough, but in 430 BC, months after Pericles had delivered his Funeral Oration, ships arrived, carrying in their holds an unwelcome cargo: plague. Rapidly it spread through the crowded city, and by the time it had eventually abated some four years later, it had claimed the lives of a third of Athens' population. Among its victims was Pericles.

'Life', as Oscar Wilde observed, 'imitates art far more than art imitates life'. Euripides could not have foreseen the extent to which his grim warning would come true. Yet, for us, who have the benefit of hindsight (albeit coupled with the disadvantage of having lost the other plays from the original *tetralogy* and thus being unable fully to appreciate its context), *Medea* can seem almost prophetic: just as welcoming the infanticide from Corinth would threaten to destroy Aegeus' household and risk the life of his son, Theseus, so embracing war with Corinth and her allies would lead to plague, the loss of countless Athenian lives and, in the end, the defeat of Athens herself. Pericles (who was undoubtedly present at the City Dionysia of 431 BC) would not be the only father in Euripides' audience, who would soon be burying his sons.

As for Medea, the princess, whose story predates Homer, she continued to inspire both fascination and fear, the leading character in further plays and epic poems, the heroine of operas and films, but always remembered above all as the protagonist of Euripides' great tragedy, the subject of the chapters which follow in this book.

1

Murder in the Family – Medea and Others

Jasper Griffin

Medea and the world of myth

The myths and legends of the Greeks, like those of most peoples, reach us only in the form which they were given, and which was enduringly preserved, by men. There were also, hardly less importantly, stories that were told and retold by women. They certainly existed, and they were repeated by mothers, both to their sons and also, and (no doubt) especially, to their daughters. Those stories have very rarely come down to us in anything like an original form or colouring. They are now merely a part of that huge and haunting subject: the lost literature, or the lost literatures, of Hellas. Of the very large mass of literature in Greek that once existed, we must always remember that we possess, and that we can read, only a small fraction.

Very often, no doubt, such mythical stories were never written down at all. When they were, their female versions were drowned out for posterity by the usually narrated forms, and by the generally accepted versions. That, consequently, dictated the shape in which they came to be embodied, sooner or later, in the standard works of high and serious literature; and that was how they made a crucial step: on to the syllabus of works that were read in schools.

The beginnings of the Medea story seem, in outline, to be very simple. A dashing young prince, oppressed by his wicked uncle – and uncles in stories all over Europe are all too often wicked – was sent off on a deadly mission: he must sail to the very edge of the world, passing various terrific perils, there to find, and to bring home, a marvellous Golden Fleece. The possession of a fearsome tyrant, it was guarded – to make the situation apparently quite hopeless – by a dragon which never slept. From such an adventure, clearly, the young man was not expected to return.

But the fearsome Eastern tyrant has a daughter, and she will be his fatal weakness. There is a secret that every tyrant should know: however powerful you may be, and however formidable to your subjects, you cannot really control, and you cannot completely trust, your own womenfolk. Women are, by nature, emotional and volatile creatures. Careful and inscrutable in handling, in expressing, and (still more) in concealing, their thoughts and their feelings, they do not show their emotions in the naive and unguarded way that is so touchingly, so pathetically, common with men. They do not speak their minds, which are more complex, more emotional, and much more unpredictable, than the minds of those simpler creatures: the male persons who, whether they like it or not, have no choice but to trust and to depend on them. The typical tyrannical father only finds out about his daughter's passions when it is already too late. Ariadne's father, King Minos, was one such father; Scylla's father, King Nisus, was a second; Medea's father, King Aeëtes, was just one more.

Yes, it is only too true: females are emotional, and they are also secretive! That, of course, is a very dangerous combination. Women store mysterious things in their cupboards, and in their chests, and in their trunks: things, which may include not only the medicines and cosmetics, that rightly and properly belong there, but also both love-charms and poisons – two categories, indeed, which are very closely related, and which alarmingly overlap. (In Sophocles' *Women of Trachis*, Heracles himself falls victim to that grey area.) Above all, as the stories tell us over and over again: a young woman may suddenly fall in love with the wrong man, and her passions may mislead her, inducing her to oppose, and to frustrate, the well-laid plans of her papa, who is tyrannical and oppressive, certainly, but who is also - and fatally – masculine, short-sighted, credulous, and obtuse.

In the stories, that opposition to the father is, on the whole, a good thing, and all turns out, in the end, for the best. It is the hero – young, glamorous, and adventurous – who is the natural focus of our attention and our sympathy. Nobody wants to identify with the grumpy elders: with the tyrannical old fathers and the wicked uncles, who exist, as they do in the fairy stories, only to be defied, and frustrated, and (in the end) defeated; but there is, inevitably, a dangerous ambiguity about such tales. When we are not under the spell of the storyteller, we observe, with a colder and more analytic eye, that such passionate unions rarely turn out well in the end.

Why, the girl has, after all, deceived her father, and betrayed him, and injured him: she is capable, then, both of inscrutable emotions and, in action, of dangerous and unpredictable secretiveness and deceit. What else may she not be capable of, before her ambiguous career is over? What deeds, and what deceptions, may her powerful, unpredictable, and inscrutable emotions not lead her to commit, or to condone? As Desdemona's father says to the all too credulous Othello:

> Look to her, Moor, if thou hast eyes to see:
> She hath deceived her father, and may thee.

> Shakespeare, *Othello*, I ii 292–3

In that particular case, of course, such suspicions were notably unjust; but we see that they were not unnatural. We cannot doubt that many wiseacres in Shakespeare's audience, at that point in the play, nodded their heads in sympathy and in general approval.

What is the original colouring of the Jason-and-Medea story as a whole? Clearly, it is romantic, and also upbeat. The two nasty old men, Jason's wicked uncle and Medea's tyrannical father, are both defeated – as we, in the audience, naturally want them to be. They are frustrated, and they fail, quite properly; while the glamorous young lovers sail away in triumph, carrying with them the marvellous Golden Fleece, into a life of love and happiness. We see the story ending, naturally, with a romantic fade-out, as the victorious young couple advance, hand in hand, into that golden future. 'And they lived happily ever after': such is the natural and satisfying conclusion that such a tale seems to demand, and that such a romantic pair of lovers certainly seem to deserve. It is, indeed, much the way in which the *Argonautica*, the third-century epic on their adventure, does fade out.

But someone, sooner or later, insists on pressing the story and its characters a little further. Jason, the dashing prince, who carried off the wonderful Golden Fleece and the beautiful princess, and who brought them home in triumph from the distant edge of the world: is he, really, quite satisfactory as a hero? After all, when you come to reflect on the story, it was Medea who made it all possible for Jason. It was she who put to sleep the fearsome and ever watchful dragon which guarded the Fleece; and it was she again, by her uncanny medications and her powerful interventions, who enabled Jason to yoke the fire-breathing bulls, to plough the fatal field, and to cope with the armed men who arose from the sowing of the dragon's teeth. It was even she who threw the pursuing Aeëtes off the track of the fleeing lovers by chopping up, and sprinkling in their wake, the body of her young brother, Apsyrtus. In fact, it was she, really, who did all the crucial things!

So – what kind of hero, after all, can this Jason have been? A little further reflection, a little more meditation, and we come up, very soon, with a rather unflattering result. He was very good looking; that is clear – why, Medea fell passionately in love with him at very first sight; fell so deeply in love, that she betrayed her father for the 'extravagant and wheeling stranger' (*Othello* again), and so made his heroic exploits quite easy! He was, in all probability, just the sort of young man who is handsome and charming, and who is perfectly conscious of his own good looks and powerful charm; who is well aware of his own success with women (those dear trusting creatures!), and who thinks he will always get away with it, whatever it may be, because he always has got away with it, and because he is – after all – so handsome and so charming. His career – when you came to think of it – had not really shown much heroism at all! The original tale had presented the journey of the good ship *Argo* as the first of all sea voyages, and her entry into the Euxine, the dreaded northern sea, with its euphemistic and all too hopeful name ('friendly to travellers' is its actual meaning), as an action of epoch-making daring and resolution. Euripides turns the focus right away from all of that; and the daring journey, with all its perilous adventures en route, is now kept far from our minds.

Medea has betrayed her father and stolen his cherished treasure; she has killed her brother Apsyrtus; and she has run away to a foreign land with a handsome foreigner, her father's hated enemy. She did it for love: yes, all for love! What sort of person, then, must *she* be? Obviously, she is – clearly, she must be – a passionate and headstrong woman, who follows her passions, wherever they lead; and who, unreflectively and rather naturally, imagines that other people are, essentially, just like herself. Yes, no doubt they are passionate and headstrong, too! Jason, of course, is a hero, and he, especially, must be just like that! Yes, of course: he must be just like her!

On that point, unfortunately, she is badly wrong. Jason, we soon see, is very different from Medea: very different indeed. Through the lines of his self-defence (522–75), his history clearly emerges. Cool and calculating, he accepted her advances, when he was in distant Colchis, far from home, because he found himself in a very tight corner. At that moment, he desperately needed her help. Now, though, he doesn't need it any longer. Now, in fact, she has become a nuisance: yes, now she is a positive burden. But for her tiresomely persistent presence, he would be free to marry the Corinthian princess, who has been so conveniently offered to him by her father, and then he would be at perfect liberty to settle down in Corinth: no longer a glamorous but slightly disreputable middle-aged adventurer, married to an exotic and formidable wife, with kindred blood on her hands, who can never revisit her fatherland. On the contrary, he would be quite safely, quite comfortably, and very advantageously placed: in a middle age of well earned dignity, respect, ease, opulence, and comfort. There would be no more hardships; no more knocking about the world. And his children – *their* children – would be much better placed. The Athenian audience of the play, sitting in the theatre of Athens, will have taken for granted the current Athenian law, which restricted full citizenship to the offspring of two full citizens. Under such a law, the children of Jason and Medea – offspring of a foreign mother – would not be eligible to be full citizens. They must remain for ever dubiously legitimate and not fully accepted.

So: why can't Medea understand? It's all so straightforward; it's all so childishly simple! Why must she persist in being so absurdly and tiresomely unreasonable? There will be some provision, there will be a nice comfortable granny flat, for her; while as for him, he will be absolutely in clover, for the rest of his life! Her whole career has shown that Medea simply is not, and never was, that sort of character; but Jason has never understood anything at all about Medea. He cannot imagine that she is not, really, someone exactly like himself. Given a little time, and some careful explanation, she will, surely, see and accept the obvious advantages of this new marriage of Jason's. That estimate is, of course, just as wrong as her estimate of him. It is, in fact, *his* disastrous mistake.

The story of Jason and Medea is set in a distant and exotic past, of dragons and the marvellous Golden Fleece; but Euripides has chosen to play down the supernatural elements in the story, and to present his Jason and Medea as two perfectly intelligible human characters, whose marital squabbles, and wrongdoings, and grievances, and mutual reproaches, are rather uncomfortably lifelike: are all too close, in fact, to our own. We are confirmed in this view by remembering Aristophanes. He bitterly complains, in *Frogs* in particular, that the characters who appear in Euripides' tragedies are just too ordinary; that they are too like us, and that they are altogether too deficient in the good old tragic distance, and remoteness, and glamour. Aristophanes could have pointed to Euripides' Jason as a perfect example of his point.

It is quite important, I think, to realize that Jason is perfectly sincere in what he says, and in what he offers Medea in their first confrontation (lines 446–626). In her place, we can assume, he would be perfectly content – would, indeed, be only too happy – to accept such an offer. After all, one wife, and one princess – either Medea or this Corinthian young lady – is, if we are honest about it, very much like another; while comfort and security are very, very different from insecurity and dependence. Jason tries, quite conscientiously, to explain all of that to Medea. Surely she must see it! But no: she insists on refusing to understand what is, to Jason, perfectly obvious and, really, quite self-explanatory. After all, sex can't matter that much – not to a woman, or to the sort of woman he thinks he knows.

Of course, we can see that Jason is not, in truth, being nearly as sensible as he thinks. Under the pressure of urgent and perilous events, he has incurred great obligations to a woman of a nature radically different from his own. He has, indeed, fatally entangled himself with her. He has failed to understand his own position or his own story. To put it in another way: what was originally, perhaps, a *Märchen*, a fairy story – 'so the beautiful princess saved the dashing prince from his imminent peril, and they defeated her wicked father, and they sailed away together, to live happily ever after' – is developed and transformed, into a darker, grittier, more realistic tale: into a story, in fact, of actions eminently unromantic and unheroic: of ageing and bitterness, of ingratitude, of cold-heartedness, and of disastrous misunderstandings.

Medea *paidoktonos* (child-killer)

So: are we saying that the audience are wholly on Medea's side: that they
endorse her actions, in this dark situation, faced with such monstrous
ingratitude and with such coldness of heart? The answer to that question
must be an emphatic 'No'. The killing by a mother of her own children is a
monstrous action, and the Athenians felt that no less strongly than we do.
Consider here the reactions of the chorus – women, like Medea, and on her
side from the start. In her first bitter altercation with Jason, the chorus makes
it clear where its sympathies lie: What you say may sound convincing, they
tell him; but in my opinion, you are betraying your wife (lines 576–7). But
when she announces her change of plan – I won't kill him: I'll make him
suffer, forever, by killing *my children* – the chorus is unequivocal: I oppose
this plan! (line 813). The playwright, in fact, has arranged his action in such a
way that we are suddenly brought up short: that we, like the chorus, are
suddenly forced to stop, to change gear, and to reconsider.

Medea was, indeed, a victim, shamefully mistreated and betrayed by Jason,
after saving his life and giving him her love. We had entered into that situation,
and we had accepted her point of view. But we cannot, we will not, accept as
justifiable, and even as laudable, the murder of the innocent children. 'But we
didn't realize!', we want to shout, 'that you meant to do THAT!' The killing of
young children by their own mother is an action of ultimate horror and
shock: it is the brutal denial of everything that we take to be implied by the
very conception, by the very words, of mother and motherhood.

The story of Medea was not, it seems, a very familiar one at Athens, and it
is not even clear that the version in which she is a deliberate infanticide was
known to the Athenians at all, before this play: in earlier versions, as it seems,
the children were killed by Corinthians, after Medea's murder of their
princess – or by Medea herself, but by mistake. Euripides has so written his
tragedy that we have no hint of this horrid action until the middle of the
drama. It comes then as an appalling shock. The children are innocent; they
have done nothing wrong; and (above all) she is their mother – a word that
implied for the Athenians, as it continues to imply for us, emotions and
actions of love and protection and, even, of self-sacrifice. It implied the
absolute opposite, in fact, of the unnatural and horrendous, of the absolutely
unheard-of, action of their murder. And even if we failed to remember this,
Medea herself, steeling herself to the deed, will remind us: *Do not remember
how dear they are, how you gave them birth . . .* (line 1247).

One should, perhaps, emphasize at this point that Euripides plays
absolutely fair here. At the very opening of the play, we heard the Nurse and
the Tutor express great anxiety about the safety of the children, and about the

intentions of their mother. Medea is a character capable – evidently capable
– of violence. After all, Jason might have reflected that she abandoned her
own country, and her family, too; and that she accepted her brother's killing,
in her flight with Jason from her home, when he stole the Golden Fleece and
sailed away with it, and with her, for Hellas. She is no quiet, gentle, helpless,
home-loving woman, as Jason has very good reason to know, from her past
performances. If she is injured, she is capable of hitting back, and to powerful
effect. But the poet has taken pleasure in presenting – emphasizing, indeed
– her feminine side. She knows how to wheedle and to beg, when her urgent
needs, and her final plans, demand that course of action; and she easily
deceives and makes fools both of the Corinthian king and of her own
unfaithful husband, when we see her succeed in wheedling them, to allow her
the extra day of residence: the vital time, which she needs for her revenge, and
for their ruin, and for their reduction to final and irremediable misery.

The poet here, of course, allows himself, and also allows us, the pleasure of
seeing a plausible woman using her apparent feminine weakness to entrap
and destroy the strength of the men who oppose and menace her: the men, of
course, who seem to hold all the power, and who seem able to decide exactly
what to do with her and with her children. In fact, they did have that power:
they could have expelled Medea at once, without giving her the vital time to
organize and prepare her revenge. Doomed King Creon even knows, at some
level, that he is making a mistake (line 350). This human weakness – the
decent reluctance of the king to exert his full power, and so to get Medea out
of Corinth, and out of the way of doing harm, at once and completely – that
is what makes it possible for her to destroy both him and his family, before
leaving his city of Corinth in her final and shocking triumph.

Medea and the world of fifth-century Athens

Allow me, now, to make a little polemical point. Corinth, the scene of these
terrible events, was an implacable and long-standing enemy of Athens. Now,
some of our own contemporaries, when they interpret the literature of the
fifth century BC, want to read into it some politics and antagonisms that
all too closely resemble those of our own day, in places where they are not,
in my opinion, really to be found. We do not, I think, detect any pleasure
here at the thought of Corinthian sufferings and horrors: pleasure which
could, quite easily, have been invoked and inserted, had the tragic poet
wished to display it, and to enjoy it, in company with his Athenian audience.
Politics, I think, are not meant, here, to be anywhere near the forefront of the
audience's minds.

There will be some plays, composed in the last desperate years of the Peloponnesian War, in which hostility to Sparta, and to Spartans, is expressed with a ferocity, and indeed (sometimes) with a hatred, that are not called for by the dramatic events or situation. Such passages are included, no doubt, in order to cater to, and to gratify, contemporary feelings, outside the theatre and outside the plays, of hostility and hatred for Athens' great antagonist, now increasingly menacing, in the endless War. It may be that we should be right to imagine, in those places, outbursts of patriotic rage and of passionate applause in the theatre; but feelings in Athens have not yet, we infer, reached such a pitch of hatred, and such frankly hostile sentiments are not yet present, and are not to be intruded, in this passage.

What we can, perhaps, allow ourselves to see, is the almost magnetic attraction of a setting in Athens, and in Attica, for more and more of the mythical stories, and for the great and famous persons, for the kings and queens and heroes, who figured in them.

Every year, in Athens, fresh tragedies were produced. It followed that more and more stories were constantly being drawn into the circle of those which one or another poet had treated and developed in this, the newest and most exciting of poetical and musical forms. It followed from that process, of course, and from its Athenocentric focus, that more and more of the great men and women of the myth, and more and more of their stories, were brought into close connection, and into lasting relations, with Attica and with the people of Athens.

Why, both Oedipus the Theban and Orestes the Mycenean, or possibly the Argive, came to Attica! In fact, it was there that both of them had the culminating and crowning experiences of their fascinating careers – experiences which delivered them from supernatural sufferings and from apparently insoluble chains of disaster. Orestes was finally acquitted of the intolerable guilt of matricide by an Athenian jury – no other jury could do it, and even the prophetic god Apollo of Delphi had declared himself to be helpless in the matter; while Oedipus underwent his final supernatural cleansing, and his eventual deliverance and his passing from this world, nowhere else but (of course!) right here, among us, in Attica: in the Attic deme of Colonus. And it was Athens, not Boeotia, that produced the great poets whose works would be read, and read universally, by boys at school; so that these Athenocentric versions tended to become the standard ones, universally known, for the later world. So it was that Cicero, proud of his Roman citizenship, but a man of very high Hellenic culture, found it natural and inevitable, when he happened to be at Colonus, to be mindful of *Oedipus at Colonus*, Sophocles' final play, and to recite a noble chorus from it.

In the tragic theatre, in fact, we hear both those heroes as they devote their last words to thanking and blessing the city and democracy of Athens, ever generous and ever god-fearing. Oedipus even promises his posthumous assistance to the Athenians, against any future attack from his own ancestral city of Thebes. So close, so very close, was the link between politics, and poetry, and myth. It would be Athens, too, that offered its shelter and its protection to Medea, the exotic and sinister enchantress from the distant edge of the world. She abused it, of course, attempting to murder the young prince Theseus, who was fated to be the supreme Athenian hero. She was unmasked in the nick of time, fortunately, and had to mount her dragon chariot and go off again on her travels. But this play ends with the magical departure of Medea for Athens – the home of the audience.

It may be tempting to speculate about a different but not entirely dissimilar kind of contemporary relevance: about foreign erotic entanglements, lightly entered into, but not so lightly escaped from, by Athenian men, both soldiers and merchants, in the real, contemporary, fifth-century world. There must, surely, have been plenty of them. Men of Athens were travelling, nowadays, all over the Aegean and beyond; their adventures might bring them into contact with native rulers and potentates and families, half Hellenized or wholly barbaric; but we are not well informed about their *vie passionelle* and about any such unfortunate, or scandalous, entanglements and affairs.

We can do no more than point, rather generally, to the likelihood that such entanglements, and such stories, were by no means something purely unknown, or exotic, or literary, or even remote, for the Athenian men who were seated in the Theatre of Dionysus to watch a tragedy by that notoriously difficult and upsetting tragedian, who, nonetheless, was – undeniably – so strangely fascinating: Euripides.

The majority of the men of Athens, evidently, could never quite rid themselves of the feeling that there was something about those plays that was not right. They fascinated and gripped, admittedly, but they also disconcerted and disturbed the Athenian citizens who sat in his audience, and who formed the juries that judged him and his fellow tragic poets. Better, at any rate, they evidently felt, not to give first prize, at a religious festival, to this obviously brilliant but unpredictable fellow and his strangely disturbing plays, and thus to crown him and his work with the mark of public acceptance and approval by the city of Athens! And so they very rarely did. Unlike Sophocles, of whom we are told that he was never ranked lower than second, Euripides seems to have experienced this quite often – for the trio of plays that included *Medea*, the scholiasts, or ancient commentators, tell us that he was ranked third. That must have been intensely galling for him; and perhaps we are not surprised that he ended his life in voluntary exile, far from his own ungrateful city and from his own natural audience of his Athenian fellow citizens.

But it would be wrong to make too much of the fact that he died in foreign parts. Why, the irreproachably patriotic Aeschylus, so eminently acceptable, whose *Oresteia* is (among other things) a supreme endorsement of Athenian democracy and of the Athenian constitution, had also died far from home, while working in Sicily; and while working there for a tyrant, at that. The Attic tragedians were born into a tradition which had always been rich in travelling poets and travelling musicians, whose line extended right back to the myth and to the figure of Orpheus, itinerant poet and singer. And we must never forget that it would have been quite easy for the Athenians to silence Euripides, by simply refusing him the right to a chorus at the dramatic festivals. The Athenians did not take that simple step, which would have made it impossible for him to present a tragedy. On the contrary, they continued, year by year, to commission his plays, and they flocked to watch them.

Conclusion: Medea in Athens and beyond

There is an analogy to be made, perhaps, between the situation of the first Athenian audience and that of Aegeus, king of Athens in the play. We see – as they saw – how he is talked by Medea into allowing her sanctuary in his city. By the time she arrives, she will be stained with her own children's blood. Oedipus, welcomed by Athens in Sophocles' play, was *miaros* – a polluted man; a man accursed. And yet he was also a hero, a mysterious, larger-than-life figure, from whose presence blessings may come. What about Medea? Before Euripides, other stories had been told about her, and about her sinister powers. It appears that practitioners of magic would invoke her name, as they chanted or mumbled their magical spells. The Roman poet Ovid, some 400 years after the play, would give Medea magic spells which Shakespeare would adapt for his hero, Prospero. Traditionally, Medea was a magician, but she was not (it appears) a child-murderess. That Medea, the Medea who would fascinate and eventually monopolize the minds of posterity, was the creation of Euripides, in this play. He does not make her a witch, in the conventional sense: she is described, more disquietingly, as *sophē*, clever – a good quality, usually; at least, in a man.

She gave form to a universal male anxiety: what is going on, back home, in my house, while I am away, out at work, or on business, or in the army, or on my travels? I must trust my wife, the mother of my precious children: I have, in fact, no alternative to trusting her with them. But just suppose—! The story of Medea, as developed by Euripides, gave to that horrid fear a definite shape and form: in the Shakespearean phrase, a local habitation and a set of names. Here, at last, and in blatant fact, was that ultimate horror: the mother who murders her own children.

Literature has only very rarely had the courage, or the prurience, to peer into that dark realm, and to report what is to be seen there. With Clytemnestra and her man-slaying axe, Aeschylus' *Agamemnon* made his Athenian audience face the grisly horror of a wife who kills her husband, and who does it – to make it, if possible, even worse – with the defining weapon of a man: with a weapon of steel. Medea enacted another appalling horror: the mother who turns against her own dependent children and, instead of nurturing them, kills them with the sword. His creation was one of the most famous plays of the tragic theatre of Athens. Although ranked last out of three by the squeamish original audience, it would still be one of those that survived, when most of the plays of the Athenian theatre were lost. It still commands our attention, horrified but fascinated. An archetypal and universal fear was raised, powerfully and lastingly, to the status, and to the enduring power, of a great work of art.

2

Medea Before and (a little) After Euripides

Carmel McCallum-Barry

In Euripides' *Medea* the action opens with Medea's nurse and trusted companion setting the scene for us, explaining how they have come to be in Corinth, the current situation and the psychological nuances of Medea's mood. Jason has made a new marriage with the daughter of Creon, ruler of Corinth, betraying Medea and their children. She is alerting the audience to the points that Euripides is going to emphasize, and the way that the characters are likely to react to the situation. This is very necessary, as the many stories that are woven into what we can call the myth of Medea cover action over many parts of the Greek and non-Greek world, and she appears in the early myths of Athens, Corinth and Iolcus. The myths involve several families, and are linked with hero stories, folk tales and divine mythology. Most famous of these stories is that about the voyage of the Argonauts and their quest for the Golden Fleece, and the most commonly told version of Medea's story begins with her part in that.

The hero Jason was sent on a dangerous expedition by his uncle Pelias, king of Iolcus in Thessaly, to fetch the Golden Fleece from Colchis, a territory at the furthest end of the Black Sea. (In some versions Pelias had usurped the throne of Iolcus from Aison, Jason's father.) Jason gathered a group of heroes to sail with him on this expedition; the ship that was built for them was named *Argo*; and they were the Argonauts. After a journey full of danger and adventure, they arrived in Colchis where the king, Aeëtes, received them with suspicion. However, he promised to hand over the Fleece on condition that Jason accomplished some dangerous, seemingly impossible, tasks, the chief one being to yoke the fire-breathing bulls belonging to Aeëtes and plough with them. Jason was successful, but only with the aid of the king's daughter, Medea, who gave him powerful ointments to prevent his being harmed by the bulls. She also helped him to seize the Fleece from the sacred grove, where it was guarded by a dragon, and, with the quest accomplished, she escaped with Jason to sail back to Greece; on the way, she killed her brother Apsyrtus, and threw his body into the sea to delay pursuit by the Colchians. The

Argonauts returned to Thessaly where Pelias was still king and, in versions given by Pindar and Euripides, Medea was responsible for Pelias' death by persuading his daughters to attempt to rejuvenate him. Some time after this, Medea and Jason came to Corinth, and there are several accounts of events there besides the story we have in Euripides' play.

This is the commonest version of the myth of Medea; it makes a sequential narrative, which is how we like to read a story, but does not include different or conflicting accounts of, for instance, her brother's death or her connections with Corinth. The audience for the play probably knew of variants and episodes that were not all compatible with one another and did not fit into a neat time line, so they must have been prepared to see Euripides' personal choice of episodes and still could wonder 'will he put in the bit about . . .?' We can try to piece together what the audience might have known or expected from the play by looking at the literary sources available to us prior to 431 BC, and we can often add to this information by considering pictorial representations of the myth which come mostly from Athenian and South Italian vases.

Much of the literary source material in which Medea makes an appearance is fragmentary, but even so we can identify several strands from which poets could choose in order to make their own creative statement about her. She was known to the poets of the seventh century BC, and already then some key elements of her identity appear. In the divine genealogies at the end of the *Theogony*, Hesiod tells us that her father, Aeëtes, and his sister, Circe, were children of the sun god, Helios, and that Medea's mother, Idyia, was a daughter of Oceanus (956–62). We are also told that Jason took Medea from Aeëtes after he had completed the tasks laid upon him by the arrogant king, Pelias, and brought her on a swift ship to Iolcus (992–99).

Other later fragments mention her help for Jason in winning the Golden Fleece and her using drugs to rejuvenate Jason's father. So from the seventh century at least, her divine ancestry, connection with Jason's quest and expertise with herbs and rejuvenation are part of her mythological portrait.

Another aspect of her identity that appears at an early stage is her complicated and confusing affiliation with Corinth. According to Pausanias, writing a travel guide in the second century AD, Eumelus, in a poem called *Corinthiaca* (c. 730 BC), related that Medea was invited by the Corinthians to be their queen and that she was unintentionally responsible for her children's deaths. Notes by scholiasts (later commentators) on *Medea* line 264 cite a tradition that the Corinthians killed them, either in revolt against Medea as queen or in retaliation for her murder of Creon; they also add that that her children were honoured by a cult in Corinth. In versions from the Archaic Period there must have been at least two traditions concerning the children's death; either that Medea killed her children unintentionally or that the Corinthians did. This seems to be one of the haziest areas in the stories about Medea and therefore one where Euripides was most free to innovate – and he did!

Although the early evidence is scant, it still gives us a picture of Medea that we can recognise in Euripides. In the fifth century there are some further developments in her portrait. An important source of information is Pindar, who composed poems (*Olympian, Isthmian, Pythian* and *Nemean Odes*) to celebrate the wealthy men whose protégés and horse teams were victors at the great games. The poems were commissioned, and praised not just the current success but the victor's family and their achievements in the past. By his use of mythology Pindar linked the ancestral family of the victor to the great events of the glorious past, as we see in *Pythian* 4, composed for the victory of Arcesilas of Cyrene in the chariot race at the games of 462 BC. Arcesilas' ancestor, the founder of the city of Cyrene, was one of the Argonauts, so the poet deploys the famous myth to enhance the glory of the moment and associate his patron with the semi-divine heroes.

The poem begins with the homeward journey of the Argonauts and how Medea foretold the events leading to the founding of Cyrene, before moving further back in the story to the expedition itself. In Pindar's version, Jason was sent to get the Fleece because King Pelias had been given an oracle to the effect that he would be destroyed by a man who came to Iolcus wearing only one sandal, and Jason was that man. Pindar also mentions that Pelias had usurped the throne and possessions due to Jason, but promised to surrender them if Jason brought him the Fleece.

After he arrived in Colchis, Jason was helped by Aphrodite to win the love of Medea, and he persuaded her to disregard the natural love and respect for her parents, so that she appears almost as a victim of Jason and Aphrodite. She prepared oils and ointments to help Jason through the trials her father set for him; with these he successfully yoked the bulls and ploughed with them, 'the fire did not keep him back, because of the instructions from the foreign woman skilled in all kinds of drugs' (233–5). Aeëtes then told Jason where to find the Fleece, but was still hoping to destroy him, as the Fleece was guarded by a fierce dragon. But Jason killed the dragon 'with pale eyes and mottled back', and stole away Medea. Pindar does not say that Medea helped in killing the dragon, but calls her 'the death of Pelias' (251), one of the earliest mentions of her involvement in his death. A few years later the story was current, as the summary of Euripides' *Daughters of Pelias* of 455 BC tells that Medea was instrumental in the death of Pelias.

The audience at the first performance of *Medea* derived some of their knowledge of the myths from plays performed in Athens at the great dramatic festivals and in repeat performances in the smaller towns around Attica. From the middle of the fifth century, myths in which Medea played a part, were used frequently by Athenian dramatists; clearly the issues addressed in the stories had some relevance for the contemporary Athenian public.

Little survives of these plays except summaries (*hypotheses*) or fragments, but we do know that Sophocles produced several plays on different parts of the story. *Women of Colchis* (*Colchides*) dramatized events at the court of Aeëtes in Colchis; another called *Rootcutters* (*Rhizotomi*) dealt with Medea's special skill with magic herbs. A fragment of his *Scythian Women* (*Scythai*) shows that its subject was the return of the Argonauts and their escape from Colchis, and that the murder of Medea's brother en route was part of the subject matter, as the fragment mentions that Apsyrtus and Medea did not have the same mother.

Euripides also used the stories more than once; his first play, in 455 BC was *Daughters of Pelias* (*Peliades*), in which Medea induced the daughters of Pelias to kill their father. The plot summary tells that she herself killed a ram and boiled it with herbs in a cauldron, from which it emerged rejuvenated. Her demonstration persuaded the women to try the same process with their aged father – unfortunately they were unsuccessful. Perhaps Pindar in *Pythian* 4 and Euripides were responsible for making this the canonical version of Medea's rejuvenation magic, because there are earlier mentions of the treatment being given to others besides Pelias. A fragment of the *Nostoi*, late epic poems on the returns of the heroes from Troy, says she rejuvenated Jason's father, Aison, with drugs, 'stripping off his old age' (fr. 7). The plot summary for *Medea* comments that according to Simonides (fr. 548) and Pherecydes (3F) she used her rejuvenation techniques for Jason. Obviously he shouldn't have needed it, but there could be confusion over names here, as in Greek spelling the two are very similar (Aison and Iason). As we shall see, the early vase paintings allow differing interpretations. Nevertheless, the ability to make men or animals young must have been an integral part of her story from earliest times and, as in the case of the children's deaths in Corinth, there was no fixed version.

Both Sophocles and Euripides wrote *Aegeus* plays, which probably involved Medea after she left Corinth and took refuge in Athens with King Aegeus, where, in keeping with her other dramatic portrayals, she tried to poison Aegeus' illegitimate son, Theseus, when he came to Athens to claim his birthright. The frequency of her appearances in fifth-century drama marks the significance of her deeds and characterization for the Athenian audience.

The Argonautic expedition and Medea's story were also a favourite subject for vase painters, and in the earliest paintings two scenes predominate. One is the actual taking of the Fleece from the grove where it is guarded by the dragon; the fantastical, fairy story aspect of the encounter with the dragon appealed to the artists' imagination, and to that of their customers. The most famous example is a cup by Douris dated c. 480 BC which shows a magnificent dragon with Jason sliding out from its gaping jaws while Athena, patron of heroes, looks on; apparently he has been swallowed and disgorged, as Heracles was by the sea monster. This peculiar situation must have been long established in the repertoire, as it also appears on two Corinthian pots at the end of the seventh century. Another vase a little later in date shows Jason cautiously approaching the Fleece as it hangs on a tree; to one side we have Athena, an Argonaut and the prow of the *Argo*. These early fifth-century paintings focus on Jason. There is no Medea; only after 425 BC does she become a standard element in depictions of the dragon scene, rather than Athena, so it seems that after Euripides' play she is more interesting than the heroic Jason.

The other very popular scene is that which illustrates Medea's ability to rejuvenate someone or something, and this is how she most frequently appears before Euripides' play. From around 530 BC a series of vases in Attic Black Figure show a ram in a cauldron with women standing around it. On some of them an old man sits or stands at the side of the picture; other depictions show women leading an old man towards the cauldron. Such scenes continue into the fifth century until after 450 BC (Euripides' *Daughters of Pelias* was produced in 455 BC, keeping interest alive). The focus of attention is always the ram in the cauldron with women standing round it. In these scenes Medea is sometimes distinguishable from the other women by the *polos* headdress she wears, which is perhaps a comment on her divine ancestry, as this headdress is usually seen on goddesses. However, after the production of *Medea* in 431 BC, although scenes showing the seizing of the Fleece and the dragon are still frequent, the Pelias episode is no longer important, and scenes based on events in the play take over, especially on the vases from South Italy.

The shift of attention away from the Pelias episode, and the fact that Euripides had already treated it in *Daughters of Pelias*, make it hard to guess what the audience would have expected to see in his *Medea*. They would have been familiar with Medea as a foreign princess, from a strange faraway land, a descendant of Helios, the sun god. She was known as the helper of Jason in seizing the Golden Fleece from Colchis and then escaping with him and the Argonauts. It is noticeable that the vase paintings show only Jason encountering the dragon, but Medea's skill with magic herbs and drugs was part of her help for him in taming the bulls and perhaps also in taming the dragon. For love of Jason she worked against her father, left her family and killed her brother, and so came to Greece. There her expertise in magical

Figure 2 The rejuvenation of a white-haired male: a ram springs from a cauldron towards Medea who is sprinkling the ram with a magic potion. (© The Trustees of the British Museum)

herbs was highlighted in the vase paintings, which showed her attempts to rejuvenate a person or animal, and through these and Euripides' play she was famous for causing the death of Pelias at the hands of his daughters.

At each stage of Medea's journey in myth from Colchis to Iolcus, a recurring motif is the betrayal of traditional family loyalties, as she harms those close to her (betraying her parents, killing her brother) or leads others to cause the death of loved ones in their own family, like the daughters of Pelias. In the next stages of her journey, in Corinth and later in Athens, the pattern continues.

There was a wide choice of story elements here for the plot-maker, so the Athenians might have wondered: would Euripides put it all in and could he do something new? In fact he did both. The standard elements of the myth are acknowledged but not emphasized as part of the action. Medea herself deals with them almost dismissively in her first speech to Jason, where she lists what she has done for him:

> I saved you then, when you were sent to yoke the bulls, whose breath was fire, and sow the field of death. And I killed the dragon, which was coiled around the Golden Fleece, tight in a stranglehold, its guardian, unsleeping …And I betrayed my father and my very home and came with you back to Iolcus and Pelias' land, so eager, so naïve, uncalculating, killed Pelias – such a painful death at his own daughters' hands – and devastated utterly his house. You let me do all this for you and then, you worst of men, betrayed me for another woman's bed, though we had children. Oh yes, if you'd been childless still, I might have pardoned you for lusting after this new bedding …
>
> 476–91

Medea mentions only the killing of Pelias, not fantastic rejuvenation, and she refers to the dragon only to claim that she killed it, not Jason. As he plays down the magical and bizarre parts of her story, Euripides concentrates on the issues that can disturb or destroy a family – betrayal, childlessness, murder. All his major innovations in the play proceed from this focus, so that Medea's past as a woman who betrayed her father and killed her brother, and induced other women to kill their father, is not part of the plotting but forms an atmospheric background for the drama. Euripides builds on her past rather than retells it, and in the present it is Medea herself who is the victim of betrayal, 'you betrayed me for another woman's bed, though we had children'. Unlike her victims in the mythological past, she will take her revenge

All this is clearly signalled in the Prologue by the nurse, whose description of Medea's mood warns the audience to be prepared for something strange.

She is afraid Medea may kill her children or even Jason and his new wife (36–43); to make sure that the audience take notice, she repeats a little later that Medea may harm her children: 'I saw her just a little while ago, staring at them full of hate' (92–3). The nurse's final song emphasizes that her mistress in her inconsolable rage is ready to attack all those close to her in the household (187–9). Medea herself threatens that she may kill the king and his daughter and Jason too, wondering whether to set fire to the house or to stab them, but concludes, 'The strongest way's the most direct, the way in which I am by nature most experienced – to poison them' (384–5). So the audience know that she is going to kill someone, but it is not clear at first exactly who or how; they must wait to see just how she will achieve her revenge.

A series of encounters with male characters, in which Medea persuades them to grant her wishes, shows her constructing this revenge. The encounters emphasize family imperatives, in particular men's need and love for children and the respect that should be given to a wife, especially if she has produced children.

She persuades Creon to give her an extra day in Corinth to make arrangements for her children, by appealing to his love for his daughter, even though he knows Medea is a danger to him, 'I love my family more than I do you' (327). In her meeting with Aegeus, king of Athens, she wins his sympathy immediately, because Jason has not given her the honour due to a wife. Her promise to cure Aegeus' childlessness, 'I am familiar with certain drugs and medicines' (718), encourages him to offer her refuge in Athens, when she leaves Corinth. Having gained time to act and a refuge afterwards, in her next scene with Jason she convinces him that she has become reconciled towards his new marriage and insists on showing her goodwill by sending the two children to his new wife with gifts of a valuable robe and golden garland. The poisoned gifts kill the bride and, in a sinister echo of the daughters of Pelias, the bride is the cause of her own father, Creon's, death as he tries to take the deadly robe from her body. Once the deaths of Creon and his daughter have been reported, Medea knows that the die is cast and that she is going to kill her sons; despite the nurse's earlier warnings, this must have been a shock in the theatre. We know that there were several traditions about the circumstances of the children's deaths; before he knows that they are dead, Jason even refers to another possibility, that Creon's relatives might kill them in retaliation for their mother's deeds (304–5). A reminder of other versions serves to underline Euripides' innovation in this crucial area, and it is generally agreed by scholars that he was the first to make Medea the intentional killer of her children. In doing this, her revenge on Jason is perfect, as she leaves him without children or hope of others, as his new wife is dead too.

Medea hits at everyone she encounters in the play where they are most sensitive, in their concern over household and family, *oikos*. Despite this, she gets our modern sympathies and, to a large extent, those of the women of the chorus. The role of drama as a forum where all sorts of problems could be examined, can help explain this. Drama is still a place to air difficult issues; in soaps we constantly get personal and family problems up for inspection – child-bearing and rearing, parent-child tensions, husband-wife tensions, adultery, incest, relationships between members of families and outsiders. These were the topics of Greek tragedy too. In presenting family problems it also examined wider issues and values important to the city of Athens, and these were often sensitive issues, such as a hero who commits suicide, or women who kill their husband or children. Such subjects were not easy to deal with in front of a large and emotionally charged audience, but, by setting drama in the mythical past, a distance could be created between the disturbing events on stage and those watching them. Another way of confronting terrifying possibilities or extreme cases was by viewing them through female characters. Women in tragedy were not meant to be realistic portrayals, but the transgressive character and actions of Medea and others, women who fight back or act for themselves, allowed the dramatists to comment on their own society and its concerns.

One of these concerns was that of identity. After 450 BC, Athenian citizenship and its privileges were jealously guarded. Only those with both parents Athenian born could be citizens. This meant that non-Athenian Greeks as well as non-Greeks were foreign outsiders, and we see the problematic relationship between these groups addressed frequently in tragedy. Medea is the ultimate foreigner, a barbarian from the edge of the civilized (i.e. Greek) world. Her nurse makes this clear in the Prologue, but says her mistress is accepted and popular in Corinth; however Medea herself frequently emphasizes how she has rejected her home and family and is a foreigner everywhere.

The Athenian audience were familiar with the serious disadvantages of this situation, and no doubt many shared the prejudice against foreigners, but the chorus of local women in Corinth are puzzlingly sympathetic towards the foreign barbarian. They can feel for her because all (married) women are foreigners, strangers in their husbands' household, frequently regarded with suspicion as outsiders; Medea's situation is an exaggerated example of the common female experience. Sophocles, too, draws attention to the problem in his *Tereus*, where, in one of the remaining fragments, Procne says she has seen that grown women count for nothing; as children they have a happy life in their father's house but once mature 'we are pushed away and sold away from our ancestral gods and those who gave us birth, married to foreigners,

some to barbarians, some to happy homes and others not' (fr. 584). Procne
was not a foreigner like Medea, but an Athenian woman, who killed her child
to punish her husband's rape and mutilation of her sister; her chilling
appraisal of the only life choice for Athenian women explains why the chorus
can spend much of this play expressing sympathy towards a barbarian
murderess.

Besides her foreignness, the other disturbing aspect of Medea's traditional
character is her ability to concoct magic potions, with which in her past she
helped Jason survive the fire-breathing bulls and engineered the death of
Pelias. In this play she uses her skills as herbalist to offer Aegeus a fertility
medicine and to make the deadly ointment that kills Creon and his daughter,
but the appearance of these motifs in other plays shows that strange potions
were not unknown to Greek women. In Sophocles' *Women of Trachis*, the
gentle Deianeira tries to win back her husband Heracles' love for her by
making what she thinks is a love potion. She smears it on a robe, which she
sends to him as a gift, but the mixture is deadly and kills him. Phaedra's nurse
suggests special medicines and magic spells for her mistress's lovesickness in
Euripides' *Hippolytus* (478, 509, 517). Clearly it was not unusual for wives to
seek out love potions to win back straying husbands, and Greek tragedy
shows that one of the most common areas of danger for Athenian men was
the home. Medea as ever is the extreme case; she does not seek to bring Jason
back to her with her drugs, but to destroy his future.

We have noted that the city of Athens was extremely protective of its
citizenship and special identity, which included the city's achievements and
material resources; the male members of the *oikos* were similarly protective
of its integrity, reflecting the exclusive state approach. Threats to this entity
form much of the subject matter of tragedy, and the myths about Medea
highlight concerns that appear frequently in fifth-century drama, such as the
need for children, sexual problems, and a wife's need for respect and honour
in the household. So how does Euripides make a new and memorable version
of the well known story?

The main part of the story, where there seems to be least certainty for
myth-tellers, concerns events in Corinth, and Euripides focuses his
innovations around the stay of Jason and Medea in the city. Already at the
beginning we have the new theme of Jason's marriage to the king's daughter,
and later the horrible death of Creon and the new bride provides a graphic
and poignant messenger speech. We can also see the unheroic portrayal of
Jason and the embarrassing (for Athenians?) discussion of Aegeus' infertility
as a new way of presenting the myth.

But Euripides' major innovation is that Medea actually kills her own
children, after long and anguished hesitation, and in addition is able to escape

from Corinth without punishment. The shocking deed makes dramatic sense in the context of her portrayal as a woman who has betrayed and killed within her own family and led others to do the same; her character has been taken to the limit and gone beyond humanity. But her escape is also shocking as it seems to indicate her deeds have divine approval, since she appears in the chariot of the god Helios, her grandfather. Medea's divine ancestry has not been emphasized during the play, except for her own significant remarks that the robe and garland she sends to Jason's bride were bequeathed by Helios to his descendants (954–5). The final scenes must have been doubly disturbing for the audience; not only does a woman get away with killing a king and her own sons, but a god helps her!

We cannot know how Euripides' innovations in Medea's story were received in Athens, but it is interesting to note that these new episodes do not appear on any Attic vase paintings, as if the events were too disturbing for public taste. However, they became favourites with the painters of South Italy, who produced scenes not previously seen on vases, which reflect Euripides' play. The murder of the children appears frequently: sometimes they are shown lying on the ground, but several vases show Medea killing them at an altar. There are representations of the death of Creon and his daughter and more of Medea in the chariot of the Sun; sometimes all three elements are put together on the same vase like a comic strip. On a vase in Cleveland, Medea in oriental dress rides in a chariot drawn by dragons, the chariot is enclosed in a circular frame with the rays of the sun around it, the boys' bodies lie below on an altar, and a helpless Jason looks up at her (see illustration, p. 9).

What next? Medea announces that she intends to bury her children at the shrine of Hera outside Corinth, and institute a festival in their honour to atone for what she admits is a sacrilegious murder (*dussebēs phonou*, 1378–83). Then she will go to live with Aegeus in Athens. As for Jason, he will die dishonourably, struck on the head by a piece of wood from the *Argo*. It would be obvious to all that, in giving these prophetic words to Medea, on high in her chariot, Euripides puts her in the role usually given at the end of his plays to a god who foretells the future and it reinforces the impression of Medea as a divine being.

So, in the next phase of the myth after the events of this play, this female threat to Athenian peace of mind is in Athens with Aegeus; when his son Theseus comes to make himself known to his father, Medea persuades Aegeus that he is an enemy, and with Aegeus' agreement tries to poison him. Scenes which show the dangerous female barbarian as the would-be killer of the national hero do appear on Attic vases in several forms. But Aegeus recognizes Theseus before it is too late and all is well – or is it? The audience, familiar with the myths or their own city's past, knew very well that Theseus, the great

Athenian hero, would eventually be the (unwitting) cause of his own father's death.

Euripides has made some startling innovations in his treatment of Medea, which could have been unwelcome to his audience, and he ends his play leaving them with even more unsettling thoughts about what is to come.

3

Otherness and Exile: Euripides' Production of 431 BC

Ioanna Karamanou

To the memory of Professor Eric Handley

Medea was produced in 431 BC as part of a *tetralogy* which also contained *Philoctetes, Dictys* and the satyr-play *Theristae* ('*Reapers*'). Euripides won the third prize, which is suggestive of his lesser popularity during his own lifetime. Nonetheless, ever since antiquity, *Medea* has remained a highly influential play, while there is concrete evidence for the reception of *Philoctetes* in later literary criticism and of *Dictys* in fourth-century iconography.[1]

As with most Euripidean *tetralogies*, the three tragedies belong to different myths (unlike Aeschylean *tetralogies*, whose tragedies derive from successive phases of the same legend). This chapter sets out to explore certain common underlying themes, which, despite the plot differences, pervade the plays of this *tetralogy*. I shall argue that the tragedies are conceptually interrelated by means of the key notions of exile and otherness and shall investigate the manner in which these ideas are embedded within their contemporary sociopolitical and cultural context.

While exploring the treatment of these ideas in the *tetralogy* of 431 BC, it should be borne in mind that the typical Greek way of defining the Athenian 'self' was by negative polar opposition to a whole series of 'others'. The 'other' was mainly represented in drama by disempowered individuals marginalized by gender, ethnicity, social class and physical factors, such as deformity or advanced age.[2]

Medea's multifaceted otherness emerges from a combination of features. The first element, which is shared by all three tragedies, is the notion of exile. The theme of Medea's exiled status is displayed right from the outset in the Nurse's prologue (12) and permeates the first part of the play until the implementation of her revenge-plan (255, 273, 280–81, 359–61, 502–3, 512–15, 604, 704, 706, 711–13). In the second *stasimon* the Chorus refers to the anguish and isolation which exile incurs, and goes as far as asserting that death itself is preferable to the calamities of exile:

> O my fatherland, my home!
> I would that I might never lose my city
> and so know that yawning life of helplessness that cannot be endured –
> of all the sorrows in the world, most pitiable.
> No! I would sooner die
> and put an end to all the long days of my life,
> for there is no grief greater
> than to lose your native land.
>
> 645–53

Medea's utter isolation emerges from her own description of herself as deserted (255; see also 604) and bereft of her homeland, and is underscored through a powerful juxtaposition of words:

> If I am to be driven out in exile,
> cut off from all friends, from all family, and all alone with my poor lonely sons.
>
> 512–13

Medea is a foreigner and as such she should make herself agreeable to the city (222–24) by acting with the caution expected of foreigners, who are in need of protective refuge (386–90). At the same time, Medea's social inferiority arises from her abandonment by Jason, for whom marriage to a barbarian woman does not provide sufficient status (591–92).

Medea's otherness is further enhanced by her gender. The famous passage from her monologue, in which she asserts that of all living creatures women are the most abject (230–51), highlights the superlative state of their wretchedness and alludes to the unfair social structure and the social imperatives which underlie the female predicament. In this speech Medea starts from the immediate situation of her own plight and moves on to identify herself both with the sympathetic female Chorus, and on a larger scale with the whole female sex.[3]

Hence, Medea's vulnerability in the first part of the play arises from her status as the 'other'. Subject to injustice and humiliation (20, 26, 692, 696), she is forced to succumb to the power of her enemies:

> And though I've been ill-used, I shall keep quiet.
> Those who are stronger than I am have beaten me.
>
> 314–15

Her precarious position further emerges from two supplication scenes. Medea assumes the role of suppliant first towards Creon (324–51) – a 'suppliant-enemy' confrontation, in which Medea pleads with Creon to delay her exile – and then towards Aegeus (709–13) – a 'suppliant-rescuer' scene, in which she extracts Aegeus' oath of protection.

According to Edith Hall, the concept of ethnic 'otherness' tends to be embodied in the monstrous or the supernatural.[4] Thus Medea's supernatural qualities and her status as a sorceress further demonstrate her wildness and ethnic otherness. This emerges from Jason's final utterance:

> There was no woman ever in the whole of Greece
> who could have done such things, and yet I did not marry any Greek.
> I married you. I married hatred, spite, destruction,
> not a woman but a lioness unleashed
> and more inhuman than the sea-snakes circling Scylla.
>
>   1339–43

Her supernatural qualities, which are downplayed in the first part of the play, are highlighted at the end by means of her overpowering presence (especially in 1317–22). Medea turns herself from victim to agent, punishes Jason for breaking his sacred oath to her through an appalling retribution of tragic justice and disappears upward and out of sight.[5]

The themes of exile and otherness similarly pervade the fragmentarily-preserved *Philoctetes*. The play aroused literary interest towards the end of the first century AD, when a treatise on the *Philoctetes* tragedies by Aeschylus, Sophocles and Euripides was written by the critic Dio of Prusa (*Oration* 52). Dio also provides a paraphrase of the prologue-speech and the ensuing scene of Euripides' *Philoctetes* (*Oration* 59.2–11).

As in Sophocles' extant *Philoctetes*, the dramatic setting is in Lemnos and the façade of the stage-building represents Philoctetes' cave-dwelling. Odysseus delivers the expository prologue revealing that he has come transformed by goddess Athena to recover Philoctetes, following the prophecy that Heracles' invincible bow (now owned by Philoctetes) will bring down Troy (frr. 787–89, 789a Kannicht; henceforth abbreviated as K.). He then encounters the crippled and ragged Philoctetes and gains his sympathy by pretending that, like Philoctetes himself, he is an outcast from the Greeks (frr. 789d, 790, 790a K.). In the *parodos* the Chorus of Lemnian men apologizes for neglecting Philoctetes over a long period of time (fr. 789c K.), while (presumably in the first episode) Euripides introduces a shepherd, Actor, the sole Lemnian to support the tormented hero – an innovation in the treatment of the legend (Dio of Prusa *Oration* 52.8, Hyginus *Fabula* 102.2).

Probably in the second episode a Trojan embassy arrives, attempting to recruit Philoctetes and his bow through bribery. Their representative becomes involved in a formal debate with Odysseus, who appeals to Philoctetes' patriotism by urging him to resist the barbarians (frr. 794–97 K.). After the departure of the Trojans the hero is likely to have suffered a seizure of pain from his wound (for which, see fr. 792 K.), which arouses the Chorus' pity (fr. 792a K.). The evidence for subsequent events is meagre. Dio refers to the entry of Diomedes (*Oration* 52.14), presumably to assist Odysseus in carrying out his mission, and the fragmentary evidence is suggestive of Odysseus' effort to persuade Philoctetes to come to Troy (frr. 798, 799, 799a K.). According to the papyrus-*hypothesis* of the play (Papyri Oxyrhynchi 2455, fr. 17.21), Philoctetes was finally compelled to accompany Odysseus and Diomedes on board ship, which suggests that he was reluctant to follow them.[6]

As with Medea, Philoctetes' otherness is extensively defined through his exile. The *hypothesis* (P. Oxy. 2455, fr. 17.3–8) attests that he was bitten by a viper and in his extremity of pain was abandoned by the Greeks on Lemnos, where he lived in misery for ten years, arousing pity in those who encountered him. No Lemnian ever approached or showed any concern for him, and no one ever received him in his house or tended his wound, because it was intolerable (Dio of Prusa *Oration* 52.8). Unlike the Chorus of *Medea*, which is initially sympathetic towards the tragic heroine, the indifference of the Lemnian Chorus towards Philoctetes' plight is a further indicator of the hero's physical isolation in the island of his exile.

Like Medea, Philoctetes underlines the injustice and humiliation he has suffered from his companions (fr. 789d.18–19 K.), which underscores his exclusion from and incompatibility with his social context. Accordingly, he points out that 'when a man does badly, friends keep out of his way' (fr. 799a K.). At the same time, he is sympathetic towards the contrived story told by the disguised Odysseus – believing him to be deprived of friends and resources, Philoctetes regards Odysseus as one of his own kind (fr. 789d.48–55 K.). Philoctetes' status as a humiliated and oppressed outcast is reinforced by the ending, where he is reported to have been compelled by the Greeks to follow them to Troy.

Philoctetes' otherness is indicated visually through his disability and dreadful appearance, which is vividly described by Odysseus (fr. 789d.1–5 K.). His plight is obvious, as he walks with difficulty and in pain. He is physically deformed, and his appearance is appalling due to his affliction. His attire is unnatural, as he is wearing hides of wild beasts, which are further suggestive of his wildness and remoteness. His wretchedness and poverty (see fr. 790a K.: 'There is no pale silver in the cave, stranger') were so effectively staged as to be parodied by Aristophanes in *Acharnians* (423–24).

The manner in which Philoctetes first addresses Odysseus is abrupt and arises from his plight and alienation from the community (fr. 789d.6–12 K.). Philoctetes lives in grim conditions, and his cave provides a miserable sight full of bandages and tokens of his affliction (frr. 789d.48–55, 790 K.). The agony of his wound is portrayed in strong language in a line commended by Aristotle (*Poetics* XXII 1458b.19–24) as ingenious: 'An ulcer, which feasts on my foot's flesh' (fr. 792 K.). Accordingly, in a powerful lyric fragment, the members of the Chorus pray not to face the misfortune which Philoctetes endures, thus stressing the hero's misery and isolation even further:

Life, enough! Make an end
before any mishap
comes to my property and my own self here.

fr. 792a K.

In *Dictys* Euripides reiterates the theme of exile through the presentation of Danaë's predicament. Danaë, daughter of Acrisius, king of Argos, was impregnated by Zeus and gave birth to Perseus. Upon finding out about the child, Acrisius enclosed her and baby Perseus in a chest, which he cast adrift. The chest reached the coast of Seriphos, where it was fished up by a fisherman named Dictys, who took Danaë and Perseus under his protection, treating them as his own family. When Perseus grew to manhood, Polydectes, king of Seriphos, enamoured of Danaë, asked Perseus to bring him the Gorgon's head, so that, in his absence, he might win Danaë. Helped by Hermes and Athena, Perseus manages to decapitate the Gorgon and returns to Seriphos to find his mother and Dictys as suppliants, trying to escape from Polydectes' violence. Perseus asks Polydectes to gather his friends in a feast to see the Gorgon's head and, consequently, turns them to stone.

A rough account of the supplication of Danaë and Dictys and their rescue by Perseus is provided in the *Bibliotheca* of Ps.Apollodorus (2.4.3) and in Theon's *scholium* on the *Twelfth Pythian* of Pindar (P. Oxy. 2536.1–12). The scene is also shown on an Apulian vase-painting dated to 370–360 BC.[7] In the centre of the representation is the altar of Poseidon (complete with cult-statue), where Danaë and the white-haired Dictys have sought refuge. On the left, Polydectes, holding a sceptre in his right hand and a sword in his left, is looking at them. All three characters are dressed in stage-costumes. On the right, Perseus, arriving at Seriphos and carrying the pouch with the Gorgon's head, is depicted in heroic nudity. Danaë and Dictys are looking at the hero with surprise, hope and relief, and Dictys is making a 'speaking' gesture towards him. This vase-painting is likely to have been inspired by a revival of *Dictys* in South Italy and presumably aimed to offer its viewers a recollection of the main themes of the play, such as the dramatic tension of the supplication scene, Polydectes' violence and the crucial moment of Perseus' return.

According to the aforementioned testimonies and the most substantial fragments, the plot structure of *Dictys* seems to have been constructed upon the patterns of 'supplication-return-rescue-revenge', which were later similarly represented in the first part of Euripides' *Heracles* (1–814). The island of Seriphos is clearly defined as a dramatic locale – probably in the first line of the expository prologue (fr. 330b K.).

Like Medea and Philoctetes, Danaë and her son Perseus are in exile and thus in a precarious position. Perseus has been sent by Polydectes to accomplish the supposedly impossible task of decapitating the Gorgon, while Danaë resists the king's amorous passion. Danaë's suffering emerges from the consolation addressed by Dictys to the lamenting mother, who, in view of his long absence, regards Perseus as dead:

> Do you think that Hades is concerned at all for your laments,
> and will send your son back up if you will go on grieving?
> Stop! You'd feel easier if you looked at the troubles of those near at hand,
> if you'd be willing to consider
> how many of mankind have been exhausted by struggling with bonds,
> how many grow old bereft of children,
> and those who are nothing after ruling in the greatest prosperity:
> these are the things you should contemplate.
>
> fr. 332 K.

This fragment reproduces typical themes of consolatory speeches, such as the futility of lament and examples of other people's suffering, urging the addressee to consider the adversities of human life and the necessity to bear them. These lines might have been part of a wider discourse between the two suppliants on how to act under these circumstances and bear their misfortune, which could be paralleled in the exchange between Amphitryon and Megara in *Heracles* 60–106, 275–347. Accordingly, Danaë's reluctance to raise herself up is suggestive of her psychological weariness and frustration (fr. 342 K.: 'Why make me stand up, old man, when I have forgotten my miseries?')

Danaë is a victim of Polydectes' oppression. She is doubly marginal, since her otherness and, in turn, her vulnerability arise not only from her exile, but (as with Medea) from her gender as well. She is a victim of male violence, being constrained by Polydectes to succumb to his intentions, according to the accounts of both Theon (P. Oxy. 2536.5–6: 'being pressed hard by Polydectes') and Ps.Apollodorus (2.4.3: 'because of Polydectes' violence'). To evade his pressure, she resorts to supplication along with her protector Dictys.

As in *Medea*, the fragments of *Dictys* are suggestive of a 'suppliant-enemy' confrontation. Unlike Creon in *Medea*, Polydectes does not yield to the suppliants' cause. This 'suppliant-enemy' encounter seems to have taken the form of an *agon* between Dictys and Polydectes, intensifying the power-gap and dramatic tension, which is a practice followed by Euripides in the debates within the supplication scenes of *Heraclidae* (134–287), *Andromache* (147–273) and *Heracles* (140–251). This scene is clearly signposted as a formal debate (fr. 334.3 K.: 'contest of words') and it is probably Polydectes who declares that, though it is beneath his dignity to argue with a person of lower status, he cannot tolerate being offended by a social inferior, i.e. the fisherman Dictys (fr. 334 K.). Polydectes' loquacity is criticized (fr. 335 K.), while the Chorus-leader dissuades Dictys from arguing with the king (fr. 337 K.). Despite the suppliants' disadvantaged status, it is possibly Dictys who declares his faith in the power of justice (fr. 343 K.), which he regards as a prerequisite of nobility (fr. 336 K.). Dictys is a fisherman, thus an 'ordinary' man, who, like Actor, his equivalent in *Philoctetes*, supports the character representing the 'other'. He also belongs to a group of elderly, morally assertive Euripidean characters including Peleus (in *Andromache* 547–765) and Amphitryon (in *Heracles* 170–326).

The satyr-play *Theristae* ('*Reapers*') may have been lost as early as the fourth century BC, to judge from the complete absence of quotations and evidence for its theme. Its title suggests that it comprised a Chorus of harvesters. The most famous myth about reapers is that of Lityerses (attested in the scholium on Theocritus 10.41–42 Wendel), who killed passers-by after forcing them to compete with him in a reaping contest, and who was finally overpowered by Heracles. At the same time, it has been assumed that *Theristae* may have been an alternative title of the satyr-play *Syleus*, in which the name-character forced people to dig up his vines before killing them. It should be noted, however, that *theristae* in Greek refers to harvesters of wheat, corn or grain, not of the vine, which makes Lityerses' story a likelier theme for this play than the legend of Syleus. Satyr-plays tend to be only loosely associated with the tragedies of the same production, even in connected Aeschylean *tetralogies*. Considering the lack of evidence, this satyr-play may be only generally linked with the three preceding tragedies through the shared theme of otherness, which is also a distinctive feature of satyrs. In view of their very nature as part man and part beast, as well as of their boorish and unrestrained behaviour, satyrs were regarded as antiparagons in relation to humankind and thus as manifestations of the 'other'.[8]

The dominant notions of exile and otherness permeating this *tetralogy* should be explored within the Athenian sociopolitical framework of mid-fifth century BC. As mentioned at the outset, the definition of 'self' and 'other' relies on the distinction between the Athenian male citizen and socially marginalized groups, such as women, slaves, foreigners and disabled people. The characters representing the 'other' in all three of our tragedies belong to this disempowered group and are all facing male political power. They are excluded, oppressed and vulnerable.

The tension between the Athenian 'self' and the 'other' was enhanced after the victory in the Persian Wars, which produced the idea of a collective Panhellenic identity and the notion of non-Greeks as the 'other', thus engendering the polarization of Greek and barbarian. This polarizing ideology underpinned Athenian supremacy within the context of the Delian League, which was subsequently transformed into the Athenian Empire. Moreover, Pericles' citizenship law of 451/450 BC restricted Athenian citizenship to men whose parents were both Athenians (see [Aristotle] *Constitution of Athens* 26.4, Plutarch *Pericles* 37.3), thus creating a limited privileged citizen-body, which corresponded to the self-image of the Athenians as rulers of an empire.

The Athenians drew a tight line around their civic membership, closing their descent-group to outsiders and posing a clear boundary between citizens and non-citizens, which is suggestive of an increasing development of Athenian identity. Hence, this construction of Athenian ideology against a series of 'others' assumed a clearly political complexion. It may also provide an insight into the making of civic identity and the development of Athenian self-consciousness.[9] Considering that the mythical material of these tragedies belongs to the Heroic Age, the political allusions introduced by Euripides seem to involve oblique anachronistic references to the ideology and values of Classical Athens.

The politically nuanced notion of otherness corresponds to the similarly political resonances carried by these plays, which were performed on the cusp of the Peloponnesian War. In the third *stasimon* of *Medea* (esp. 824–45) Athens is praised as the traditional protector of suppliants and as a sanctuary for victims of oppression. The Athenian self-image is represented through harmonious music, moderation and *sophia* (wisdom), as opposed to the Corinthian disorder displayed before the Aegeus-episode.

Likewise, *Philoctetes* is described as a 'political' play *par excellence* by Dio of Prusa (*Oration* 52.11, 52.14). In more specific terms, the figure of Odysseus seems to represent the popular Athenian politician of that era, who is concerned for common welfare, as well as for his own success and reputation (frr. 787–89 K., Dio of Prusa *Oration* 59.1–2). He is a man of affairs, resourceful and eloquent, reproducing the politically charged, polarized stereotype of Greeks and barbarians in his rhetorical contest with the Trojan representative (fr. 796 K.).

Odysseus' quest for political action within the context of a highly competitive public life (frr. 787–88 K.) stands in sharp contrast to Philoctetes' resigned life in Lemnos. The latter behaves like a hermit, driving the intruders away (fr. 789d.6–12 K.), and shows no interest at all in leaving his exile, to judge from his final reluctance to follow the Greeks. Accordingly, it is evidently Odysseus who seems to be making a call for action as against quietism addressed to Philoctetes, by arguing that a citizen's prosperity is dependent on the city's welfare (fr. 798 K.). This idea was embedded in contemporary political thought and is consistent with Pericles' emphasis on the interrelation between state and individual (Thucydides 2.60.2–3), as well as with his disparagement of political apathy during the second year of the Peloponnesian War (2.40.2, 2.63.2). It should be noted in passing that the polarity between active and quiet life intensified throughout the course of the War and its consequent sociopolitical crisis and was later represented in *Ion* (595–606, 625–32) and *Antiope* (frr. 183–202, 219–20 K.).

Similarly, *Dictys* contains a fragment in which an unsympathetic character (perhaps Polydectes) is disparaged for showing contempt for his own native land (fr. 347 K.). Such a reproach would have strongly appealed to the civic sensitivity of the Athenian audience, especially in the period of stress at the outbreak of the War.[10] All these political allusions are thus further suggestive of the shaping of a civic conduct and of the construction of a robust civic identity demonstrating the self-image of Athens as an imperial power. In turn, these references may shed light on the process leading to the demarcation of the Athenian 'self' from the 'other' as a means of determining Athenian self-consciousness.

The political and cultural debate on otherness was given a sophistic spin in the second half of the fifth century BC, as the inferiority of the 'other' was put into question on the basis of the opposition between nature (*physis*) and convention (*nomos*). In a famous papyrus fragment Antiphon the sophist argues in favour of the unity of mankind, asserting that the human race is fundamentally akin and expressing his belief in universal, 'natural' laws of human behaviour (DK 87B44). By undervaluing the significance of cultural differences between Greeks and foreigners and leaving no room for assertions of cultural superiority, he demonstrates the natural similarity of all human beings. Likewise, Hippias of Elis distinguished nature from convention, arguing in favour of the natural kinship of individuals wrongly divided by convention and pointing out that '*nomos*, tyrant of mankind, violates nature in many ways' (Plato *Protagoras* 337c–d). Further passages deriving especially from orators some decades later reveal that discriminations against the 'other' were often counteracted by the position that it was shameful and insensitive to exercise one's power in order to triumph over the weak.[11]

Euripidean drama evidently reflected its contemporary intellectual milieu by challenging the inferiority of socially marginalized groups on the basis of the principle that they are inferior only by convention, but equal by nature, as for instance in *Andromache* 636–38, *Ion* 854–56 and *Helen* 728–31.

A final question concerns the issue of audience's response towards Euripides' treatment of otherness in this *tetralogy*. As Ismene Lada-Richards has plausibly argued, audience-reception of tragic suffering is a complex process attained in emotional as well as intellectual terms. The fundamental source for tragic emotion is Aristotle's *Poetics*, where pity is said to be aroused by the undeserved suffering of the tragic hero (XIII 1453a4–5). The spectator's empathy is thus dependent on the sufferer's deservingness or undeservingness, as well as on the similarity of their situations, since, by attending a tragic performance revealing the fragility of human condition, the spectators fear for themselves (*Poetics* XIII 1453a5–6).

Accordingly, the tragedies of 431 BC involve vulnerable women (Medea during the first part of that play and Danaë) and disabled persons (Philoctetes) living marginalized lives in exile and wretchedness. The vulnerability of their otherness expressed with stark poignancy arouses the audience's sympathy and pity for their precariousness and for the injustice which they suffer. At the same time, their plight is likely to strike a chord in the spectators' cognitive evaluation of the world, offering insight into the frailty of human nature.

Nonetheless, it is also feasible that the very marginality of certain tragic characters representing the 'other' may give rise to an intellectual process, shaping an intensified awareness of the Athenian male citizen's sense of self. For instance, the ramifications of Medea's radical otherness as Eastern, sorceress and murderous mother, which are particularly underscored at the end of the play, would have evidently increased the gap between the Euripidean heroine and the average Athenian male spectator. This example may well be suggestive of the shifting and mixed reactions which Euripides perhaps wished to evoke through the open-endedness of this tragedy. The dramatist thus seems to create a primary channel of contact between himself and the audience through the communication of emotion as well as reasoned argument.[12]

Euripides explored the notion of otherness throughout his dramatic career. Among several Euripidean figures portrayed as representing the 'other' are Andromache and Hecabe (who are both barbarian and slaves), the suppliants seeking protection in *Heraclidae* and *Suppliant Women* and the female Choruses of Trojan captives in *Hecabe* and *Trojan Women*. Even more characters from fragmentarily preserved tragedies, such as the exiled Hypsipyle (in *Hypsipyle*) and Melanippe (in *Captive Melanippe*) or the crippled and ragged Telephus and Bellerophon (in *Telephus* and *Bellerophon* respectively), could provide articulate parallels. Yet, *Medea* and its companion tragedies constitute an early, fine and eloquent example of Euripides' systematic treatment within the same *tetralogy* of the vulnerability of otherness and its political and cultural ramifications.

Notes

1 I am grateful to David Stuttard for valuable comments. For the date of this production, information on the competing poets and the result of the dramatic contest, see the Alexandrian hypothesis on *Medea* by Aristophanes of Byzantium in Diggle (1981–94) I 90, ll. 40–43. Euripides' victories amount to five in total, according to the Byzantine encyclopaedia, Suda (ε 3695 Adler). For the vast influence of *Medea*, see for instance Mastronarde (2002) 64–70, Hall, Macintosh and Taplin (2000), McDonald (1983) Ch. 1-2.

2 Seminal works in this field include Cartledge (2002) with a rich bibliography, Loraux (1993) and Zeitlin (1996), both focusing on gender, Hall (1989) with regard to ethnicity; see also Cohen (2000) 3–12.

3 For Medea's alterity, see Sourvinou-Inwood (1997) 253–62 and Rehm (2002) 261–69; for her precarious position as a woman, see for instance Foley (2001) 257–68 and Knox (1989) 311–16.

4 Hall (1989) 51–53. See also Page (1938) xviii–xxi, Griffiths (2006) Ch. 4.

5 See Boedeker (1997), Luschnig (2007) Ch. 3, Zeitlin (1996) 348.

6 For the reconstruction of the play, see Müller (2000) 83–124, Collard (2004) 3–8, Jouan (1966) 308–17. The cited passages from *Philoctetes* and *Dictys* follow the translation by Collard and Cropp (2008).

7 For the reconstruction of the play, see Jouan and van Looy (1998–2003) II 73–92, Karamanou (2006) 134–39, 155–63 and Fig. 1, Collard and Cropp (2008) I 346–49, Karamanou (2002–2003).

8 For the plot of *Theristae*, see Pechstein (1998) 284–86 and Krumeich, Pechstein and Seidensticker (1999) 476. For the otherness of satyrs, see for instance Padgett (2000) 43–48, Lissarrague (1990) 66.

9 See Hall (1989) 6–13, 56–60, 160–65, 175–77, Zeitlin (1996) 2, Patterson (1981) Ch. 4, Davies (1978) 111–12, 118, 121.

10 For the political overtones of these tragedies, see Mastronarde (2002) 304–5, McDermott (1989) 98–106, Olson (1991) 278–83, Scodel (2009) 50–55, Müller (1997) Ch.1, Adkins (1960) 191, n. 13.

11 See Guthrie (1962–81) III 148–63, Kerferd (1981) Ch. 12, Pendrick (2002) 351–56 and for rhetorical sources, see Dover (1974) 279–83.

12 See Lada (1993) 106–09, 122–125, Easterling (1996) 173–180, Lada (1996) 406–09.

4

Staging *Medea*

Rosie Wyles

Ancient Greek tragedies were written to be performed, and it is only through careful analysis of staging that a playwright's talent for dramatic effect can be fully appreciated. Thinking about staging is not merely a question of imagining what the play looked like, when it was performed in the ancient theatre (though this is an important part of the process), it is also about understanding the stage actions, blocking, costuming/props, and scenery in relation to what had already happened on stage. (I use the term 'on stage' figuratively to mean 'in performance' – I am not implying that there was a raised stage in the fifth-century theatre. On this issue see below.)

In this chapter, I will look at the staging of *Medea* in the context of the other productions which (to use Marvin Carlson's image) 'haunted' the Athenian stage and informed the audience's interpretation of this performance. By the time Euripides produced *Medea* in 431 BC, he already had twenty-four years' experience of competing at the Dionysia – he first competed in 455 BC with a tetralogy, which included one tragedy (*The Daughters of Pelias*) related to the Medea myth. Furthermore, as the dramatic festival itself had been running for perhaps a hundred years, this offered Euripides a rich performance history to exploit in his tragedy.

When Carlson explored the concept of the 'haunted stage', he was not thinking specifically about ancient theatre.[1] But the idea that past productions can hover in the background of subsequent plays and be exploited for dramatic effect works, arguably, even better in the ancient theatre than it can on the modern stage. The cultural institution of the City (or Great) Dionysia, the annual dramatic festival in Athens, offered the ideal conditions for the development of a consciously exploited performance history.

The continuity of performance space and audience ensured that allusions to past productions could be appreciated by the audience and exploited by both tragic and comic playwrights to create particular dramatic effects. The parodies of tragedy in comedy, especially those which play on a visual element of staging, depend on exactly this performance memory on the part of the audience. The continuity of performance space (the Theatre of Dionysus) could be used to reinforce the allusion to the former production as it does, for example, in Aristophanes' *Women at the Thesmophoria* (1060–1) when Echo, a parody of a tragic character from Euripides' now fragmentary *Andromeda*, tries to prompt performance memory by saying that she had been in the same place the year before. Similarly tragedians could allude to earlier productions, even if less explicitly, to add another level of dramatic meaning to a performance. Euripides' use (or abuse?) of allusions to Aeschylus in this respect has been well established.[2] It is my suggestion, however, that the extent of performance history's potential for creating dramatic meanings within tragedies in general has not been fully explored. Certainly in the case of *Medea*, a consideration of all the potential echoes of former productions created through the staging can invite new ways of thinking about the play.

Before analysing the staging in *Medea* and the performance history, which might be significant to understanding the ancient production, it is worth establishing the basics of the performance space and the nature of the audience, both of which have been subjects of contention in scholarly debate. The iconic image of the curved stone theatre with a capacity for 17,000 spectators has been put under serious scrutiny in the last few decades.[3] In fact, a plausible case has been made for the use of wooden benches, set around a trapezoid or rectilinear performance space in the fifth-century theatre. The estimated capacity of the theatre has also been reduced to somewhere between 4,000–7,000 or, less conservatively, between 10,000–15,000 spectators.

Modern points of comparison can be helpful in imagining the scale of difference involved: it is roughly equivalent to the Royal Albert Hall (5,272 seats) in comparison to Wimbledon's Centre Court (15,000 seats). While, of course, there is a significant difference to the envisaged experience of ancient theatre depending on which estimate is accepted, at the same time even the most conservative estimate considerably outnumbers any current theatre capacity in the UK – the Edinburgh Playhouse comes closest with just over 3,000 seats, but other major theatres have a capacity of about 1,000 seats. Nonetheless, whether there were 4,000 or 15,000 spectators (and, with no way to determine the precise numbers with certainty, as a working hypothesis I assume an audience of about 10,000), the experience was a collective one and on quite a different scale from a trip to the National Theatre today.

The second point of contention is whether women were included in the audience.[4] Again the nature of the evidence makes a conclusive argument impossible. I accept the model which envisages women (citizen women included) as part of the audience sitting at the back (separately from the men). This still allows for exploration of collective male identity through the plays (since men sitting together creates a comparable experience to being an all-male audience) but is also consistent with the general inclusivity of ancient festivals.

A final point to consider is whether the performance space included a raised stage or not. On this issue, I follow the working assumption that, if there was a stage, it was low enough to enable actors to step down easily to interact with the chorus during performance.[5] The less controversial assumptions are that the Theatre of Dionysus also included a building (*skene*) with a central door at the back (from at least 458 BC), a roof that could be used in performance, entrance/exit paths on either side of the building, portable painted scenery panels, the *ekkyklema* (rolling-out platform to display a tableau from inside the building) and the *mechane* (crane).

Crying inside

While the opening of *Medea* would hardly have surprised the audience, Euripides' treatment of the entrance of the protagonist and the chorus is unusual and potentially shocking. The cries of a character from within the *skene* were not an innovation by Euripides, but Medea's sung cries from backstage at lines 96ff are unusual since they go on for an extended period of time and also interfere with the *parodos* (choral entrance song). Often cries from within are used at the point of murder or suicide (indeed Euripides offers an example of this later in *Medea*, 1270f), but these cries from Medea fall into a different category. In fact, there are only two parallels in extant tragedy: Sophocles' *Ajax* (333) and Euripides' *Bacchae* (585). *Bacchae* is a much later play but *Ajax* can be dated to the 440s. The character Ajax, then, is potentially one of the ghosts, from the performance history of the theatre, evoked by this staging. The comparison is an important one since Medea, like Ajax, will demonstrate an almost unflinching conformity to the heroic code.

The echo of this former production also brings out the exceptional situation in *Medea* in which the audience hear the voice of the protagonist before even seeing her on stage. In *Ajax* the dramatic scenario for the off-stage cries is rather different since the audience has already had a glimpse of Ajax in his interaction with Athena (91f), when the goddess calls him from the *skene* (here representing his tent) for Odysseus (and by extension the audience) to view him in his madness. As a result, his disembodied cries at line 333 cannot have had the same impact as Medea's – since the audience have already seen Ajax on stage, their suspense will only be over whether he is still mad or not when they see him next, whereas in *Medea* the audience are still waiting to see the protagonist for the first time.

The audience's first engagement with Medea is through hearing her anapaests, first despairing and then threatening, sung from inside the *skene*. The use of the anapaestic metre together with her change in mood suggests her charged emotional state and builds tension, which adds to the suspense over her entrance. By the end of the fifth century, Aeschylus had the reputation, in comedy at least (Aristophanes' *Frogs* 908–29), for creating tension by delaying the protagonist's first words in a tragedy. Here Euripides uses precisely the opposite staging tactic to create suspense – as he allows the audience to hear the protagonist's first words but not to see her on stage. The anticipation over what Aeschylus' characters were going to say must have been great, but the apprehension created by these lyric outbursts from inside the house is arguably even greater for the audience of *Medea* (who are being tantalized with the emotionally-charged sung lines of a character whom they have not yet seen on stage).

Here the allusion to Ajax is important, since in that play the audience have witnessed a mad man, as Athena calls him, appear on stage (91f). In *Medea* the memory of Ajax, evoked by the cries from within, invites the audience to consider the possibility that they will see Medea, too, raging on the stage. This possibility has already been raised by the nurse's comment (just before the off-stage cries are heard):

> I saw her just a little while ago, staring at them full of hate, smouldering like a bull, as if *they* were to blame. I know well enough her fury will not cease until she's found some victim, swooped and made her kill.

The performance memory of Ajax (who, at lines 320f, is also described as a bull and, like Medea, refuses food) raging on stage makes the possibility that Medea might behave in this way all the more real. By taking the Sophoclean performance model and inverting the order (so that the protagonist appears for the first time only *after* the off-stage cries), Euripides is able to exploit the tension that the memory of the production of *Ajax* can create.

Ajax is revealed to the audience (for the second time in the play) soon after his first off-stage cry (just twelve lines later); by contrast the audience of *Medea* have to wait through her exchange with the nurse and the *parodos*, 117 lines in total, for the protagonist to appear following her first off-stage cry. The staging of the *parodos* has an essential function in preparing for Medea's arrival. Its content is, of course, important for heightening suspense over Medea's state and whether she will appear. Even more crucially, however, its form (the way in which it is staged) establishes a sense of Medea's world before she appears on stage.

Creating chaos

As Ioanna Karamanou outlines in her essay in this present collection, *Medea* was performed as the first play in a tetralogy with the (now lost) tragedies *Philoctetes, Dictys*, and satyr-play *Theristai*. In the opening of *Medea*, Euripides was creating the atmosphere of the playworld from scratch. Through his choice of staging for the *parodos*, he is able to create the sense of chaos in Medea's world through a dramatic effect almost analogous to the literary concept of pathetic fallacy. The importance of the regularity of choral entrances to an ancient audience is made clear from the (apocryphal) anecdote about the apparently shocking effect of an Aeschylean *parodos*: 'Some say that in the performance of the *Eumenides*, he [Aeschylus] gave the chorus [of Erinyes, or Furies] a scattered entry, which so stunned the audience that children fainted and women miscarried' (*Life of Aeschylus* 9).

Though this anecdote is drawn from later sources, it records what is taken to be a plausible attitude towards the chorus on the part of the fifth-century audience. They are stunned, literally struck out of their senses, not by the costuming or masks of the Erinyes (as we might have assumed given the descriptions of them in the play) but by their scattered entry. Did this mean that Aeschylus allowed only a few to enter at a time? If so, it is difficult for us to understand what was so terrifying. The shock seems to be at the breaking of a convention of entering in ordered formation and so confounding an audience expectation. A similar surprise awaited the audience with the staging of *Medea* in which the first entrance of the protagonist would be a disembodied voice, and the chorus' entrance song would take the unusual form of a dislocated dialogue.

This playworld is characterized by the disturbance of the usual order of things. One of the ways in which Euripides conveys this is by disrupting a well-established form of entrance for the *parodos*. The appearance of a chorus at the sound of a cry or through general concern for the protagonist was conventional. In *Medea*, however, the chorus' singing of the *parodos* is actually interrupted through interjections from the nurse (chanting) on stage and Medea (singing) from off-stage so that the usual choral ode becomes a three-way exchange. It is, however, an uneven 'exchange', in which there is a distinctive disjunction created through Medea's interjections, which do not, in fact, correspond to the words of either the nurse or chorus.

Even before the *parodos*, Medea's isolation has already been suggested by
her heightened emotional state in contrast to the nurse's through the
difference in the delivery of their lines (Medea sings, while the nurse chants).
Despite the potential solidarity suggested by the chorus joining Medea
through singing too, the jarring dislocation of Medea's cries serves to
emphasize her emotional distance (already expressed spatially through her
positioning within the house) from those on stage. The uniqueness of this
parodos should not be underestimated. Nowhere else in extant tragedy does a
character interject in the *parodos* from within the *skene*. Ever since Jason's
breaking of his oaths, Medea's world has become one of disturbance and
disjunction and Euripides shows it through the disruption of the expected
form of the *parodos*. Thus the audience encounters the world of Medea, and
her sense of disruption, even before she has come on stage.

Beyond preparing for Medea's entry, the staging of the *parodos* also has
important thematic significance for the tragedy. Medea, like Clytaemnestra
in Aeschylus' *Oresteia*, has symbolic control over the house and the *parodos*
demonstrates her influence on the action on stage even from within. Later,
she will take the gifts which begin the tragedy's chain of violence from inside
the house. She remains fully in control of this space right until the end when
she chooses to leave it.

The second theme introduced by the staging of the *parodos* is the idea of
disrupted order. Euripides exploits the sense of order suggested by the formal
symmetries of his tragedy's structure and staging in order to emphasize the
disruptive force of Medea's emotion. Throughout the tragedy the audience
will experience this tension between this structural order and the emotional
forces of disorder, which finally gives way at the end of the tragedy to the
complete inversion of power between the genders (again represented
disturbingly within the formal framework of a familiar convention, the *deus
ex machina* – see below).

Enter the woman from Colchis

The anticipation for Medea's first entrance is built up both through the nurse's
anxious anticipations of how she might behave and through the unusual
tactic of off-stage cries before the protagonist's entry. The audience's
expectation, or fear, of what they might see could have been partly informed
by Sophocles' previous stage presentation of the mad Ajax (as explored
above). Another production may also have played in the audience's mind in
anticipation of Medea's entrance – it is just possible, if we accept arguments
for its new dating earlier than 428 BC, that the extant *Hippolytus* had already

been performed and if so, it offers an important point of reference for Medea's entrance.[6]

In *Hippolytus*, as in *Medea*, the chorus arrive through concern over the female protagonist, having heard that she is wasting away and refusing food (132f). It is not unreasonable, given the similarity of the preparation for the entrance of Medea and the information that the audience have been given, that, if she does not appear raging like Ajax, then they might fairly expect that she could make her first entrance, like Phaedra, lying on a stretcher (170f). Both expectations (or 'ghosts') are aroused only to be frustrated, when in the event Medea calmly enters at line 214 and makes her 'closely reasoned' speech to persuade the chorus.

The costuming of Medea is another potential surprise to the audience. Since tragedy used mythological material, the same characters were presented time and again on stage, and so elements of their costume (mask, signature props, or particular garments) developed a performance history or a 'stage life'. It was not the first time that Medea had appeared on stage and Euripides could have chosen to exploit the existing 'stage life' of this character in his production. The iconographic evidence, however, suggests that Euripides, rather than opting for continuity, chose to surprise his audience's expectations at the entrance of Medea by presenting her as a barbarian for the first time in the history of the Dionysia (in earlier myth, Medea's family came originally from Corinth).

Recent commentaries have been strangely reluctant to entertain the possibility that Medea was costumed as a barbarian. The shift in iconography following Euripides' production, however, weighs heavily in favour of her stage presentation in oriental costume. Beyond the evidence of vase paintings, it would seem characteristic of Euripides to choose to invert previous theatrical treatments, where Medea seems to have been presented as a Greek amongst barbarians, by portraying her in this play as a barbarian amongst Greeks. If making Medea a barbarian was an innovation by Euripides, then why would he not wish to exploit the available theatrical means of reinforcing this visually through costume? This could be achieved most obviously through the use of the pointed hat (*tiara*), which had already been used on stage to mark Darius as a barbarian in Aeschylus' *Persians* and which is also evidenced as stage costume on the Pronomos vase, or the *kidaris* (floppy cap), also depicted in vase painting in a theatrical context. It is possible that Medea's mask could also have been dark-skinned to indicate her origin, though the iconographic tradition tells against this. Dramatically there could have been value in alluding to previous productions through offering a visual continuity in the features of Medea's mask: the contrast of her costume would put emphasis on Euripides' innovation of making her barbarian (although the word 'barbaros' is used only four times – if the term had never before been applied to Medea, then each of these four utterances would have had a deep impact on the audience); it would also play on the dynamic of her ability to 'play the Greek' (if the audience is made constantly aware that she is a barbarian through her costume, it makes the effect of her Greek-style oratory all the more terrifying).

It is striking that in their very first reference to Medea, the chorus do not use her name but refer to her as the unhappy Colchian woman, an address which 'emphasizes her exotic origin'.[7] This acts as a form of embedded advance entrance announcement and is, I would suggest, the first hint to the audience of what she will look like. Equally striking is the choice of Medea to address the chorus not simply as women, but as Corinthian women. The very first words of both the chorus and of Medea (once on stage) draw attention to the ethnic difference between them; an emphasis which could have been visually supported by Medea's costume. The rhetoric of Medea's following speech is changed if we think that she was dressed in barbarian costume – while it risked undermining her arguments of solidarity, it would certainly drive home her play for sympathy in her point about being taken from a barbarian land and now having no home.

Possibilities for dramatic effect (and meaning) open up at every reference to ethnicity throughout the play, if Medea's origin is visually reinforced through her barbarian costume. It is especially important to the impact of the play's ending which changes considerably depending on whether Medea is dressed as a Greek or a barbarian. Some years ago now, Sourvinou-Inwood recognized this and made the very attractive suggestion that Medea could have changed her Greek-style costume for a barbarian costume at the end of the play when she is in her chariot.[8] While it is true that costume changes are usually verbally acknowledged, it may be that the *tiara* or *kidaris* was such a striking element of costume that it required no comment. It seems to me to remain an intriguing possibility and preferable to the assumption that Medea appeared costumed as a Greek throughout the play. Costuming Medea as a barbarian would have had the theatrical advantages not only of surprising the audience but also of subsequently contributing to the central thematic exploration of ethnicity in this play. The use of this costume is supported by the iconographic record and its dramatic value becomes clear when considering its potential effects in performance. It seems to me the likeliest choice of costuming.

Poisoned gifts

The poisoned gifts of a *peplos* (robe) and golden crown, brought out of the house at Medea's command at 950–1, set in motion the sequence of events

Figure 3 The Pronomos Vase, showing a *tiara* on an actor's mask, top left
(© Leemage/UIG via Getty Images)

which will end in Medea killing her children. As she puts it, on hearing about the deaths her gifts have caused: 'My friends, the die is cast. I must lose no time now, but I must kill my children and so flee this land' (1236f).

The audience's response to these significant objects could have been mediated through the performance history of the Dionysia and the previous use of both *kosmos* (finery) and poisoned gifts. In Sophocles' *Women of Trachis*, Deianeira unwittingly kills her husband (Heracles) by sending him a poisoned *peplos* (which she had mistakenly believed to be infused with a love potion). This play is likely to have been performed before *Medea* and is therefore one of the plays which may have haunted this production.

While the general context could recall this earlier play, if the casket used for the gifts in *Medea* were made visually similar to the stage prop in *Women of Trachis*, then this would reinforce the allusion. Any audience member who had watched Sophocles' play would have seen the terrible effects of a poisoned robe, as Heracles is brought on stage in agonizing pain after putting it on. The casket symbolizes very graphic suffering for these audience members by evoking memories of that performance. Their anticipation over what will happen when the gifts are taken is therefore heightened and it may even arouse an expectation of seeing the princess' suffering on stage. Even though that death is, in fact, only described, one of the effects of the allusion to Heracles' on-stage suffering is that the already graphic messenger speech in *Medea* lines 1136–230 presumably becomes even more vivid in the minds of some audience members (who have seen the equivalent staged in *Women of Trachis*).

The possible allusion to *Women of Trachis* also invites a comparison between Medea and Deianeira whose 'gentleness and innocence' have been described as 'unique among major tragic heroines'.[9] Just at the moment when Medea's destructive plan is about to gain momentum, her lack of innocence is emphasized by contrast to Deianeira.

A second layer of symbolic meaning is added to the gifts through reference to them as *kosmos* (finery). This particular term has the power to suggest both wedding and funerary contexts. In Euripidean drama, its symbolic ambiguity (as a term alluding to both contexts) is exploited to create *pathos* for young female characters who, through dressing in the finery associated with their wedding day, evoke great *pathos* for their imminent death. Seven years before the production of *Medea*, Euripides had already portrayed Alcestis, a young woman dressed up in what is explicitly described as *kosmos* (finery), dying on stage. While her suffering is not as graphic as Heracles', her finery (which should be worn for festive occasions, such as weddings) creates a deep sense of *pathos* at her death. The allusion to this dramatic exploitation of *kosmos* may have been supported by a visual similarity between the fabric of the *peplos* in *Medea* to the finery worn by Alcestis, though to evoke the symbolic meaning established in the earlier production it need not have been: the verbal reference and context would offer a sufficient signal.

The comparison between plays, which this allusion invites, is instructive since in *Medea* Euripides goes even further in exploiting the wedding motif (evoked by both the term *kosmos* and *peplos*) than he himself had in *Alcestis* or than Sophocles had in *Women of Trachis*.[10] It has long been noted that the inclusion of both a *peplos* and crown as the gifts had to be significant since one or other of them would have been sufficient for Medea's purpose. I would argue that it enables a far more poignant allusion to bridal wear since a bride in fifth-century Athens would have worn *both*. There is emphasis on the princess as a bride both at the initial bringing out of the gifts, in the subsequent choral ode, and finally when she is described putting on this *kosmos* (finery) by the messenger (e.g. 985, 1002, 1137, 1179).

The true meaning of the gifts and the *kosmos*' full symbolic potential is shown through her death: the fine garment and crown are equally appropriate to a corpse. In fact this layer of symbolic meaning for the gifts, the potential of which is already apparent to the audience from previous stage productions, is vocalized by the chorus (and confirmed for the audience) who juxtapose in a single line (985) the idea of 'dressing up as a bride' (expressed in a single word in the Greek) and being amongst the dead. The underlying ambiguity and symbolic potential of the *kosmos* is here made explicit, and the comparison to Alcestis, which it naturally invites, could only make the fate of the princess in *Medea* all the more pitiful: in *Alcestis*, the death *kosmos* will in fact attain a bridal symbolism by the end of the play whereas the opposite development in symbolism occurs here.

Dying inside

Following tragedy's convention of off-stage violence, Medea kills her children inside the *skene* at 1270f. The build-up to this moment in the play is considerable – in fact, the first hint that Medea may harm the children comes as early as line 95. It is possibly Euripides' innovation to make Medea the murderer of her own children (in other versions it is the Corinthians who kill the children). The use of off-stage cries during the murder, however, is not new (see above) but I would argue that dramatically they function quite differently from any other example in Greek tragedy.

Oresteia offers an important forerunner of off-stage cries and the murder scene of *Agamemnon* (1343–71) is neatly alluded to by Euripides here through the general pattern of the scene and the chorus' deliberation over whether they should go into the house. But in *Medea* there are significant differences to the handling of this scene, which push it beyond the limits of a conventional pattern and suggest that it would have produced a unique dramatic effect in its original tragic production.

The choice to make Medea the murderer of her children offers dramatic potential for new levels of *pathos* to the off-stage cries since in this case they can include the desperate question of how the victims can escape the attack of their own mother. Euripides could have drawn inspiration from elsewhere in *Agamemnon*, since the chorus report how Iphigenia cried out 'Father' (228) before she was gagged and sacrificed. In *Medea*, the *pathos* of this reference to the killer parent is heightened through its dramatization – the audience actually hears the child cry out.

The actual off-stage cries in Aeschylus' play at the death of Agamemnon (1343f) are also crucially different to *Medea* in two other ways. Firstly the structuring of the cries in Euripides' play is carefully manipulated to produce a unique dramatic effect: '*Medea* achieves its most powerful climax of violence by having the child's cry break into what begins and ends as a regular choral ode', which 'forces the chorus into a shockingly direct contact with the crime that it has reluctantly abetted'.[11]

The second major difference in this staging is that the victims inside actually respond to what the chorus say. This is unparalleled in extant Greek tragedy. Here it adds another aspect of the unexpected and exploits the uncomfortable tension caused by the convention of the chorus being unable to enter the *skene*. The chorus, like the audience, can do nothing to stop the dramatic actions from unfolding. The powerlessness of the spectator is emphasized to an even higher degree in this play where the convention is pushed to its limits by the response from one of the children imploring the chorus to act. This cuts short the Aeschylean-style deliberation and forces the point of the inevitability of violence in a passage which has already implicated the chorus more closely in the 'crime'.

This difference is also perhaps Euripides' means of drawing attention to his independence and ability to innovate. The hopelessness of expecting choral intervention is further underlined through their return to the singing of a final stanza which metrically corresponds to the cries of the children and completes the ode. A mother may have just killed her children (and reversed the natural order of the universe) but the formal structures of tragedy will nevertheless continue to impose an ordered world on this chaos.

The structure of the scene also offers a form of dramatic correspondence on another level. The 'extraordinary arrangement'[12] here actually mirrors the unusual structural form of the *parodos*. The cries from within, which disrupt the opening choral ode, create a sense of chaos and the emotional turmoil of

Medea's world, which will lead her to this point in the play where she murders her children. The unusualness of the chorus' opening and last ode, both of which include off-stage cries, makes the murder of the children a form of 'mirror scene' to the *parodos*. This creates a frame around the action between the *parodos*, where Medea first expresses her wish to see Jason and his bride crushed (163–5), and its effective fulfilment (albeit perhaps in a different form from what may have been initially expected).

This mirroring therefore produces a disturbing sense of closure which sits in sharp disjunction to the sense of horror at Medea's actions. Reflection on this earlier scene at this point in the play can only inspire a further sense of distance from Medea as the children's cries make it clear that it is possible to hear from inside the house and it becomes apparent that Medea's earlier failure to engage with the words of the nurse and chorus in the *parodos* was perhaps a deliberate choice.

Serpents to Athens

In the final scene of the play, Medea appears above the house in a chariot supplied by her divine grandfather Helios (as she tells us at 1321–2). This seems to have been another Euripidean innovation and her appearance is carefully managed to produce maximum surprise.

After the choral ode incorporating the children's death cries, Jason appears, ironically expressing his concern that the Corinthians might harm his children (1293f). Once Jason discovers that they have already been killed, he demands that the palace doors should be opened (1314–5). Convention would lead the audience to expect that the doors will open and the *ekkyklema* (platform) will be rolled out to show a tableau with the corpses on it. In fact, the chorus assume this too since they are the ones to suggest that Jason will see the bodies of his children if he opens the doors (1313).

Instead, of course, Medea will appear above the *skene*, lifted by the stage crane, with the corpses in her chariot. Beyond the surprise of this entrance, the staging offers significant dramatic effects, which contribute to the audience's interpretation of the play at its conclusion. Medea's spatial superiority to Jason in this final scene symbolizes the dominance and victory which she has gained over him. Assuming that the crane was already in use before *Medea* and that the appearance of gods by this method was an established convention, her appearance on the crane and her reference to the future (both Jason's death and the establishment of cult) also suggest her disturbing usurpation of the place of a tragic deity. While both of these interpretations of dramatic meaning have been established by scholars, the potential further resonances with the Athenian audience have not yet been fully explored.

Medea's spatial superiority over Jason in this final scene can also be understood to have implications beyond the world of the play. If the audience included women and they were seated at the back (i.e. higher up than the men, see above), then Medea's final appearance offers a reflection and radical reinterpretation of their positioning. Relegation to seats at the back with a worse view would presumably under normal circumstances be understood to represent and reinforce the inferiority of women's position in society. The ending of *Medea*, however, invites an interpretation which sees the women, higher up the slope, as dominant. It is, in effect, as though the chorus' ode (410f) about the reversal of order has been put into action, both on stage but also through the temporary shift in perception of the meaning to the theatre's seating arrangements which this invites. The potential identification of the connection between Medea and the women of the audience makes Jason's claim that no Greek woman would have acted as Medea had (1339f) all the more necessary. Though this potential audience resonance remains speculative (since we cannot know for sure if women were in the audience), it certainly seems worth taking into consideration.

The second possible element to resonate in a particular way with the Athenian audience is the use of serpents to draw Medea's chariot. The iconographic tradition shows Medea in a serpent-drawn chariot from c. 400 BC. It is not certain whether this was part of the original staging for Euripides' production in 431 BC since it is not referenced in the text. There seem good dramatic reasons, however, for Euripides to have included these serpents in his staging, even if he does not refer to them directly. While commentaries have considered whether it makes sense for serpents to draw Helios' chariot, and Medea's connection with serpents (as a way of explaining their inclusion),[13] the Athenian perspective has not been taken into account.

If serpents were drawing Medea's chariot, what did it mean for an Athenian audience? Serpents played a central part in Athenian ideology and were essential to the city's identity. Their patron goddess Athena was a 'serpent-mistress' *par excellence*: the association was deeply entrenched through mythology and reflected in iconography. The culturally iconic statue of Athena which stood in the Parthenon showed a snake rising up by her side. Not only that, but she could also be shown in vase painting driving a serpent-chariot.[14] So when Medea appears above the *skene* with her distinctive headgear (which, being equivalent to Athena's helmet, could even make the silhouette similar) in a chariot drawn by serpents and acting like a deity, some of the audience could have interpreted this as a disturbing travesty of Athena.

Medea does not simply usurp the role of a tragic deity by appearing in her serpent-chariot, but she appropriates the position of the patron goddess of Athens. This offers a means of visually symbolizing the disturbing implications of Aegeus' earlier agreement: Medea, a child-murdering barbarian, will come to Athens and threatens to disturb its very core. Euripides probably invented the Aegeus scene and, through it, shows his interest in making this tragedy challenging for his Athenian audience. It is striking that, at the very moment that the horror of her actions should be revealed to Jason and her cold lack of remorse is expressed, Medea should remind the audience that she is on her way to Athens. Moreover, she invites them to reflect on none other than their mythological founding hero Erechtheus (1384–5) who was represented by the city's guardian snake! All this would, I suggest, be made even more disturbing through the visual contamination of Athenian iconography, which fuses Medea's connection with serpents to their own and creates a disturbing symbolic representation of her future infiltration into their city, while the formal structuring of the end of the play (and particularly the engagement in a 'mini-*agon*') resists offering a sense of closure and reinforces this sense of anxiety for the future.

Other suggestions for the appropriateness of the serpents are possible, for example, that the chariot corresponds visually to the chains of imagery presented through the reference to earth and sky; symbolically Medea has control of both. A second interpretation of the serpent-chariot is through reference to Triptolemus, who is shown in iconography with a serpent-chariot and may already have appeared on stage with one in an earlier play of Sophocles. This point of reference would also have disturbing implications for the Athenian audience as Medea would be usurping the place of Triptolemus, who was worshipped as a hero at Eleusis.

In my view, however, the primary point of reference for an Athenian audience would be the iconographic associations of their own city. This interpretation would also be consistent with the interest Euripides later demonstrates in exploiting the dramatic potential of precisely this Athenian serpent association in his *Ion*, a play which is even more closely involved with the question of Athenian identity (had he tried it out in his *Medea* first?)

Conclusion

Medea holds a special place in the assessment of Euripides since (if we keep the traditional date for *Hippolytus*) it is his second earliest tragedy to survive. An analysis of its staging shows both the influence of what had gone before (and, if more of his plays survived, we could say even more about the ghosts of earlier productions or Euripides' 'recycling' of former stage strategies) and hints at what was to come in his later plays.

After its production in 431 BC, *Medea*, too, would become an important haunting influence not only on subsequence plays on the Medea myth (and iconographic responses to this) but also on Euripides' own work; the ending of *Hecuba*, for example, offers some very interesting (and dramatically meaningful) correspondences to *Medea*. Above all, this play's staging demonstrates Euripides' characteristic trait of presenting his audience with the unexpected.

On the semantic level, Euripides emphasizes the novelty of this play through the frequent occurrences of the Greek word for 'new' in its script.[15] I would suggest that much of the 'novelty' was felt through the experience of the production and the unexpected staging effects, particularly at the entrance of the chorus, the entrance of the protagonist, the death of the children, and the close of the play. Euripides also produces the maximum dramatic effect through an exploitation of audience expectations created through existing staging conventions or the evocation of previous productions.

Medea was clearly intended to be a challenging play for the Athenian audience and must have been a disturbing one too. The invention of the Aegeus scene and the subsequent contamination and appropriation of Athenian iconography (through the use of serpents to draw Medea's chariot) suggest a very serious warning to the Athenians (or at the very least a desire to disturb their tranquility). Whether this was a warning about an ill-wind from Corinth or the risks of trading with the Black Sea, or simply about women, is difficult to say, but what can be determined (and this play makes particularly apparent) is that staging is essential to appreciating not only the experience of an audience watching a tragedy but also their understanding of the meaning of it.[16]

Notes

1 Carlson (1994a) and (1994b).
2 Torrance (2013) and Bond (1974).
3 Csapo (2007) and Moretti (1999–2000).
4 Goldhill (1994) and Henderson (1991).
5 Taplin (1978), 11.
6 Hutchinson (2004) suggests, based on metrical arguments, that our extant *Hippolytus* may in fact be the earlier of the Euripides' two Hippolytus plays.
7 Mastronarde (2002), *ad loc.* (line 132). Mastronarde goes on to modify this statement with the comment that features in the drama downplay the importance of Medea's foreignness.

8 Sourvinou-Inwood (1997), 290–4.
9 Goward's introduction to Jebb (2004), 31.
10 Lee (2004), 272.
11 Segal (1997), 170–71.
12 Mossman (2011), note on lines 1251–92.
13 Mastronarde (2002) and Mossman (2011), 1317n. On Medea's association with serpents see Ogden (2013), 198f.
14 Athena is shown in a serpent-chariot on a vase-painting from c. 440 BC depicting the judgement of Paris (*Lexicon Iconographicum Mythologiae Classicae* s.v. Paridis iudicium 40). Although the arrangement of serpents on Athena's chariot is slightly different, Ogden (2013), 200 acknowledges that the image gives a similar impression to Medea's chariot, but he does not push the implications of this further.
15 Torrance (2013), 224.
16 The choice to set the play in Corinth, which was at this time an enemy of Athens, cannot be coincidental (I do not agree with Mossman's claim that the setting was 'apolitical'; Mossman [2011], *Introduction*). For Athens' exploration of trading with the Black Sea at this time, see Hall (1989), 35. I am grateful to David Stuttard for pointing out to me the significance that Medea, as a threatening force on her way to Athens at the end of the play, should be coming from Corinth.

5

The Nurse's Tale[*]

Ian Ruffell

The focus of most of Euripides' *Medea* is on the figure of his compelling protagonist and her interactions with Jason, Creon and Aegeus. It is not, however, how an audience is introduced to her struggles. The play is set up through the extensive use of the nurse, who introduces Medea's predicament, discusses her situation with another subordinate figure, the tutor (*paidagōgos*) of Medea's children, responds to Medea's anguished utterances within the house and provides further commentary to and with the chorus. This is not the first (and will not be the last) time that such low-status figures were used in Greek tragedy, but their role in *Medea* in setting up the plot is striking, not only for their sole occupation of the stage for such a long time and the extent to which the play is set up from their point of view, but in terms of the set of associations which they bring. In addition, the nurse shapes audience expectations and emotional response through three filters: the nurse as a faithful servant, going back at least to the *Odyssey*; the nurse as confidante of the tragic heroine, not least in relation to transgressive sexuality; and the broader run of low-status and slave characters in Greek tragedy.[1] Yet the nurse is also a moral agent in her own right and it is her tale and her moral predicament that grounds the play.

The involvement of the nurse

The nurse's contribution falls into four parts. The first part is a prologue speech, which shares common features with prologue speeches elsewhere in tragedy, not least in Euripides. Rather than a god (as in *Alcestis* or *Hippolytus*) or a central character (as in *Telephus* [438] or *Stheneboea*, or *Heraclidae* [Iolaos], or *Andromache*), the nurse is lower in status and has played less of a role in what she relates. She wishes that Medea had never met Jason, that Jason had never arrived in Colchis to win the Golden Fleece, that the *Argo* had never been built, and that Medea had never arrived in Greece with Jason. She refers to the daughters of Pelias, whom Medea induced to chop up and boil their father to death under the pretext of rejuvenating him – a topic that was the subject of one of Euripides' first set of plays, *Peliades* (*Daughters of Pelias*) – and which is the reason for their arrival in Corinth. The nurse presents Medea as wronged – dishonoured, in terms that evoke traditional heroic ideology. She tells of Medea's emotional reaction to being thrown over for the daughter of the king of Corinth, and worries about what she will actually do in response.

Following this soliloquy, Medea's children (who remain silent) and their tutor arrive. The second part of the opening scene (49–95) is a dialogue between the two slaves, with a certain amount of needling of each other. Their initial conversation is about how a good servant should behave in safeguarding their master or mistress. The conversation turns to Medea's predicament, and the tutor is induced by the nurse to reveal an overheard conversation that suggests that Creon, king of Corinth, will exile Medea and the children, and that Jason will not do anything to prevent it. Expressing concern for the children's future, the nurse urges the tutor and children inside.

At this point (96), Medea's cries are heard from inside. An exchange (in anapaestic metre) ensues, as Medea laments her lot and the nurse continues to urge the children inside and to worry about their future. As Medea's anger escalates, she wishes death on her children as well as on Jason. The nurse stresses the innocence of the children, how they have been caught up in circumstances for which they have no responsibility. Finally, the chorus enter (131). They have heard Medea's cries and have come to investigate and ask the nurse what is happening. As Medea's cries continue, turning towards oaths and imprecations, the chorus join the nurse in responding. The chorus urge the nurse inside to ensure that no harm comes to those within and to bring Medea out to talk to them. The nurse departs with doubts about the likelihood of success and of curing such passions as these.

There is some debate as to whether the nurse returns with Medea, as one of her attendants, at 214 or not. If she does return, then she remains a silent character from this point on, with the speaking actor swapping costume and mask with a mute actor. This would be an unusual technique for Euripides. If she stays, then she is brought into Medea's plan to kill her own children at 820–3, without making a reply, and she will go off at 1076, taking the children to their ultimate fate. I will return to this problem at the end of the chapter. For now, I will concentrate on her role as a speaking character.

The lost boys

The use of the nurse in the opening scenes of the play, prologue and *parodos*, is not only to articulate the back-story, but to illustrate Medea's character, to explore the predicament of her children, to situate the dispute between Medea and Jason in terms of the wider household, and to set up the audience's expectations and emotional responses. In doing so, however, the nurse draws upon and evokes a range of poetic precedents, which further colour the interpretation of her commentary. Most fundamental, perhaps, is the tradition of the nurse in heroic narratives, the kinds of heroic narratives that the nurse's account of Medea's treatment evokes. Medea, according to the nurse, has been 'dishonoured' (*ētimasmenē*, 20, 26) by Jason (*sphe... atimasas ekhei*, 'he has dishonoured her', 33). Just as her mistress will do later when she appears, the nurse evokes the categories of masculine heroic ideology. In addition to *timē*, 'honour', the language of oaths and betrayal also evokes relations between male *hērōes*.

The role of the nurse in such narratives lies elsewhere. The fundamental example is Eurycleia in the *Odyssey*. When Odysseus has returned to Ithaca alone after twenty years to find his house beset with suitors, his critical task is to discover who in his household (*oikos*) remains loyal. After staying with the swineherd Eumaeus and revealing himself to his son, he visits the palace in disguise, masquerading as a Cretan refugee, who claims to have heard of Odysseus' death. In book nineteen, he is recognised by Eurycleia, when she washes his feet and glimpses a scar that he gained on a boar hunt in his youth. Demonstrating her loyalty, she remains quiet about his identity, even to her mistress Penelope, until Odysseus finally reveals himself, when she assists them to prepare for the battle in the hall. After the battle, she identifies the disloyal servants for execution and glories in the return of her master (22.390–432). In Odysseus' restoration of his *oikos*, Eurycleia is the conspicuous example of loyalty among the female staff, loyal both to her master and mistress.

In Greek tragedy, this theme of servant loyalty is picked up in the *Oresteia*, which like the *Odyssey* is a tale of (multiple) homecoming. In the second play, *Libation Bearers*, Orestes has been exiled by Clytemnestra and has returned from Phocis to avenge the death of his father, Agamemnon. Just as Odysseus reported his own death, Orestes reports to Clytemnestra that he has died in exile. Clytemnestra sends the nurse, Cilissa, to inform Aegisthus of what is, to Clytemnestra, good news. The nurse emerges to give a despairing account of her task to the chorus (734–82). She is distraught at the supposed death of Orestes, and in her grief gives what is certainly the most detailed account of childcare in Greek tragedy (*Libation Bearers* 748–62):

I drained the dregs of misery in every respect
except for my dear Orestes, trouble dear to my heart,
who I received from his mother and brought up
along with the howls before dawn that made me wander the house at
    night,
frequent, troublesome, and no good for me
who endured them.[2] Whatever has no reason, just like an animal,
needs to be nursed (of course) according to its mood,
for a child, when still in nappies, can not speak at all,
if hunger or thirst or the need to wee takes hold.
Children's bowels, when young, are a law unto themselves.
I was the one to watch out for this, though I think I was often
misled, the cleaner of his nappies:
cleaner and nurse performed the same function.
It was with these twin roles that I received him in his father's service.

Notwithstanding perhaps, an element of humour in the juxtaposition of bodily functions with the grander plot in which it is embedded, this physical care is at the heart of the nurse's loyalty and the concomitant disgust for the current rulers of Argos. This description of a more unified *oikos*, when husband and wife were likewise concerned for their child's welfare, also sets up the immediately following confrontations, both Aegisthus' arrival to enter the palace and die and Orestes' killing of Clytemnestra. Although in both we see crucial steps towards the restoration of the household (*oikos*), the nurse's reminder of the physical experience of child-rearing sets up the physical mother-son relationship that Clytemnestra will seek to exploit at the death: baring her breast in a direct evocation of the physicality of childcare.

In both cases, the nurse is loyal to the restoration and preservation of the male *oikos* and thence the broader social order, which depends on this royal household. The distinction is that Eurycleia's interests are aligned with those of Penelope, whereas Cilissa is antipathetic to Clytemnestra. The nurse in *Medea* is operating in this tradition of the preservation of the patriarchal *oikos* and its travails, and calling attention to an even more dysfunctional household than even these two accounts. Whereas, for these other nurses, domestic considerations had political implications, the nurse in *Medea* explicitly adopts broader political language to emphasize that the *oikos* only stands where there is no dispute between husband and wife: 'this is the greatest security [*sōtēria*], when a wife does not stand in dispute with her husband' (14–15).[3] The irony, of course, is that Medea and Jason's *oikos* is far from political power: indeed, it is in order to join the royal *oikos* that Jason is in the process of dissolving his own household. The nurse's loyalties are also in conflict. Although she speaks initially of her mistress and regards Jason's acts as those of betrayal (17), she nonetheless acknowledges that he is her master (83–4), and that her loyalty is to the *oikos* as well as to her mistress, a point that the *paidagōgos* emphasizes in their dialogue (49).

The element of pathos, that can be seen particularly in Cilissa's reminiscences, but also (somewhat more grimly) in Eurycleia's meeting with the disguised Odysseus, is not lacking from the nurse in *Medea* either, but it changes focus over the course of the prologue and into the *parodos*. Initially, her concern is with Medea. The children are mentioned with her as the victims of Jason's betrayal (17), but in Medea's rage she has turned on her children: 'She detests her children and she takes no pleasure even in seeing them. I am afraid that she may devise something unprecedented' (36–7).[4] The text from this point on is contested: as transmitted, it suggests the nurse has an inkling of Medea's future actions against Jason's new bride and in-laws; what is not contested are the nurse's comments on Medea's feelings for her children and the proximity of these to the nurse's nameless fear.

As the scene progresses, attention shifts much more towards Medea's boys, who enter with their tutor. In the dialogue between the two slaves, they are mute and innocent witnesses to the situation. They are oblivious to Medea's troubles (or misdeeds: *kakōn*, 48). Whereas Cilissa was worried about young bowels (*nea nēdys*, *Libation Bearers* 757), Medea's nurse is worried about the young mind (*nea phrontis*, 48), that does not enjoy pain. The tutor reveals that he has overheard more news: that Creon plans to exile the children along with Medea (67–72). The nurse denounces Jason to his children, but hustles them inside with reassuring words. To the tutor, however, she suggests that he keep them isolated from Medea in her savage mood (80–2). Medea is clearly planning something; the nurse hopes that it will be enemies, not friends or family (*philous*) that she targets (95). As Medea is heard from the inside, the nurse reiterates both the urgency and the anxiety she feels in relation to the children. And not without reason, as Medea's focus on herself turns (as the nurse has predicted) towards others (111–18):

Medea (*Screaming*) Look what they've done to me! Look what *he's* done to me! Misery! Pain! Oh! I curse you, my children! Yes! May you die with my hatred, your mother's, you and your father! And let all the household crash down to ruin!

Nurse Oh, my mistress, so ill-used and yet so cruel! What have your boys to do with the sins of their father? Why do you hate them? My poor, poor children! I am so worried something will happen to you.

For the moment, however, further thoughts in this direction are cut off by the arrival of the chorus. Medea's exclamations, too, turn in yet another direction, towards suicide and then to the oaths that supposedly bound her and Jason, and the gods' supposed guarantee of such things.

Sexual passion

From a post-classical and modern perspective, however, stories of loss (and return) are not the kind of role for which nurses in Greek tragedy are most well-known, and the responsibility for this alternative perspective and role can largely be laid at the door of Euripides. It is all too easy to think of the nurse as something of a stock character in ancient drama, as the confidante of and go-between for women of royal rank, rather than as a slave involved in childcare (or indeed wet-nursing). To be sure, both Eurycleia and Cilissa have something of this role, too, but it is in Euripides that the nurse's ubiquity and role as a confidante and conspirator become paramount. The nurse in such a role featured also in later Sophocles (*Women of Trachis*) and then on into Senecan drama (*Medea, Phaedra, Hercules Oetaeus* and even *Octavia*).[5] It was largely from Euripides, too, that the nurse entered into the comic tradition. From there, the nurse continued into the drama of the early modern period, notably in Shakespeare's *Romeo and Juliet*. The nurse of Euripides' *Medea* is clearly related to this character type and even contributed to it. Yet to see the nurse in this company is to miss the specific connotations of the nurse in 432/1 BC.

The most obvious points of comparison for the nurse in *Medea* are the parallel characters in the series of plays that were picked upon by Aristophanes as examples of Euripides' unhealthy interest in women and in sexual morality – or immorality. In *Frogs*, the Aristophanic Aeschylus claims that Euripides' women, who explored sexual desire, such as Stheneboea and Phaedra, were notorious (1043–4). These scandalous women all belong to plays of roughly the same time as *Medea*, and all seem to have been accompanied by a nurse, who was a speaking and very active character, and deeply implicated in the psychosexual problems of their mistresses. The nurse of *Medea*, I suggest, is not only parallel to these but actively *draws upon* their example. Or, to put it another way, audience expectations would have been framed by this cluster of Euripidean interest – much more recent, indeed, than Cilissa.[6]

Thus in Euripides' *Stheneboea*, which probably dates to the 430s and is most likely earlier than *Medea*, the eponymous queen propositions her guest, the Corinthian prince, Bellerophon, and on being spurned she accuses Bellerophon of rape. Her husband, Proitos, sends Bellerophon to Lycia with a letter that urges the king of Lycia, Iobates, to have the bearer killed. Iobates does so creatively, by sending Bellerophon to hunt the Chimaera, but Bellerophon survives and returns to confront and gain revenge on Proitos and Stheneboea. The nurse's involvement comes at the beginning of the play. Bellerophon describes how the nurse is acting as a go-between, secretly urging him to accept the queen's advances, and suggesting he will gain the kingdom (fr. 661.10–14). In two fragments, the nurse describes the queen's passion for Bellerophon (frr. 664–5); in another she offers abstract reflection on the nature of sexual passion (*erōs*, fr. 663). At some point, Bellerophon seems to be attacking the nurse as *pankakistē* ('utterly wicked in every way', fr. 666) for her role in propositioning him. Euripides' *Cretans*, a play of uncertain date, but probably belonging to the earlier part of his career, presented the passion of Pasiphaë, the queen of Crete, for a bull, and her giving birth to the Minotaur (and the aftermath). The nurse here is deeply implicated in Pasiphaë's schemes, and especially in covering up the birth of the monster. She it is who is interrogated by Minos about the birth, and she is condemned to being walled up in a dungeon with her mistress, as her accomplice (*synergon*, fr. 472e.47–50).[7]

The only fully surviving (extant) play of this type is Euripides' *Hippolytus*, where the nurse plays the pivotal role. This is the second of Euripides' *Hippolytus* plays, the so-called *Hippolytus Garland-Wearer* (*Hippolytos Stephanēphoros*). It was the earlier play that was particularly notorious, as it was there that Phaedra apparently propositioned Hippolytus directly, leading her stepson to cover his head in shame – leading in turn to the play's title, *Hippolytus Veiling Himself* (*Hippolytos Kalyptomenos*). In the later play Phaedra is represented more as the innocent victim of divine disfavour (just as, in fact, Pasiphaë presented herself in *Cretans*), and the nurse must have played a correspondingly different role in the surviving *Hippolytus*, where her actions precipitate the crisis. When Phaedra is wasting away, it is the nurse who wheedles the truth of Phaedra's condition out of her, who promises certain remedies, and who betrays her mistress by approaching Hippolytus herself. In prompting Hippolytus' disgust (like Bellerophon earlier) and his tirade against women, the nurse is culpable for Phaedra's decision to hang herself. Unlike her counterpart in *Cretans*, however, she does not obviously suffer any punishment in the play.

Somewhat similar functions are offered by other female characters of a similar social status. In terms of plays earlier than *Medea*, the female slave of Euripides' *Alcestis* (438 BC) is likewise used to bring a report, like a messenger, on the state of mind and actions of her mistress, who has chosen to die on behalf of her husband (*Alcestis* 141–212). The choice of a female servant clearly plays upon the separate male and female social spheres, and the flip-side of the idealized presumption that women should be inside the house (alluded to by the tutor in his opening words to the nurse at *Medea* 50-1) is that women share secret talk to which men are generally not privy. Yet, in the case of the anonymous servant of *Alcestis*, the events she describes are private, in the sense that they are happening indoors, but they quite explicitly involve the entire household (*Alcestis* 192-3) and are no secret. The nurses in these plays of adultery and sexual transgression, however, play upon male anxieties much more strongly and can be distinguished from other anonymous servants. They take a much more prominent and active role as an agent in the plot and have a much closer, more intimate and private relationship with their mistresses, which allow for discussion and advancement of transgressive sexual relationships. It is just that sort of intimacy to which the tutor sarcastically refers (52).

Of course, any female retainer could do the job, but the choice of a nurse to fulfil this role points to a particular intimacy, whether by virtue of being the noble character's nurse in childhood, or through sharing childcare duties (as in the instance of Cilissa, earlier). The connection between the one type of intimacy, care of the product of sexual relationships, and the negotiation of another, in the managing of illicit sexual relationships, should not need spelling out, and is at a fundamentally physical level. In the nurses of these plays, it is not always clear which type of nurse is being meant. In *Hippolytus*, at least, the nurse is clearly that of Phaedra's own childhood. In other instances, the nurse may be that of the queen's children. Certainly, this latter kind of role was evoked in *Cretans*, where the nurse is interrogated by Minos as to the nature, circumstances and care of Pasiphaë's monstrous offspring. The nurse replies to him that the ones who bore it are raising it (*trephousi*, fr. 472bc.39, cf. *trophos*, 'nurse').

The nurses of this strand of Euripidean dramaturgy are clearly drawn upon in *Medea*, particularly in the prologue speech, where the nurse describes Medea's passionate relationship with Jason – being struck senseless with love (8) – and her equally passionate response to being spurned by Jason in favour of the king's daughter. These emotional responses are clearly related, and the symptoms of her loss or rejection are expressed in terms very similar to the nurse's account of Stheneboea's passion for Bellerophon. The ineffectiveness of any sensible advice in *Medea* 28-9 echoes the counterproductive attempts to gainsay *erōs* in *Stheneboea* (fr. 665), using the same verb (*nouthetoumenē*). In both cases, an obsessed gaze reflects loss (27–8, fr. 664). Both nurses relate *erōs* to poetry, albeit with different emphases: in *Stheneboea* to talk of the power of *erōs* as a teacher of poets (fr. 663), in *Medea* to comment on the lack of power of song and celebration to counter *erōs* (190–203). The characterization of sexual passion and the loss that is moved by it, as a form of sickness or illness or pain, is common to these plays (*Medea* 16, cf. 24–5; *Stheneboea* fr. 661.6; *Hippolytus* 176–361 *passim*), including the motif of self-starvation (*Medea* 24, cf. *Hipp.* 274–5).[8]

The nurse thus combines elements of both types of elderly servant, the personal confidante and the carer for infants. This combination of role reflects a certain lack of definition over the nurse's actual status and household function. Although she is routinely described as a nurse, going back as far as the ancient scholars (she is listed as a nurse in the *hypothesis* to the play), nowhere is this explicitly said by any character in the play. Although the tenderness she shows for the children would support a suggestion that she was their nurse earlier in their lives, this is not categorically stated (nor indeed would costume and mask have been decisive here). Even less supported in the text is the suggestion that she was Medea's own childhood nurse. She certainly regards Medea as her *mistress*, but unlike, for example, the nurse of Phaedra in *Hippolytus*, she never addresses Medea as *teknon* or *pai*, 'child', or refers to any experience of bringing up the younger woman.[9] Nor indeed is it ever suggested that Medea has brought the nurse with her from Colchis, as scholars have often supposed.[10] Although her loyalty is in the first instance to Medea, and she is able to comment on her feelings from a position of proximity, and while she is condemnatory of Jason, she articulates a broader loyalty to the household, and she articulates feelings that, if anything, are more for the children than for her mistress. Although she has privileged access to and sympathy for Medea, it becomes increasingly clear that she is no unthinking partisan of her mistress' interests. Rather, her intimacy with Medea is sufficiently close to gain a clear idea of her character, but sufficiently distanced to articulate anxieties about that character, and sufficiently close to others (the children) to express concern about the impact of Medea's reactions on the rest of the household.

Class and realism

Thus far, then, the nurse can be seen to be exhibiting multiple loyalties, which are potentially or actually at odds with each other. This reflects the dysfunctional (indeed, terminal) nature of the Jason–Medea household (*oikos*), but the nurse goes beyond simply expressing alternative loyalties (and sympathies). However complex these might be, such a servant would still largely be in the mould of a Cilissa from *Libation Bearers*, whose loyalty is to Agamemnon and Orestes, or Eurycleia from the *Odyssey*, whose attempts to show a certain ruthless initiative in restoring the household herself are brusquely slapped down by her returning master (*Odyssey* 19.495–502). Euripides' technique, in giving such a prominent role at the beginning of his play to a female slave, is not only to have her reflect upon the nature of her mistress, the behaviour of her master and her anxieties about the dangers that might befall the children, but also to reflect upon the nature of servitude and mastery themselves.

Indeed, Euripides presents not only one servant's reflections on these matters, but a dialogue and debate between two servants, the nurse and the tutor (*paidagōgos*). On being challenged by the tutor, the nurse argues that a good slave should feel for and give thought to the (mis)fortunes of her masters, something that is implicit in much of the earlier representations of slaves. Even when the tutor callously lets slip the news that Creon intends to exile both mother and children, the nurse refuses to wish Jason dead, even though she sees him clearly in the wrong (84); the tutor is, however, entirely cynical about human relationships. Self-interest will always triumph over concern for one's neighbour (85–8). The tutor's words question the implicit alignment of slave and master in the ideal household, but in his pragmatism he prefigures the cynicism of Jason.

While the nurse, as I have suggested, draws upon more idealizing figures, such as Eurycleia, she also questions the nature of masters and mistresses. Before the chorus' arrival and after hearing Medea's anguished cries from within the stage-building, the nurse expresses fear for the children's future. She then opens out the nature of the problem beyond the individuals and the household (119–24):

> The tempers of lords (*tyrannoi*) are terrible, and, perhaps because
> they are controlled in few ways but exercise power in many,
> they are quick to anger, with grievous results.
> Being accustomed to live on an equal basis
> is better. At any rate, I wish to
> grow old securely in humble circumstances.

The nurse here presents Medea's emotional responses to her predicament and indeed her psychological disposition as socially determined rather than being essential or natural. Medea's class position, the nurse argues, renders her liable to extreme swings of mood or behaviour. The fragility of the temperament of the individual ruler (*tyrannos*) is something that we find elsewhere in Greek tragedy, as notably already in Sophocles' *Ajax* and *Antigone*, and again in the near-contemporary *Oedipus Tyrannos* (*Oedipus the King*). And while the term *tyrannos* earlier on in Greek history is more neutral, it is a term which is heavily ideologically loaded under the Athenian democracy, which defined itself against the earlier tyranny of Peisistratus and his sons. *Antigone* (probably late 440s) is a particularly interesting parallel, as

Creon's increasingly despotic behaviour is indicated in large part through the trepidation of a low-status character, the guard, and the response from the king to the news that he brings. Yet it is a mark of how Sophocles presents such a character that modern directors are frequently inclined to play that character for laughs.

There is no such humour or potential for humour in the nurse's comments or the style in which she offers her reflections on her masters, which is no different from those of a much higher social status in tragedy. Her language makes the political connotations explicit, however, by opposing the psychology of *tyrannoi* to living on equal terms (*ep' isois*). Although she goes on to make more conventional observations about moderation and not overstepping the mark (125–30), the application of this political language to the social and personal predicament is striking, the characteristic of an individual of royal extraction generalized to the class of *tyrannoi*, who are in turn associated with those who mark themselves out from the crowd. The fact that this is coming from a slave only makes it even more pointed.

After the following three-way song/recitative dialogue between Medea, the nurse and the chorus, the chorus urge her to go indoors to pass on the goodwill of the chorus and invite Medea out. The nurse departs after another long passage of recitative, in which she expresses reservations, or more properly fear (*phobos*) as to the likelihood of persuading Medea, and then she again generalizes the situation. In a perhaps surprising set of concluding remarks, the nurse attacks earlier generations for being 'stupid and not at all wise' (*skaious ... kouden ti sophous*, 190) in supposing that grief such as Medea's might be cured by song of the sort that takes place at feasts and festivals. Here, perhaps, high-status epic traditions are particularly brought to mind.[11] The nurse's alternative is rather more robust and practical (201–4):

> But where there are feasts that
> provide a great meal, why do people make their voices shrill?
> The ample supply, close to hand, from the feast
> brings mortals joy.

Such an emphasis on the material and the bodily in this way is a common tactic in deflating the pretensions of an elite culture, although it is something more commonly associated with (often self-consciously) lower forms of cultural expression.[12] The sentiment would not be out of place in Aristophanes, for example. It is not as jarring or as potentially humorous here, because the nurse strikingly expresses this view while maintaining her tragic style and register. The point is nonetheless one that proceeds from her own background and her emphasis on humbleness and equality, which is set up in her first long passage of recitative. Focus on the power of song is simply the wrong element in such elite entertainments: what is effective in fostering human happiness is something much more fundamental, namely the food. Conversely, the wailing and lamentation that Medea has been engaging in is pointless in the context of the comfort provided by a square meal.

This was not the only time that Euripides was to give such expression to and exploration of characters from lower down the social spectrum. Indeed, his moves in *Medea* are replicated in such characters as the poor farmer, to whom Electra is married in *Electra*, or Creusa's old retainer in *Ion*, or even the eponymous character in the same play, or offstage characters whose words are reported in the assembly debate in *Orestes*, not to mention the other nurses I have mentioned above. Indeed, such presentation of social diversity is the source of well-worn humour about Euripides in Greek comedy. Thus, in the debate between Euripides and Aeschylus in Aristophanes' *Frogs*, Euripides prides himself on using characters from a range of backgrounds and giving voice to all of them, a practice upon which both Aeschylus and Dionysus seize (*Frogs* 948–52):

> **Euripides** Next, right from the very beginning I'd not have left any character idle, but I'd have the woman speak and the slave no less, and the master and the girl and the crone.
>
> **Aeschylus** Shouldn't you have died first, for daring this?
>
> **Euripides** I did it on a democratic basis.
>
> **Dionysus** Let this go: talking about *this* is no good for you.

Such diversity is one of a series of related complaints about Euripides that Aeschylus makes in that play, including presenting kings in rags (memorably spoofed already in Aristophanes' *Acharnians* with reference to Bellerophon and Telephus among others) and the shameless women, who so often have nurses in tow (*Frogs* 1007–88). The argument over those women is over the moral and didactic function of tragedy. In response to Euripides' protest, that he is representing real life and its moral complexities, Aeschylus concedes that such things as adultery and incest do happen, but that the good poet should not present them, but instead present a good moral example. In the passage I have quoted, Euripides starts off from discussing poetic technique in making maximum use of his characters and not taking refuge in formulaic or stereotyped dramaturgy, but his explanation, that he presents a socially diverse range of characters 'on a democratic basis', suggests that Aristophanes is here exploiting a similar idea of a more realistic representation of society in Euripidean tragedy. Yet the extension of *dēmokratikos* to cover both free and non-free and both men and women is quite remarkable in a context where political rights were restricted to male citizens alone. Euripides' claim does, however, resonate with the nurse in *Medea* using the language of political equality, and specifically democratic equality against *tyrannoi*, despite being a female slave. Euripides is clearly going *beyond* what is realistic in having the nurse articulate these thoughts. In other respects too, as I have noted, the nurse remains in the tragic register, and there are distinct limits to Euripidean realism: contrast the nurse of Aeschylus' *Libation Bearers* with her concern for dirty nappies.

What is also surprising in *Frogs* is Dionysus' warning Euripides off the claim of being *dēmokratikos*. The reasons for Dionysus' objection are not entirely clear. It might be because Dionysus is simply endorsing Aeschylus' position in *Frogs*, that tragedy ought to remain unambiguously in the heroic past and avoid blurring the boundary between the mythical and actual world. Such Euripidean movement as there is towards realism is, along with other elements such as extravagant displays of emotion, one of the reasons why his plays are said to be attractive to the mass of Athenians – who are characterized, further, as the lowest sort: robbers, father-beaters and burglars (*Frogs* 772–4). Going beyond what is democratic may, however, be the point at issue: an allusion to Euripides' adventurous social thinking, particularly under the influence of contemporary philosophical ('sophistic') trends. In these terms, the nurse's preference for humble equality represents a challenge as much to the restriction of the franchise and the practice of slavery as to the pretensions of the elite.[13]

To consider the effect of Euripides' technique, we can again compare Aeschylus' *Oresteia* (458 BC), where the whole trilogy is introduced through a character of similarly low status. *Agamemnon* opens with a watchman, who has been keeping vigil on the roof of the palace for the signal that shows that Troy has been captured. In addition to bemoaning the discomforts of such night-time watch-duty, he drops heavy hints that all is not right with the household (*oikos*). The queen has instructed him, a queen with a heart that plans like a man (*androboulon kear*, 11), and his nightly wish for a turnaround in the house's fortunes are on the ominous, if obscure, grounds that it is 'not administered in the best way'. The sighting of the beacon leads to joy, but before departing to let the rest of the household know, his final words are full of foreboding (*Agamemnon* 36–9):

> As for the rest, I keep quiet: a great ox has come to stand
> on my tongue. The house itself, if it acquired a voice,

would tell you very clearly. I speak readily
to those who understand; to those who do not, I forget.

In contrast to the nurse in *Medea*, the watchman in *Agamemnon* works
through hints and implications, rather than through explicit reflection. He
has much to say about the rigours of watch-duty, but the unhappy state of the
household is not spelled out. The dark and empty mutterings about the *oikos*,
however, rapidly take a fuller and rounder shape. The nurse in *Medea*, as well
as being far more developed, is much more direct and is used, like many
parallel characters in Euripides, to generalize and offer abstract reflections,
including on the status of slaves themselves. Yet for all the satire on Euripides
in Aristophanes' comedy, it may be that Aeschylus (in particular) is more
realistic, even if Euripides is more sympathetic and interested, and allows
such characters to have a moral complexity and to take a stand on the broad
issues of the play, in a way in which similar figures in Aeschylean and
Sophoclean parallels do only indirectly.

The function of the nurse

There are, then, a number of important consequences to Euripides' decision
to open his harrowing tale of the choices open to Medea through the eyes of
the nurse and to set up Medea's decision to kill her own children through the
nurse's observations about the family and their history. Through the nurse's
own words and through the expectations set up by earlier appearances of
nurses in Greek tragedy (not least Euripidean tragedy), attention is called to
four elements which combine to provide both sympathy for and apprehension
about Medea, and a worrying prospect for her children.

First, the nurse is unequivocal in assigning blame for Medea's predicament.
Jason is clearly in the wrong for abandoning Medea, described by the nurse
as an act of betrayal. The slaves are clear that Creon is taking advantage of the
situation to drive Medea out. To the extent that the nurse is sympathetic to
Medea and the tutor has a cynical view of human nature, which explains
Jason's actions, the pair of slaves anticipate the argument between Medea and
Jason, but are by no means limited to that function. The tutor's account of
self-interest could as easily extend to cover other players in the drama that
unfolds; as we have seen, the nurse's sympathy is not without its complications
and ambivalences.

Second, the nurse evokes a pathetic image of the vulnerability of young
children and even stories of their neglect (or worse) at the hands of mothers
(notably Clytemnestra). The prospect of harm coming to the children is one

that is explicitly considered by the nurse, and even though the decision of Medea to kill her own children is likely to be a Euripidean innovation, which escalates earlier accounts, the fate of the children in those pre-Euripidean accounts is cause enough for concern.[14] However much both Jason and Medea attempt to rationalize their behaviour in the play, the nurse's pathos, and the memory of other infants, is set up as a reproach to the adults from the very beginning.

Third, parallels to the nurse in Euripidean tragedy of the same period point to stories where sexual passion is the focus, a sexual passion which leads women to all kinds of transgressions. Taken together with the comments the nurse (in particular) makes about Medea's fearful rage, that brooks no gainsaying, a worrying picture emerges of a woman on the edge and not entirely in control. Together with the concerns that are expressed by the nurse about the children's safety, the prologue and *parodos* are full of ominous prospects. It is striking, then, that Medea fights on other grounds, that are anticipated by the nurse, of justice, honour and betrayal, rather than sexual passion, and implicitly rejects Jason's accusations of jealousy and sexually-motivated affront (555, 568). The connotations around the nurse in Euripidean tragedy, however, would tend to support Jason's contention. Initially an audience might be led by Medea's behaviour to reject that suggestion, but it is a lingering possibility of an uncontrollable emotional intensity, that Medea's subsequent actions will reawaken with a vengeance.

Fourth, the generalizations about social class and political power become particularly pointed in the light of what follows. It is a common observation that Medea deals in the language of traditional (especially Homeric) male heroes, in her desire to maintain honour (*timē*) and reputation (*kleos*), and an equally traditional ethic of helping friends and harming enemies. In particular, there are striking parallels between Medea and some of the heroic individualists of Sophocles, such as his Ajax.[15] This adoption of heroic language and ideology by Medea is undercut by the nurse's attribution of individual and social problems to the behaviour of an elite. The problem, from this point of view, is not so much the transgression of Medea adopting a primarily masculine language and ideology, but the problem of that ideology in general. The tutor may attribute human actions to self-interest, and thus set up Jason's cynical pragmatism, but both manifestations of elite behaviour are, for the nurse and her egalitarian outlook, problematic.

The parallels with other nurses in Euripidean tragedy also suggest a further possibility, that the nurse is ultimately, and notwithstanding the concerns she expresses for the children, the one who most helps Medea

bring about the destruction of Creon's family and the murder of her
children. This suggestion turns on whether the nurse returns with Medea at
214 and stays on stage to be brought into the plan at 820-3, and exits
with the children at 1076 to take them to their death (and perhaps fetches
Jason at 866, and is involved with the gifts for Creusa at 951). It is somewhat
difficult to reconcile these actions with the figure of the opening scene, with
her concern for the children and anxiety about Medea. Medea addresses an
attendant at 821 as being her best advisor and threatens her to stay silent,
if she is loyal (823). These qualities (and demands) would certainly suit
some of the other nurses of Euripidean tragedy, that I have discussed,
although less obviously the nurse of *Medea*.[16] Nothing the nurse has said
suggests that she is an unthinking accomplice of her mistress, nor is there
anything formally to prevent Euripides from using the nurse as a speaking
character, since there are only ever two speaking characters on stage at the
same time in the play. Yet it would be even more odd to remove the nurse
and then single out an entirely silent character as a particular confidante.
Clearly, this is something for any director to resolve in practice, but if
the nurse is to be understood as becoming a silent character, then that
silence demands interpretation, as does the failure to respond to Medea's
revelation at 823.

The effect of the mute witness to the confrontation between Medea and
Jason in the first instance serves as a reminder of the issues raised and
stances adopted by the nurse: sympathy for Medea, anxiety for the children
and a reminder of their fragility, an awareness of the depth (and origin) of
Medea's emotion and generalized reflections on the distorting and
undesirable effects of class and status. This is similar to Sophocles' *Ajax*,
where the debate over what to do with the hero, once he has committed
suicide, would seem to take place in the presence of the corpse and the
values for which it stands. Unlike Ajax, the nurse *could* intervene, so
the question remains why she does not. Here, I think, we can return to the
nurse's general reflections on class and specific reflections on Medea as a
mistress. The nurse has already on more than one occasion expressed
reluctance and even *fear* about the prospect of confronting Medea or
changing her mind (93-4, 109-10, 171-2, 184-9). If we also consider what
Medea says, then there is clearly threat here as well as the sharing of
confidences (820-3):

> Right then, go inside and fetch Jason:
> I use you in all confidential matters.
> Do not mention any of my decisions
> if you are well disposed to your owners and you are a woman.

Medea exploits both the loyalty of the nurse, as a good slave, and also female solidarity, both of which have been seen in the prologue, and the second of which is central to her discussion with the chorus. Although Medea emphasizes her habitual trust in her addressee, she does not disguise the reality of the relationship, expressed through a generalizing use of the masculine plural (*despotais*). The peremptory exclamations, commands and prohibitions of 820 and 822 do not countenance any opposition. Even the provision of being well disposed has more than a touch of implied threat. As far as the verse caesura, it would mean rather more bluntly: 'if you have sense'. Whatever the complex sympathies and loyalties of the nurse, this passage seems to point clearly to the limited options for intervention that a slave would have had.[17]

None of this is to downplay the moral problem that these lines present, or to excuse the nurse's inaction. Indeed, these lines only sharpen a question that would be implicit in the play, even if the nurse were never to reappear: what should she do given her anxieties for the children's future, and how might she have done more to safeguard them against either her mistress or any other threats? The situation in which the nurse finds herself gives the lie to the social analysis, which she essays. Even granted that the problems of the play stem in large part from different applications of elite ideology, this does not let off the hook those leading a less grand existence. The decisions facing Medea and Jason may have awful consequences, but their choices are straightforward. The nurse, while being used to construct the pathos, passion and ideology of the play, faces a much more complex set of challenges in conflicting loyalties and emotional and rational responses to the situation, and a powerless, even dangerous, social position, from which to intervene. The questions posed by the nurse's sympathy constitute the moral centre to the play and they continue to pose questions to modern audiences. As a series of high-profile cases of child deaths in the UK has recently shown, it is all too easy to stand by and do nothing.

Notes

* Thanks to Chloe Stewart for comments on a draft of this chapter.
1 On her identification as a *nurse*, see the end of the third section.
2 The text is corrupt, but the general sense is clear.
3 The term *sōtēria* could simply refer to Medea's personal safety (as suggested in Stuttard's translation), but it is often used with more general, and explicitly political, application: see, for example, Faraone (1997), 54–8. The verb *dikhostateō* is also suggestive of civil strife, *stasis*.

4 The verb *stygeō*, 'detest' or 'hate', is very strong.

5 The *Octavia*, in particular, is not generally thought to be by Seneca himself.

6 With performance of epic poetry at the Panathenaea, there is no doubt that Eurycleia would have remained current. There is some suggestion of re-performance of Aeschylus already at around this time (primarily in Aristophanes' *Acharnians* 9–11), although a recent performance of the *Oresteia* is by no means guaranteed.

7 For dates and reconstructions of the plays, including a translation, commentary and further bibliography, see Collard, Cropp and Lee (1995).

8 The theme of sickness and madness in Euripides' plays is accordingly parodied by Aristophanes in *Wasps*: see Harvey (1971).

9 See especially *Hipp.* 698; for *teknon*, see *Hipp.* 203, 223, 297, 353, 705; for *pai*, 212, 288, 473, 521. Admittedly, she addresses Hippolytus in similar terms (609–15) when trying to placate him.

10 So, for example, Allan (2002), 70 states unequivocally that the nurse is a 'fellow Colchian'; similarly, Mastronarde (2002), 43. The nearest suggestion of such a long relationship is the tutor's address of her as 'the old household possession of my mistress' (49), which is not at all decisive.

11 Mastronarde compares *Iliad* 9.186–9, Hesiod, *Theogony* 98–103, and even Demodocus in Homer, *Odyssey* Book 8.

12 See especially Bakhtin (1984).

13 For Euripides challenging or questioning social norms, see, for example, Gregory (2002) and Hall (1989). The language of *Frogs* 952, *peripatos* (literally a 'walking and talking') will later be used of Plato's and then Aristotle's philosophical practice.

14 The originality of Euripides in making Medea murder her children depends upon the date of Neophron's *Medea*, which is probably (but not certainly) fourth century. Earlier stories of Medea included death of the children, whether by accident or at the hands of others. For discussion of the mythical background, see Mastronarde (2002), 44–64.

15 See especially Bongie (1977).

16 Page (1938) on 820–1 argues that 821 and 823 point unequivocally to the nurse; Allan (2002), 63 also has the nurse as a silent character after 214. Mastronarde (2002), 43 argues that it is a mute attendant and not the nurse.

17 Accordingly, such direct intervention against an owner's actions is rare in either tragedy or comedy, major exceptions being the unnamed servant of *Helen* 1629–33 and the shenanigans of Xanthias in *Frogs*. For tragedy, see Gregory (2002), 157–60.

6

Re-evaluating Jason

James Morwood

Some ten years ago, in the *Medea* chapter of a book on Euripides,[1] I unhesitatingly joined the ranks of those who view Jason as the villain of the piece, but I none the less accorded him some audience sympathy as the orphaned father of the final scene. The structure of the play, I argued, lends ballast to this reading, with the transformation of Medea from wronged woman to horrific demon finding an echo in Jason's progress from love rat to conclusively fallen hero. A further decade of living with the tragedy has not caused any fundamental shift in my opinion; and I cannot go along with Judith's Mossman's view, advanced in her brilliant 2011 edition of the tragedy, that Jason's 'lack of self-perception' militates against any profound feeling of pity' for him in the concluding scene. On the contrary, I now feel that Euripides' concentration on the ordinary alongside the monstrous, his treatment of human beings 'as they are' (to quote Sophocles' reported dictum), can lead us to a greater understanding of his Jason. I shall certainly not be proposing, however, that to understand all is to forgive all.

While it is probably true that the most plainly 'ordinary' character in Greek tragedy is the nurse Cilissa in Aeschylus' *Libation Bearers*, who talks, for example, about having to clean the baby Orestes' nappies (759–60), the opening of *Medea* surely has the greatest claim to be ushering us into an uncompromisingly below-stairs domestic world. One slave, the Nurse, launches the play, soon to be joined by another, the Tutor, who escorts Medea's two children. The normalcy of it all is rendered the more emphatic in that they are the slaves not of a royal palace, which is the backdrop to many Greek tragedies, but of a more down-to-earth aristocratic house. The children have been taking exercise (either running or playing with hoops, 46), and the Tutor conjures up the routine of city life when he tells us of the old men of Corinth playing draughts by the spring of Peirene (68–9), on whom he has been unheroically eavesdropping (67). The sympathy shown by these two slaves towards their mistress Medea, as has often been noted, leads the audience into a ready acceptance that she has been vilely wronged. When the

Nurse discovers that the children are to be exiled with their mother, she finds her loyalty to her master Jason severely tested:

> Children, do you hear how your father is towards you? I don't wish him dead, for he is my master; but he has been caught being bad to his loved ones.
>
> 82–4

Almost halfway through the play, the king of Athens will give royal endorsement to the slaves' view of Jason's behaviour, dubbing it 'most shameful' (695).

Yet the tragedy's striking of this note of normal life, of people 'as they are' – not for nothing did the comic poets dub Euripides a greengrocer's son! – may in fact work in Jason's favour as well as Medea's. After all, he has already been stripped of his heroic carapace, the surpassing glamour with which the poet Pindar endowed him (*Pythian* 4.78–92). The glory days of the epic voyage of the *Argo*, so memorably evoked in the play's opening lines, and the winning of the Golden Fleece, are now firmly in the past. According to one ancient scholar writing on line 1387, the ship's figurehead was now in a temple of Hera, the goddess to whom it had been dedicated. Because of Medea's murderous activity in Jason's home town of Iolcus, the couple have had to flee to the harbour-city of Corinth (9–12). Here he is now adrift. His barbarian wife is no longer of any use to him; indeed, her behaviour at Iolcus has shown her to be a liability, to put it mildly. To adapt her image at line 770, he has no doubt been looking for a boat to attach his stern-cable to. Marrying the Corinthian princess, presumably with an eye on succeeding Creon as king, could provide a splendid solution (553–4). While this is not of course the actual Corinth of Euripides' lifetime, we surely find ourselves in a real world of family problems, with the go-getting husband moving on from the first wife who has seen him through the difficult times, to a new model, a dumb blonde (980) from the top family. The great hero has been transmogrified into an eminently recognizable man on the make. To acknowledge this does not, of course, render him any less contemptible, but we know the type. Some of us may well *be* the type. Certainly he is one of us.

As we find that we share our humanity with the appalling Jason, so we may grasp more fully how very different from us is the wife he is in the process of dumping. Modern readings of the play have benefited greatly from the perception that the sorceress-like elements in Medea's character are downplayed in the earlier part of the tragedy; and the Chorus of Corinthian women express solidarity with her and are only conclusively alienated late in the play when she goes off at line 1251 to kill her children. However, as early as lines 9–10, the Nurse has referred to her tricking of the daughters of Pelias into killing their father; and this devoted slave has observed that there is something animalistic about her (92, 187–8) and feels that the children should be kept clear of their mother (90–1).

When Medea first appears on stage, she is eminently reasonable, her analysis of a woman's lot, however revolutionary in its famous conclusion, proving most movingly sympathetic. Indeed, she contributes to the play's undertow of down-to-earth human experience by discussing the strains of married life and raising the subject of divorce (235–47). However, her commitment to the revenge ethic shows an uncompromisingly murderous spirit (265–6). In her determination to eliminate Jason, his new bride and her father, she wonders whether to burn down the bridal home or 'push a sharpened sword through their vitals, going in silently to the house where the bed is made for them', or – 'the way in which we women are particularly clever' – to kill them with poison (378–85). (Are we really supposed to approve of the Chorus' endorsement of her plans for triple murder in their celebrated first song, so beloved of the suffragette movement [410–45]?) 'We are women,' Medea alarmingly declares, 'most useless for good, but the cleverest contrivers of all evils' (407–9; cf. 265–6).

The figure of the woman scorned is of course as recognizable in life as in literature: hell proverbially has no fury like her. But Medea is surely parting company with humankind: she becomes something more – or less – than a woman, the fury of the proverb, in fact (1260). If it appears unreasonable to refer to the end of the play when most commentators would, I take it, agree that she has developed into a nakedly demonic force, we should remember that, when Jason at line 1342 calls her not a woman but a lioness, he is using the same word as her loyal Nurse had at line 187. From the outset we have felt with her as a victim at the same time as being aware of frightening undercurrents.

Euripides has masterfully given us an initially sympathetic figure who has the potential to grow into something monstrous – a Scylla as Jason calls her, and she does not demur (1343, 1359). In 2011 a woman called Theresa Riggi, who stabbed her three children to death for fear of losing them after her estranged husband applied for access, was said to suffer from narcissistic, paranoid and histrionic personality disorders (*The Times*, 8 March 2011). Her defending counsel asserted that 'Theresa Riggi is not evil. She is not wicked. She is not a …monster'. In a word, she is human. Compare and contrast Medea, whose understandably human feelings at the start of the play are accompanied by a deeply sinister sense of threat.

So, despite the nasty impression that we have received of Jason, we may yet feel some nervous apprehension for him when he enters at line 446. No doubt we shall be alienated further by the smugness which he projects. His dismissal of Medea's vital assistance in his epic adventures as due to Cypris (Aphrodite), goddess of love, may make more sense to an ancient Greek than it does to us. Helen uses exactly the same argument in Euripides' *Trojan Women* (946–50), and in the *Iliad* Agamemnon blames his disastrous treatment of Achilles on *Atē*, the force that blinds gods and men (19.86–138). However, Jason's words come across as a decidedly perfunctory acknowledgement of her (or even Cypris') role in the construction of his heroic identity (526–33). He may genuinely believe that his new marriage will prove of benefit to the children (562–7) (though he would be wrong to do so: stepchildren get a raw deal in Greek life as well as literature).

When he tells Medea that, in leaving a barbarian land and coming to Greece, she has encountered a legal system free from the influence of force (536–8), we may feel with Mossman that 'her experience of laws and customs has not been encouraging, since Jason has broken his oaths to her and she has in fact been exposed to force, or the threat of force, in the Creon-scene (335)' (n.536–41). However, whatever substratum of irony may be mined in Jason's words here – and at least one ancient Greek scholar was alert to it – Euripides' largely or exclusively male audience would have felt an instinctive sympathy with Jason's insistence on the superiority of Greek over barbarian civilization. Thus, when he goes on to say the following, he is surely speaking the truth:

> All the Greeks perceived you to be wise and you had a reputation; but if you were dwelling on the furthest boundaries of the world, there would not be a tale about you.
>
> 539–41

King Aegeus of Athens has heard of her wisdom and values it (677); and at this moment she has a glorious place in Greek mythology as the woman who enabled the success of the quest for the Golden Fleece. (It is she who will ensure by her later terrible actions in the tragedy that those are what she is chiefly remembered for, in large measure, of course, owing to this very play.) Without doubt Jason's behaviour is shabby, but he does not altogether disown his responsibilities. He offers Medea and her children financial support and letters of introduction to guest-friends in their exile (460–62, 610–13). Perhaps one can conclude at the end of this scene that, if Medea is not totally sympathetic, Jason is not entirely hateful.

Their second scene together is stage-managed by Medea with dazzling virtuosity. A metatheatrical dimension here shows her creating her own play and taking one of the leading roles. She knows her former husband well and can exploit his weaknesses. Like Orestes vis-à-vis Iphigenia in *Iphigenia among the Taurians* or Menelaus in dialogue with the eponymous heroine of *Helen* elsewhere in Euripides, he is not too bright. He oozes the complacent vanity of an (up till now) successful ladies' man (944–5, 1149–57), which keeps him off his guard. (Even the limited Creon realized that he was making a mistake in going along with her [316–20, 350].) Yet as he walks off, blindly trusting, to his doom, we can sympathize both with his deluded belief that a potentially horrific divorce has been amicably negotiated, and with his willingness, in letting Medea send her fatal presents, to allow her more than is wise (959–75): he even escorts the children, who carry them.

By their third scene the play has swung round. The excited feminist assertion of the Chorus' opening song has, after Medea's decision to kill her children, given way to the bleak desolation of lines 1081–115, in which they conclude that it is better not to have children at all. Medea, now appearing aloft in her crane-supported (and possibly dragon-drawn) chariot and thus usurping the elevated position conventionally reserved for the gods, has shed her humanity and hardened into a demon. The rituals she proposes to establish for her children offer little consolation (1381–3).

Jason meanwhile has lost everything. Confronted with the demonic Medea, the former epic hero now shrinks to entirely human proportions, specifically to a father whose dead children droop out of his reach from the chariot above him. In this chapter I have tried to make the best possible case for him, but the fact is that he never denies that he has broken his oaths to Medea, thus offending the Oath-god Zeus; and the most common divinely-inflicted punishment for oath-breaking was childlessness.[2] Thus Jason has suffered the appropriate penalty (802–5), and the audience may feel a sense of satisfaction that condign justice has been meted out (1352–3; cf. 1231–2). However, we also have to react to a man who challenges this sense of justice through his naked emotional agony. In the vast shipwreck of his life's esteems, he has been reduced to nothingness. It may affect our attitude that Medea has taken vengeance on Jason's impiety through what she herself freely admits is an impious murder (796, 1383). Through the totality of his defeat at the hands of this demonic creature, some glimmers of genuine audience sympathy for her victim may surely be ignited.

Notes

1   *The Plays of Euripides*, Morwood (2002).
2   See e.g. Herodotus 6.86, Andocides 1.98.

7

The Final Scene

Richard Rutherford

After infanticide, what do you do for an encore? Euripides may not have posed the question in quite these terms, but he must certainly have been conscious of the problem of how to avoid anticlimax at the end of *Medea*. In the preceding scenes the audience have witnessed Medea's agonised soliloquy, listened to the messenger recounting the horrific end of the princess and her father, and waited in suspense for the death-cries of the children within the house. A brief choral lyric precedes the concluding part of the play. How will the dramatist avoid making it a mere afterthought? His solution was bold, outrageous, theatrically stunning. Aristotle disapproved of it, but in general audiences are impressed. It is a tour-de-force, but what does it mean?

As the choral interlude ends, Jason comes dashing on, questioning the women as to the whereabouts of Medea and the children. His main concern is to protect them: he fears that the Corinthians may take revenge on them as retaliation for the deaths of their king and his daughter, destroyed by the poisoned garments the children conveyed. Jason's anxiety already shows Euripides self-consciously playing with the mythical tradition. It is clear that another version of the legend did indeed have the children die in this way. Jason does not realize the full horror of the Euripidean version: the chorus have to break the news to him that the children are already dead, and by their mother's hand. A moment later he is crying out for the doors of their house to be opened: 'Unbar the doors, slaves, now! As quickly as you can! Unlock the bolts that I might see the horror of my children's death and take my vengeance on their murderess!' (1314–16). Again the dramatist is exploiting the audience's expectations, this time with regard to theatrical convention. Demands of this kind often precede the opening of an entrance and the use of the so-called *ekkuklēma*, the 'rolling-out machine'. This was a platform or trolley device which the tragedians used in order to present events indoors to the audience: the platform was 'rolled out' with one or more actors upon it, simulating the effect of entry into the building. It was often used when the plot required the revelation of corpses or unconscious characters. Aeschylus and Sophocles had both employed it in famous episodes. Although it seems a cumbersome and artificial device to modern audiences, it was a standard feature of the Athenian theatre by the time of *Medea*.

In this play, of course, expectations are frustrated: the *ekkuklēma* is not used. Instead the doors remain closed and a voice is heard above. Medea appears on a higher level. She cannot simply have ascended to the roof of the stage building, since she refers to a vehicle, in which she is riding, together with the bodies of the children. 'My father's very father, Helios, the Sun, has given me his chariot, my tower and my defence against my enemies' (1321–2). The chariot needs to depart at the end of the scene, removing Medea and the corpses not only from Jason's view but from the audience's. This means that she can only have been moved into view of the audience on the *mēchanē*, the 'crane', which the dramatists sometimes used when they needed to represent a character in flight or descending from Olympus. Here a human character, previously earthbound, has been elevated to a higher realm, where Jason cannot touch her (1320).

This startling denouement raises a variety of questions, some of them unanswerable. Did Medea change her attire before departure: does her appearance alter as well as her position on stage? Did she, for instance, assume a more exotic or Oriental 'Colchian' dress? How much was the 'crane' adapted to its function as a chariot of the gods? Was there any attempt to represent it as drawn by flying snakes or dragons? These questions arise from the remarkable representation on the Cleveland vase, which is probably inspired by the original production of the drama. Even so, however, the goal of some critics, to recover the experience of the first presentation to an audience, is unachievable. Every director has to make decisions afresh. Still more does this apply to the shifting tones of voice and styles of delivery at each stage. Granted that the text imposes some restrictions, there is still wide scope for variation. Jason can be made more pathetic or more contemptible, Medea more vindictive or more wretched in her triumph.

If we are to understand Greek tragedy, we need to appreciate its peculiarities of form and its use of conventions which were familiar to the Athenian theatre-going public. Some of these are obvious: the constant presence of the chorus for most of the play, the long messenger speech, the alternation between speech and song. Another is the so-called *deus ex machina*, a Latinization of the Greek expression which was already used by Plato to denote a sudden and sometimes arbitrary intervention to bring a recalcitrant plot to its end. The device is typical of Euripides: it occurs in half of his extant plays (*Hippolytus, Andromache, Suppliants, Electra, Iphigenia in Tauris, Ion, Helen, Orestes, Bacchae*); it probably did occur in the original ending of the *Iphigenia at Aulis*; a novel adaptation of the technique is used at the end of the spurious *Rhesus*. Sophocles' late play *Philoctetes* also uses the device, perhaps under Euripidean influence.

As already mentioned, Aristotle had his reservations about *Medea*. He comments disapprovingly on two aspects of the plot. One complaint, obscurely expressed, relates to the Aegeus scene (unless this refers to a play of that name); he may have been disturbed at the way in which the Athenian ruler turns up out of the blue, with no preparation or causality (*Poetics* 25). If so, that would be a criticism along the same lines as his other comment, which refers specifically to the finale:

> in the representation of character as well as in the chain of actions one ought always to look for the necessary or probable sequence ... Clearly, the denouements of plots ought to arise from the representation of character, and not from a contrivance as in the *Medea* and in the episode of the flight to the ships in the *Iliad*.

> *Poetics* 15

'Contrivance' here translates *mēchanē*, and Aristotle evidently has the departure of Medea in a supernatural chariot in mind (the analogous Homeric episode also ends with a supernatural intervention: Athena intervenes to ensure that the Greek forces do not sail away). Aristotle objects to plots which do not unfold in 'a necessary and probable sequence', in which the dramatist cheats, so to speak, by introducing a completely extraneous element, something which could not have been predicted from knowledge of the initial situation or the characters. Even if we are willing to allow the tragedian more leeway than he does, we can understand the basis of the complaint, and also see why he has more difficulty with Euripides than with Sophocles in this as in other respects.

It has long been maintained that the final scene of the *Medea* is a bold exploitation of the *deus ex machina* convention. Aristotle's wording, though typically compressed, suggests that he saw it in these terms. True, Medea is not a goddess, but she is related to the sun-god Helios, and refers to this relationship in her first speech in this scene; it is he who has sent her the supernatural vehicle in which she rides. The imperious tone in which she greets Jason recalls the authority exercised by deities in scenes of this type (they often challenge the human characters and bid them cease what they are doing). Like the intervening gods in other plays, Medea predicts the future (including Jason's future demise, 1386–8), and in particular foretells the establishment of religious cult, here to commemorate her dead children (1381–3). Similarly Artemis in *Hippolytus* predicts that virgins of Troezen in time to come will cut a lock of their hair on the eve of marriage, in tribute to the virginal hero Hippolytus. Almost all the *ex machina* scenes offer parallels to this aetiologizing of future cult.

There are potential objections to this reading. One is that the crane may also be used for other purposes in tragedy. The parody in Aristophanes' *Peace* makes it likely that Euripides' *Bellerophon* used the device to represent Bellerophon riding on the winged horse Pegasus. Another reason for scepticism might be that there are no surviving cases of the *deus* scene earlier than *Medea*: can we assume that this was already established as a conventional ending for tragic drama, sufficiently so for a novel exploitation to be effective?

These objections are not decisive. *Bellerophon* probably is earlier than *Medea*, but even if it is, Bellerophon is attempting to ride to Olympus itself, a rash undertaking for which he is traditionally punished by being hurled to earth and lamed. The play would still be marking the air as the domain of the gods. *Medea* was first produced in 431 BC. We have only one play by Euripides earlier than that, but he had been a regular contender in the tragic festivals since 455. Selection and chance have conspired to give us a much fuller picture of his work in the second half of his career than in the first. But even in what we have, we see considerable continuity. Although we cannot prove it, it seems perfectly possible that he used the *deus* ending in at least some earlier plays. Such endings have been hypothesized for two plays produced in 438, *Cretans* and *Alcmaeon in Psophis*; there is no certainty, but neither can be categorically excluded. The end of *Medea* is more effective theatre if we make that assumption. The convention has become familiar, but is now subverted, even caricatured. On the other view, the novelty would be greater but also harder for the audience to comprehend; in particular, it would be hard to see why Medea could be sure of the future cult if such predictions were not an established motif in this type of scene.

If then we accept that the finale is a version of the *deus ex machina* scene, it is important to define how it differs from the norm. Several interesting aspects can lead us towards a sharper perception of the scene. It can be argued that the ways in which Medea falls short of divine status are more important than those in which she achieves it.

First, in all the surviving scenes of divine epiphany at the end of Euripidean plays, the god's first speech on appearance above the stage is the most significant, and it is always of considerable length. *Andromache* exemplifies the simplest form of this type of finale: Thetis appears and proclaims her will in a speech of forty lines, to which the leading figure on stage, Peleus, declares his grateful assent in a much shorter speech; so ends the drama, apart from a choral tailpiece, which is either spurious or routine. *Suppliants* follows the same pattern: long speech by Athena; much shorter speech of obedient submission by Theseus; choral coda. Some of the other plays involve more elaborate structures, including dialogue with the god (as in *Electra* and *Bacchae*), but the initial long speech is invariable, and what follows generally assumes the finality of the god's decrees.

In the light of this convention, the pattern of Medea's initial exchanges with Jason is remarkable. Her first speech is a mere six lines, and is followed by a tirade of invective from Jason lasting nearly thirty. Her reply, though still adopting a tone of superiority, does at any rate engage with some of his insults (1358–9). Despite her triumph, Medea does not have the complete control of the situation that a deity can command. It seems that with typical ingenuity Euripides has merged an epiphany scene with something very like an *agon*.

The abnormality of this scene continues in what follows. After Medea's second speech a passage of stichomythia ensues. This is not unknown in regular epiphany scenes, but in those the pattern is for the human characters to ask questions which the god will answer (so in *Hippolytus*, *Electra* and to some degree in *Bacchae*). Here Jason's lines are aggressive and insulting, Medea's responses contemptuous, and neither party is clearly taking the lead or asserting authority in the exchange. After this sparring match, Medea makes a longer speech, in which she predicts the commemorative cult and also Jason's death. At that point the metre shifts from trimeters to anapaests (which often phase in as the end of the play approaches), but the interlocutors revert to quick-fire insults and retailing of their wrongs. Their utterances are asymmetrical, each interrupting the other with fresh jibes. The final say is Jason's (a longer speech, 1405–14), in which he invokes Zeus and other powers as witness to Medea's crimes and his own sufferings. Despite the apparent similarities to *deus ex machina* scenes, we could not be further from the pious submission with which speakers generally accept the dispensation of the intervening god (e.g. *Iph. Taur.* 1475ff.). The reason is obvious: Medea remains a wronged wife and a murderess; she lacks the detachment as well as the power of a god.

Second, the Olympians, besides being more powerful than mankind, also know more, and are privy to the workings of fate. The gods of tragedy often make reference to divine justice or to some overarching plan. On the rare occasion when a mortal challenges a god's pronouncement, the lesser deity can disclaim responsibility, declaring that all of this is Zeus's will. Castor in *Electra* adopts this tactic when questioned by the chorus: 'fate and necessity directed her [Clytemnestra] to her destined end'; Dionysus in *Bacchae* takes a similar line: 'Long ago my father Zeus gave his consent to this.' But in our scene Medea, although she can foretell the future, has no god-given insight into the divine will. Both Jason and Medea insist that the gods are on their side, that the other is hopelessly in the wrong. The issue is highlighted at 1371–2:

Medea The gods know who it was began this conflict.

Jason Yes, and they know your mind and it repels them.

(In the Greek text each line begins with the same word, bringing out the impasse.) It recurs at a later point, where the dialogue shifts into anapaests:

Jason The furies of your children's vengeance, yes, and blood-soaked Justice damn you!

Medea There is no god or spirit hears you now, for you have broken solemn oaths and sullied all the sacred ties of friendship!

Is Medea right? If a god had stepped in to conclude the action, we might have been given clearer moral guidance (though even divine utterances on such matters can be questioned); as it is, we are left to form our own assessment. That Helios has sent her the means of escape is not decisive, for his assistance rests on a bond of kinship, mentioned several times in the drama. Earlier in the play we shared the chorus' sympathetic distress at her situation, and it was easy to condemn Jason, all the more so when he cuts so unappealing a figure in the confrontation scene; but with each successive scene Medea has become a more alarmingly complex and horrifying figure. In the finale Euripides has achieved the seemingly impossible: to make Jason deserving of our pity.

This comes out especially in the handling of the issue of physical contact, Jason's desire to touch his children:

Jason I wish so much that I could kiss my children one last time!

Medea Yes, there is so much you would say, so many kisses, yet a moment since you'd drive them out in exile.

Jason By all the gods! Let me caress their soft skin one last time!

Medea It cannot be. There is no longer any use in words.

1399–404

The lines in question possess intense pathos, and highlight the visual gap between the pair: he cannot reach up, she will not descend. They also remind us of the tenderness with which Medea herself caressed and kissed the children's soft skin while they still lived (lines 1074–5 are particularly close). Euripides seems particularly sensitive to the physical aspect of mother-child affection (there are equally touching passages in *Hecuba* and *Trojan Women*).

Some readings of *Medea* interpret the finale as showing that Medea has transcended all such emotions, that she has abandoned her humanity, become something monstrous and daemonic: that is what the startling shift to quasi-divine status signifies. But that interpretation, even if it contains some truth, has to ignore the references within this scene to Medea's own emotions. Jason tells her that her grief must be as great as his, and she does not deny it: rather, she replies that 'you cannot ridicule me now, and that soothes all my pain' (1362). Again, Jason cries out 'My sons! I love my sons so much!' and Medea responds 'Their mother loves them. You do not.' (1397: the lines do not exclude continuing affection even for the dead). These lines continue a theme which was present in the earlier scenes, when the deed was still to be done: at 1247–9, just before entering the house, Medea exhorted herself: 'For this one day forget they are your children. You will have all your life to mourn.' Here, as in the earlier monologue, other emotions conflict with and temporarily displace the grieving – hatred of Jason, bitterness at his sexual rejection, fierce pride and determination – but to deny that Medea *does* feel grief and will do so in future is to fly in the face of the text.

This argument also encourages a fresh contrast with more conventional epiphany scenes. It is not that gods in final scenes never grieve. Homer had set a strong precedent here (especially with Thetis, *mater dolorosa* of Achilles), and in *Hippolytus* the hero's patroness, Artemis, expresses her sorrow at the youth's untimely death. But that grief is strongly qualified: Artemis withdraws before the moment of death, she does not come close to Hippolytus, indeed appears to be invisible to him, and she declares that it is forbidden to her to shed a tear. The remoteness of deity is emphasized; there is austere pity but no sign of empathy. Similar points can be made about gods and revenge. The tragic gods are often vindictive (more often, indeed, than they feel pity): Aphrodite in *Hippolytus*, Athena in *Ajax* and *Trojan Women*, and above all Dionysus in *Bacchae*. Yet here too there is a sense of the vengeance being distant: the god will punish those who have offended, but this revenge is a cold-blooded affair. In the aftermath, divinity does not gloat (though Dionysus comes closest, in a play that draws god and man unusually close). Here again there is a lack of empathy: the gods seem scarcely to understand what a devastating effect their acts have on the human victims and their dependents. All this can be contrasted with the case of Medea, who even in the final scenes retains her fierce and passionate involvement with all that has taken place. Moreover, although we can find cases of gods who grieve and cases of gods who take revenge, we cannot find cases where the same deity does both, where a god does as Medea does, punishes a mortal while knowing that this will bring sorrow on himself. (Homer went some way in this direction, in portraying a Zeus who loves Troy and the Trojan leaders, but must accept the necessary destruction of Troy; but that experiment in divine complexity is a path which the tragedians do not seem to have followed.)

Finally, the normal epiphany scene naturally involves a god temporarily making an appearance before characters in the mortal world. In almost all cases the deity comes from Olympus and at the end returns there. *Bacchae* is unusual in that the god in question, Dionysus, has been resident on earth since his birth and has previously participated in the drama in human guise; but at the end he is clearly an Olympian and distances himself from the affairs of mortals as easily as his kindred gods in other plays. But neither of these scenarios suits the case of Medea. Hers is a temporary elevation, which will swiftly end – in Athens itself, as Aegeus promised and as she predicts in this very scene. Earlier in the play, the chorus of Corinthian women already expressed dismay at this outcome – how can civilized Athens shelter a polluted murderess? The Athenian audience must feel at least as much misgiving.

Medea's apotheosis, then, is no such thing. She must return to earth, and resume a human existence which will include the pain and grief that she here thrusts aside and treats as secondary to revenge. Moreover, her control over events evidently has its limits. She predicts her own arrival in Athens and her cohabitation there with Aegeus; his desire for children was made clear in the earlier scene. Perhaps she hopes for children who will replace those now dead. But her insight into the future is imperfect. Here the knowledge of the audience must be relevant, even though the future events lie outside the drama. We know less than we would like about the myths of the Athenian royal house in the fifth century, but it is clear that Aegeus, Medea and Theseus figured in a number of tragic dramas by Sophocles and Euripides. Though now lost, they evidently influenced later works such as Plutarch's *Life of Theseus*. According to the tradition, Aegeus was the father of Theseus but the boy grew up away from Athens, perhaps even unknown to his father (in Euripides' play Aegeus believes himself to be childless). On reaching adulthood, he sets out on a journey in search of his father. The mythological handbook ascribed to Apollodorus gives the following account:

> Theseus came to Athens. But Medea, being then wedded to Aegeus, plotted against him and persuaded Aegeus to beware of him as a traitor. And Aegeus, not knowing his own son, was afraid and sent him against the Marathonian bull. When Theseus had killed it, Aegeus presented to him a poison which he had received the selfsame day from Medea. But just as the draught was about to be administered to him, he gave his father the sword [which Aegeus had left with his mother], and on recognizing it,

Aegeus dashed the cup from his hands. And when Theseus was thus made known to his father and informed of the plot, he expelled Medea.

'Apollodorus', *Epitome* 1.5–6

Exactly what would happen when Medea reached Athens may not have been clear in the audience's mind, but they would naturally assume that she would cause trouble there too, and probably anticipated that she would pose a threat to Theseus, the favourite Athenian hero. Here we have yet another reason to find the end of the play disturbing in the extreme.

Greek tragedies are often open-ended. Sophocles' *Oedipus the King* ends with the hero's fate unsettled: will he remain in Thebes, or go into exile as he himself desires? The oracle must be consulted yet again. Euripides' *Iphigenia at Aulis* leaves Clytemnestra embittered: the murderous designs that will mean Agamemnon's death on his return are clearly anticipated. But when the *deus ex machina* is used, the god normally settles matters decisively: disputing parties are reconciled, subsequent events clearly marked out. In *Medea* the heroine does not possess that authority, and the opposing parties are even more antagonistic than before (here again there is a similarity to the *agon*, which rarely if ever brings those involved closer together). The gods' view of the matter is never made explicit; Jason's is obvious and extreme. The audience are thrown back on their own resources, and no member of the audience, ancient or modern, will take quite the same view of this weirdly unorthodox ending to an extraordinary play.

8

'It Wouldn't Happen Here ... Could It?' – Chorus and Collusion in Euripides' *Medea*

Sophie Mills

Perhaps more than any other extant Euripides play, *Medea* is shot through with questions, central to critical reception of Euripides since as early as his contemporaries (e.g. Aristophanes, *Thesmophoriazusae* 85, *Frogs* 1050–54): why does he portray such dangerous, transgressive women and what are these portrayals intended to suggest to his audience about the treatment of women in fifth-century Athenian society? What is the relationship between Medea's early speech to the Chorus on the unfair restrictions surrounding women (*Medea* 230–51) and the horror of what she will prove able to do when freed from those restrictions? Many scholars argue that Medea's manifesto-like speech is intended deliberately to seduce the Chorus into complicity with her plans of revenge against those who have hurt her, and that they are deceived into doing so because, like all the male characters in the play, they are no intellectual match for her – as is powerfully shown at 358–63, when their sympathy for Medea's apparently hopeless plight is rejected by a Medea who is utterly in control under an apparently vulnerable exterior. Medea herself is also often viewed as a warring mixture of elements of hero and mother, or masculine and feminine, most notably in her great monologue (1019–80), in which the ultimately heroic Medea conquers Medea the mother. Both claims can certainly be amply substantiated by Euripides' text, yet they also have the potential to diminish some of the play's more sinister aspects, which emerge from greater scepticism concerning Medea's supposed manipulation of the Chorus.

If Medea is an unusual mixture of masculine and feminine, she is formidable and dangerous, but also anomalous, so that she is easier to distance from the regular run of women. Jason himself does this at the end of the play as he tries to comprehend the process by which he has lost children, new wife and his newly-acquired status in Corinth, coming to the deeply flawed conclusion that a Greek woman would never have done this (1339–40). Of course, we know from the Chorus only some fifty lines earlier that the

Greek Ino also killed her child, and some in the audience might even remember other Greek mothers who killed their children, so he is clearly mistaken, but it is understandably easier for him to view Medea as uniquely terrible. But since he is wrong in his assessment of Greek women's powers, it is worth looking closely at the Chorus of Corinthian women in *Medea* and questioning standard interpretations of their role in the play.

The conventions of Greek tragedy mean that we should not expect complete naturalism from the Chorus, nor even expressions of entirely consistent attitudes throughout the play. The multiple functions a chorus must play mean that their perspectives can shift from scene to scene, and yet, as Greek choruses go, these are is remarkably consistent in their view of Medea. The verbal support that they offer most of her decisions means that they are implicated in everything she dares to do, even ultimately those things which they ostensibly condemn, and their acquiescence may raise disturbing questions about the nature of what a Greek woman might in fact do. I suggest that, although they are bounded by choral convention, the Chorus are actually more amenable to what Medea does than is often emphasized and that even their rejection of the infanticide is portrayed ambivalently by Euripides. This element of the play has been underemphasized for two reasons. First, Medea is supremely dominant and her individualism naturally overshadows the Chorus, but this fact need not deny them all capacity for individual response or force us to interpret them purely as pawns in Medea's game. Second, even today, a mother's murder of her children is shocking and barely imaginable: perhaps we too, like Jason, would prefer to turn Medea into a special case and separate what she does from typical or ordinary female action. But what if there is a degree of common ground and understanding between this remarkably individualistic heroine and the collective – between an abandoned and vengeful Colchian woman and fifteen ordinary Corinthian women?

'On this one day I think some spirit's clamped so many sorrows hard on Jason, but with justice' (1231–32). This is the Chorus' response to a remarkable messenger speech, which graphically describes the hideous effects on Jason's prospective bride and her father of the poisoned gifts Medea sends her. It is clear from the unfavourable reaction to him by characters such as Aegeus that Jason's behaviour has been undoubtedly unattractive and that Medea's complaints are at least up to a point legitimate. Choruses often respond to suffering individuals in ways that by the standards of modern realism seem remarkably unsympathetic (e.g. Sophocles, *Oedipus the King* 1347), but their direct and perfunctory judgement here is striking. It is, however, quite typical of the role of the Chorus in this play.

Euripides' choruses can sometimes seem rather disconnected from the action of the play as a whole (as already noted by Aristotle, *Poetics* 1456a27), and it is not always easy to see how the content of their choral songs is related to that action. In *Medea*, however, three main factors closely connect Chorus and protagonist. First, they use very few of the lengthy mythical examples that can often contribute to a sense that the choruses are detached from the immediate action of the episodes. Second, the connections between the choral songs and the actions of the protagonists are usually very clear: for example, the unfavourable stereotypes of women that Medea invokes at the end of the first episode prepare us for the first stanza of the first stasimon. Similarly, the fourth stasimon predicts what will happen to the princess (980–89) and agrees with the extended account offered by the messenger (1135–203). Connections between the stasima and the action in the episodes can even have a rather sinister effect: the end of the second stasimon laments Medea's lack of friends and a safe haven, but immediately Aegeus unexpectedly appears to offer her refuge. Third, as at 1231–32, they sometimes make direct and quite partisan moral judgements. All these factors help to create the impression that the Chorus is unusually directly connected with the events of the episodes, and their engagement intensifies their bond with their fearsome protagonist.

In tragedy, different combinations of categories of age, gender and nationality either align or alienate protagonist and chorus. Different combinations will make for a more, or less, naturally sympathetic relationship than others. Thus in Sophocles' *Antigone*, the contrast in gender and age between the Chorus and Antigone automatically creates a distance between them, that isolates her from the collective body of the Theban citizens, while there is little love lost between Clytemnestra and the Chorus in the *Agamemnon*, in spite of their shared nationality. In *Ajax* or *Philoctetes*, by contrast, the similarities in gender and nationality between Chorus and protagonist strengthen the bonds between them. Plays such as Sophocles' *Trachiniae* and Euripides' *Andromache* feature bonds between women which transcend differences of nationality, but these are more bonds of friendly sympathy than actual complicity. In Euripides' *Hippolytus*, Phaedra has a bond with the women of Troezen, whose good intentions towards the royal household are clear: they support her in attempting to uphold traditional morality against the temptations offered by the Nurse (*Hippolytus* 482–85), and though they are sworn to silence by Phaedra, they do at least try to save Hippolytus from his father's curse by urging Theseus to rescind it (891–92).

It is important to realize that Euripides had considerable freedom in choosing the identity and character of his Chorus in *Medea*, and that there is no play quite like this one, whose Chorus and protagonist frequently invoke their shared gender to further the protagonist's own interests at others' expense. Although in the play at large, Medea's nationality is given at least as much emphasis as her gender, Jason and Creon are the ones who emphasize her foreign birth, and the Chorus and Medea find common ground in their common gender. The result of this is that ordinary Corinthian women who ought, as does the Nurse (82–83), to want their city to be safe and the royal line to be continued, rather than destroyed, in fact side with Medea, and thus she carries out her vengeance. Moreover, there is something slightly off-balance in this Corinth, since the Chorus, though women and therefore not technically citizens, are in some ways analogous to the male citizen choruses so common in tragedy, but their focus is on female interests rather than those of the civic community at large.

But of course, all this does not yet address the argument invoked at the start of this chapter, that the Chorus are essentially victims of Medea's formidable powers of persuasion and superior intellect. It is certainly true that she must use all her powers to get her natural enemies, Creon and Jason, to do what she wants them to do, but the Chorus are not her enemies in the same way. If she does manipulate them at all, she is working with much more fertile ground from the start. The choral comments that precede Medea's great speech on the wrongs of women display plenty of sympathy and goodwill towards Medea (in particular 136–38, 178–83) and, while they do urge her to restrain her excessive grief, they also promise her that Zeus will have revenge (152, 157–59; cf. 208), so that she should not grieve excessively. Nothing Creon or Jason say is like this.

Moreover, the differences between the Nurse and the Chorus at the start of the play are highly significant. Both are portrayed as ordinary and non-heroic. The Nurse desires to avoid grand passions and live moderately (125–30), a wish similar to that expressed by the Chorus later (636–37), but the Nurse shows herself highly aware of Medea's destructive potential and expresses explicit loyalty to Jason as her master, whatever she thinks of his conduct (36–45, 82–83, 91–95, 102–4, 108–10, 171–72, 187–89). By contrast, although they have 'heard' (130, their very first word) the same threats from Medea that the Nurse has, the Chorus focus much more on expressing sympathy for Medea and only once express a rather vague concern for 'those inside' (182–83). In fact, they seem most concerned about the effects of Medea's grief on herself. Again, already at 205–7 they seem to share Medea's point of view by calling Jason 'the man who has betrayed her bed, her evil-hearted husband'.

Euripides suggests a depth of sympathy between the Chorus and Medea, which begins before she exercises her formidable rhetorical and intellectual skills upon them and lasts throughout the play. Medea's great speech is indeed partly designed to get her emotional and intellectual solidarity with the Chorus, so she uses the first person plural, calls them 'friends', and addresses them with notable respect throughout the play, here contrasting strongly with the rude and abrupt addresses of Creon or Jason to her (271, 446, 866), but their attitude to her before her speech suggests that they need less active encouragement to be sympathetic to her than many commentators claim. At most, we can say that she is playing to an audience already sympathetic to her, who understand (unlike Jason), both before and after her great monologue, that her anger stems not merely from sexual jealousy (though Medea does cite this motive at 263–64) but issues of status and justice (157, 208; cf. 659, 1000). She does not have to try that hard to win them over. To her request (259–63) that they should keep silence about any plan she concocts, not only does the Chorus acquiesce without any reservation, but they agree that she will have revenge on her husband 'justly', the very same word (*endikos*) that they use to characterize his loss of bride and father-in-law (1232).

Since Greek choruses are typically continuously present on stage, it is a convention of tragedy that protagonists must frequently secure their silence, but different degrees of complicity and realism in motivation are possible. Sometimes choral complicity is a natural result of a strong sympathy between the chorus and protagonist (cf. Euripides, *Hippolytus*, or Aeschylus, *Choephoroi*), while sometimes it is more perfunctory. In this play, of course, the Chorus and Medea are closely aligned with one another and it is significant, given Medea's immense interest in the sacred importance of oaths, shown most notably in the Aegeus scene (746–55; cf. 161–3), that she does not exact any formal oath from them at this point, but merely asks them to promise to keep silence. Even her formulation at this point seems quite casual – 'and so I would ask this one thing of you' – and in stark contrast to the way in which she secures Aegeus' help. Perhaps oaths are superfluous if she knows she can already trust in their extreme partiality to her.

Here, a comparison with *Hippolytus* is instructive. At *Hippolytus* lines 713–14, the Chorus swear a solemn oath by Artemis to reveal nothing of what they have heard of Phaedra's troubles, whereas Medea simply asks her Chorus to be silent. Moreover, Phaedra's Chorus promise their silence before they discover that Phaedra will attempt to preserve her good reputation as a woman by killing herself. Medea's Chorus promise silence after Medea has explicitly expressed her desire to find a means of revenge on her husband (260–67). Later in *Hippolytus*, though the Chorus keep their oath of silence, they do their best within the constraints laid on them to avert disaster by begging Theseus to take back his curse on his son (*Hippolytus* 891–92). Medea's Chorus manage to keep silence rather more effectively.

After their assent to Medea's request for silence, the very next words that the Chorus speak express sympathy for Medea's terrible plight (358), but, almost immediately, she reveals the first incarnation of her revenge, promising that this day will see the deaths of father, daughter and her husband, following this with a sustained meditation, directly addressed to the Chorus ('dear friends', *philai*, l.375, cf. 765), on exactly how she can accomplish her revenge. At the end of the monologue she appeals directly to them again in the first person plural, invoking gender solidarity in the name of evil-doing.

The Chorus say not one word against the plan, either at this time or at any other, and their next utterance is the first stasimon, in which they apparently see what Medea is about to do as something that will redress the balance of years of unfavourable utterances about women of the kind of stereotype that Medea defiantly appropriates at the end of the scene. Again, the very direct link between speech and stasimon exemplifies the way in which the integration of the choral stasima into the action of the episodes binds Chorus and protagonist unusually close. Not only does the first stasimon view Medea's projected revenge as a means of bringing honour (415, 417) to women, invoking one of Medea's greatest obsessions but, as they consistently do throughout the play, they view the situation from Medea's own perspective. They condemn Jason's misdeeds, in particular his perjury (413, 439) and dishonour of Medea (438) as a punishable offence against the gods and the whole moral order. In the last two stanzas they endorse Medea's own narrative about how she comes to be in Corinth, which conveniently omits her violent past (432–44), and elide sympathy with Medea with the violent revenge already promised. While it would be possible to see this Chorus as inspired (or duped) by Medea into expressing sentiments that support her feelings, I am not sure that this is the only explanation. They articulate the point so well that it is hard not to imagine this as a voluntary expression of thoughts that they really do espouse themselves. Through Medea's actions in avenging dishonour done to her by poisoning three people (375, 385), honour is coming to the female race, and they too will acquire honour from it (415–20). The Chorus are similarly staunch in the next episode and second stasimon, agreeing with Medea all the way about the injustice of what Jason has done. Unlike many choruses who speak with caution and deference to those in power, this Chorus even feel empowered enough to confront Jason at 577: 'even if my words now will offend you, I think you have betrayed your wife and acted all unjustly'.

When everything is at last in place for Medea's plans to come to fruition, she shares what will happen next with the Chorus, using the same language of Jason's betrayal (778) that they have endorsed all along. But then, of course, a whole new level of revenge comes into play, a revenge which Medea claims *must* be done (791). The response of the Chorus to this shocking new development seems decidedly weak: they have consistently endorsed revenge on Creon and his family and Jason too, but until now, such revenge has been in the theoretical realm because of the practical obstacles to the completion of Medea's plan. So it would have been conceivable that they might at this point have had second thoughts about the entire plan: Euripides was interested in the concept and consequences of second thoughts for his tragic characters, and indeed makes Medea question her decision at various points in the next two episodes of the play. But in fact, they simply state (812–13), 'Since you have taken us into your confidence, and as I want to help you and uphold the laws of men, I tell you: do not do it.'

It seems that they continue to accept the first part of the revenge and are opposed purely to the infanticide, but, when Medea insists that it can be no other way, they barely challenge her, merely asking her if she really will dare to kill her children and pointing out that she will be a most wretched woman if she does (816–18). Their attention, as it was at the start of the play, seems to be as much on the effect such a deed will have on Medea as on issues of morality and justice. It is true that the third stasimon, after its praise of Athenian purity, does eventually focus on the infanticide, and directly calls her deed 'sacrilege', but even here the Chorus express doubt that she will really be able to carry out the plan and even some sympathy for the pain that she will experience if she does (860–65). Again, though, there is not a single mention of the other horrific part of Medea's revenge.

It is obvious that the Chorus cannot deem the infanticide itself acceptable. Not only would doing so be far too shocking but it would also diminish the transgressive power of a truly horrific act. The Chorus of Corinthian women are needed as a background to give Medea's act its full depth of meaning, so that they can express what is right and normal (mothers should not kill their children), and horror at Medea's plan. However, they have supported the other elements of her revenge so consistently that the clarity of their condemnation of the infanticide is inevitably muddied. They have essentially condoned Medea's hideous revenge on Jason via the princess and her father, and only now tell her to go no further; but when Medea insists that the infanticide cannot be detached from the plans she has already made with their approval, they can merely say, 'But will you bring yourself to kill your children, lady?' This rather weak response makes their resistance to her plan seem more ambivalent than if they had maintained the counsel they offer at the very beginning of the play (155–57), that she should wait for Zeus to take revenge.

While it is typically the role of a chorus to be reactive to the protagonists rather than primary players in the action of the play, in the face of the horrific act that Medea is about to commit, the Chorus here seem relatively passive in their resistance and therefore complicit: while it is true that they have promised Medea to keep quiet about her plans, it is striking that they continue to be silent in the face of such horrible intentions. The chorus of *Hippolytus*, in a similar position, do at least hint to Theseus that the situation is not what he thinks it is (*Hippolytus* 891–92). After a brief expression of sorrow and general hope that the trouble go no further (*Medea* 906), the Chorus very quickly become completely pessimistic about the children's chances of survival (976–77). Such a stance has the effect of aligning them with Medea's spurious claims that she has no choice but to commit the infanticide (1013–14, cf. 814–15.)

Even when the Chorus do go on to express sympathy for Jason and the princess in the fourth stasimon, it is equivocal. First they prophesy what will happen to the princess in a relatively factual account, imagined with less horrific details than the messenger will provide later (1167ff.), though they do call her 'poor girl' and emphasize the deadliness of her new finery. However, they give a great deal of attention to the way in which the princess will be lured by the glittering, pretty items to take up her own destruction: 'The beauty of the shimmering dress, taboo in its perfection, the golden-twining coronet will so seduce her and she hug them to her.' Here they are surely representing Medea's own strategy for destroying the princess: it is the princess' beauty and charm that have captivated Jason (whatever he may claim), and Medea destroys her by using her desire to enhance that beauty with beautiful adornment. It is disturbing that the Chorus seem to echo Medea's macabre thought processes here. They address Jason as 'bridegroom of sorrows, standing proudly at the altar of the king' (990), hinting that, though he might be pitiable, his choice to abandon Medea in favour of membership of the royal house of Corinth must never be forgotten as the cause of his suffering. Lastly they turn to Medea: 'most of all, I mourn your suffering, your pain, Medea', and while they agree here with Jason's claim that sexual jealousy is leading Medea to do an unspeakable act, one of the last words in their song describes Jason as having acted 'beyond all laws of justice' (1000), throwing the blame back on him.

After the intensity of Medea's monologue of 1019–80, the Chorus' interlude from 1081–115 seems oddly calm. Whereas she is wrestling with conflict and second thoughts, they are now pondering the whole concept of parenthood. They begin by invoking female wisdom and then asserting their own claims to the Muse: in this, they are glancing back at the claims first expressed in the first stasimon, that women have been underestimated in the past. This is certainly true for Medea, and apparently also for them, since they claim, apparently as a result of their wisdom, that childless people are better off than those who have children, because children demand continual care, they can turn out good or bad, and sometimes they can be taken by the gods and sent to Hades (1096–111). Their attitude here is remarkable as they avoid any further engagement with the wrongs of what Medea is about to do and in effect support her position, albeit indirectly, since the 'helplessness and resignation' of what they say here is ultimately in tune with Medea's claims that the children simply must die (e.g. 1236 *dedoktai*, 'the die is cast', expressing fixity and finality). The Chorus invoke cases of gods killing children (1109–111), but these are just a smokescreen, since Medea is making a deliberate human choice to kill hers. In this passage, then, it seems as though the Chorus do at some level indirectly endorse the infanticide, if only by implication. For, if the trouble of having children outweighs its benefits, how essential is it after all to make sure that they live? Although many commentators are troubled by the meditation of the Chorus in this passage, considering their words irrelevant or inappropriate, if, in fact, the Chorus are a little less hostile to Medea's infanticidal plans than scholars generally prefer to think, their words at 1081–115 are all too relevant.

The moral ambivalence of the Chorus resembles that of another female Chorus several decades later, in *Bacchae*, another play of maternal infanticide, where again the Chorus are both outside the violent action of the play (which is carried out by the unseen Chorus of Theban Maenads), yet also, as strong supporters of Dionysus against the male authority figure of Pentheus, implicated in that violence, but only up to a certain point. When Agave brings in the head of her dead son and invites them to share a feast (*Bacchae* 1184), they do finally repudiate what she represents. But both choruses, in their block of female solidarity against the interests of male authority figures and their willingness to be implicated in a certain level of violence, are deeply unsettling.

Of course, the Chorus must make some attempt to avert the death of the children. In the fifth stasimon, they invoke the help of Earth and Sun to prevent Medea from carrying out her plan, and certainly at this point they express entirely appropriate horror:

> Was it all empty, then, the loving care you gave them? And all the love that they returned, was that all nothing, too? Why did you ever cross the Clashing Rocks, slate-grey Symplegades, the boundary that separates the ordered world from chaos? How can your mind be so consumed by such a holocaust of hatred, such a lust for blood? When we spill the blood of our own blood, a terrifying miasma settles, seeping from the ground, and from the sky-gods comes the curse of their anathema.

And yet ... As Medea breaks through the bonds which typically subjugate women, so Euripides pushes at the boundaries of dramatic convention in this scene, and his remarkable twist of theatrical convention here emphasizes the

ambivalence of the Chorus' ultimate response to Medea's infanticide. Though
I cannot discuss it in any detail in this chapter, a metatheatrical element is
present here: the conventional constraints on the Chorus imposed by tragedy,
in which it has limited powers of action, reflect the constraints on women's
action detailed by Medea in her early monologue. Victims murdered off-
stage typically cry out as they are being killed, whether uttering inarticulate
cries (e.g. Aeschylus, *Choephoroi* 869) or making brief factual statements that
they are being killed (e.g. Aeschylus, *Agamemnon* 1343, 1345; Euripides,
Hercules Furens 750–54; Sophocles, *Electra* 1405–18). Because of the
convention of the Chorus' continuous presence on-stage, the Chorus must
both respond to these, yet be unable actually to intervene to stop the course
of events. Thus in Aeschylus' *Agamemnon*, we hear cries and a simple
statement from Agamemnon that he is being killed, followed by a long and
impassioned set of responses from the Chorus wondering what they should
do (1348–71). While it is somewhat lacking in naturalism, there is a vigour
and engagement about their attempts to divine the best course of action: of
course, they have also had no prior knowledge of Clytemnestra's plans.

By contrast, in *Medea*, the cries of the murdered children are unusually
incorporated metrically into the Chorus' poetic utterances. This connection
paradoxically has the effect of emphasizing their inaction, because the
children, with whom they are in a horrific dialogue, unique in tragedy, are so
clear about what is going on. The convention of the absence of violence on
stage is almost broken by their explicit 'running commentary', and the
children here act as their own messengers, showing almost as much as the
preceding messenger speech does, a horrifying vision of Medea's capabilities.
When the Chorus wonder whether to enter the palace to aid the children, the
children respond directly:

Child A   Yes! By the gods, protect us!
Child B   The sword-snare closes tight.

                                                              1275–76

But the idea is abandoned at once with little motivation for its abandonment,
even though they have known for some time what Medea plans to do and the
children are directly begging them to intervene. While, of course, the terms of
their genre mean that they cannot do so, the way that Euripides has
constructed the scene draws deliberate attention to their inaction and not
only underlines that they cannot intervene but may also hint that they will
not, rendering the conventional ineffectiveness of the Chorus unusually
painful to witness and horrifying in the context of their deep bond with
Medea.

At the end of the play, Medea is adamant in the face of Jason's entreaties, while the Chorus watch their exchange silently. Their last words of substance come at 1290–92 as they lament, 'a woman's sexuality can bring many pains; it has already reaped its swathe of suffering for men', but now they have nothing to add and certainly no real comfort for Jason. Medea continues to ascribe ultimate authority for her actions to Zeus (1352), who, like the Chorus down below, makes no intervention to foil her plans.

Medea is an unusual tragic heroine in that so many of her plots come to fruition without being frustrated, and it is tempting to attribute her remarkable success to a strange and unsettling connection between heroine, Chorus and the shadowy gods. Right at the start of the play (148), the Chorus invoke Zeus, Earth and the light, while at 155ff. they assure Medea that Zeus will be on her side and punish Jason for the wrong he has done her. At 1252, again they pray to Earth and the Sun that Medea will not carry out the infanticide. While, of course, their prayer is not fulfilled, from the vantage-point of some sixty lines later, it is as though they have invoked the god whose chariot will ultimately save Medea from retribution and bring her complete triumph over Jason.

And so Medea stands at the apex of a sinister triangle with the gods and the Chorus as accessories at various levels to her murderous deeds. The motivations of the gods must remain obscure, but those of the Chorus are perhaps a little less so. Above all, they are motivated by passionate loyalty to Medea but also perhaps, in the light of the claims of the first stasimon and 1081ff., they follow their mistress' lead in seeking recompense for the way in which women are so often underestimated by men.

9

Medea's Vengeance

Hanna M. Roisman

Judging by its prominence in the extant Greek tragedies, the subject of vengeance greatly engaged the ancient playwrights and their audiences. The determination to avenge the murder of Agamemnon drives the plot of the plays on the House of Atreus (Aeschylus' *Oresteia* and Sophocles' and Euripides' *Electra*s), and the consequences of Ajax's aborted attempt to avenge an affront by Odysseus and the Atreidae drives the plot of Sophocles' eponymous play. Vengeance figures in Euripides' *Bacchae*, is an important motif in his *Hecuba*, and is the central concern of his *Medea*. The strong emotions – anger, sense of injury, and sense of righteousness – that drive acts of revenge and the intrigues and tensions involved in accomplishing them make for riveting theatre, as does the gratification of getting one's own back for an injury.

Medea differs from most of the extant revenge plays. With the exception of *Bacchae* and *Ajax*, these dramatize revenge for the murder of a family member by means of the reciprocal murder of the killer and others involved in the deed. In Euripides' *Medea*, as in the myth, the revenge is for a husband's abandonment of his wife for another woman, and the punishment is not the murder of the husband but of his prospective bride and father-in-law and of his children. There is a huge and disconcerting dys-fit between the rather banal and hardly uncommon offence and the dire punishment that is meted out. In this chapter, I will try to show how Euripides' play highlights this dys-fit in a way that forces the audience to reconsider their attitudes towards revenge.

As Burnett points out, among early Greeks, revenge 'was not a problem but a solution'.[1] It was presented in the revenge plays as a direct means of righting wrongs and obtaining justice (e.g. Aeschylus, *Eumenides* 459–69, 739–43; Sophocles, *Electra* 528–33, 580–3; Euripides, *Electra* 87–9, 1147–61). In Euripides' *Medea*, it was underpinned by the generally accepted ethos of reciprocity: of returning good for good, and harm for harm, or, as it is usually put, of helping one's friends and harming one's enemies (cf. 809). Yet revenge may also be extremely disruptive. Thus, Sophocles' *Ajax* depicts the hero's attempted vengeance as an act of madness; his *Electra* compares the avengers to the inescapable hounds who hunt down evil crimes (1385–8). In *Medea*, Euripides confronts the audience with the implications of their ethos of revenge. His strategy is first to dramatize the allure of revenge, then to dramatize its horror (764–1316), and finally to end the play on a note of uncertainty and irresolution (1317–419).

The first part of the play (1–763) leads the audience to share Medea's compelling desire for revenge and her view of it as necessary and right. To do this, Euripides made Medea a figure of identification, whose feelings and desires the audience could share. This was no simple matter. The Medea of myth was a dangerous sorceress and foreign princess from the East, whose origins alone marked her for many of the audience as a lawless, uncivilized barbarian. In her love for Jason, she deceived her father, murdered her brother, and tricked Jason's nieces into killing their father, Pelias, and cutting him into pieces. For the audience, who knew her history of family violence, her outsized revenge would have been a natural sequel in her bloody course. Yet Euripides did not depict Medea as a barbarian and evil sorceress. He made her a human woman who nonetheless inflicted a most terrible revenge that far exceeded the offence that elicited it. He turned her foreignness and her gruesome, unconstrained violence in the past in her favour; backgrounded her violent inclinations and deceitfulness to her suffering; and depicted Jason as a cad, who abandoned both her and his children, and Medea as the undisputed victim.

The play opens with the Nurse's account of all that Medea had done in her love for Jason. The Nurse frames Medea's deception of her father and grisly murder of Jason's uncle as acts motivated by love, and Jason's decision to take a new wife as an act of ingratitude for the many sacrifices Medea had made for him. She describes Medea as a good wife, who followed Jason to Iolcus and then to Corinth, and lived as a stranger in a foreign land for his sake. For this, the Nurse relates, Medea has been dishonoured and betrayed, and suffers the wrenching symptoms of unrequited love, as she refuses food, lies practically inert, and cries incessantly. The Tutor further tilts audience sympathy towards Medea by bringing the news that Creon plans to exile her and her children, and by emphasizing Jason's neglect of his house and children, whose exile he did not oppose (74–7, 84–8).

There are also ample indications in the prologue of the terrible retribution that Medea will exact. The Nurse repeatedly describes Medea as violent (e.g. 38–43) and dangerous (44) and observes that, unlike ordinary women, she will not quietly accept her mistreatment. She also voices dark forebodings about what Medea may do to her children (36–7), advises the Tutor to keep them away from her (89–95), and tells the children to beware their mother's 'savage temper and single-minded all-consuming hatred' (103–4); and we hear Medea cursing her children and declaring that she hates them (112–14). Yet, for the time being, these dark presentiments are secondary to the descriptions of Medea's suffering and the wrongs done to her. The Chorus' statement that they heard Medea's shriek from the palace gives concrete expression to her sufferings and makes them salient (131–3).

A similar foregrounding of Medea's sufferings and the wrong done her occurs in her first exchange with the Chorus. In this speech, Euripides addresses the issue of her foreign origins (214–66). The purpose of the speech is to win over the Chorus – and the outer audience – to Medea's side. In the first part, Medea lays out the affinities between herself and the Chorus of Corinthian women. As women, she tells them, they are at the same disadvantage as she in marriage, where the power resides with the man and from which women, unlike men, lack a ready escape if it doesn't work out. But, as soon as she establishes their common subjugation to men, she reminds the Chorus of their difference. While they have a country, family, and friends, she tells them, she is not only a deserted wife, spurned by her husband, but also a foreigner, without father, brother, or any relation with whom to take refuge. In ancient Athens, as the audience would have known, divorced women were returned to the protection of their father's home.[2] Since this possibility was closed to Medea, the description is designed to elicit pity for her and to bring home Jason's callousness in leaving a wife whose foreign status makes her totally dependent on him.

The speech may also be seen as a feat of rhetorical persuasion by a clever woman. In fifth-century Athens, rhetorical ability was viewed as a dangerous skill, which enabled persons to dissemble and mislead. Medea was in the company of tragic heroines such as Aeschylus' Clytemnestra and Euripides' Phaedra, whose rhetorical powers and scheming led to the violent and untimely deaths of others.[3] For the time being, though, what stands out is the Chorus' concurrence with Medea. They not only agree to her request to keep silent, should she find a way to retaliate. More importantly, they declare: 'Medea, you are right to seek your vengeance on your husband' (267–8). This statement at the close of the scene simultaneously expresses the Chorus' attitude and justifies the attitude held by the audience.

In her next encounter (271–356), Medea persuades Creon, who has just banished her and her children, to give her an extra day in Corinth – the time she will need to carry out her vengeance. We see her pretending that she hates only Jason and not Creon or his daughter, minimizing her formidable intelligence, and bending down on her knees to Creon in supplication. We hear her acquiescing to the new marriage, wishing it luck, and asserting that, although wronged, she will submit to her betters – in other words, telling Creon exactly what he wants to hear, although the sentiments are utterly unnatural under the circumstances. But even if we see her here as a manipulative woman, who abuses the ritual of supplication and exploits Creon's kindness, the primary impression is still of a badly wronged but resourceful woman, who has been forced to humiliate herself before a powerful ruler so as to obtain justice.

The Chorus continue to affirm the rightness of her revenge even after its grisly contours begin to emerge. After Creon exits, Medea chillingly tells the Chorus, and the outer audience, that she will use the day Creon granted her 'to make corpses' of Creon, Jason, and his bride (374–5), considers in detail the means she will employ and her need for an exit strategy, and vaunts her ability to do 'every form of harm'. Nonetheless, the Chorus' song at the end of this speech reiterates, in lyric form, their earlier approval. They sing of an inverted natural order, in which the springs and rivers flow backwards to their sources, men's minds breed deceit, and their oaths by the gods 'do not hold fast' (412–13).[4] The message is that revenge is needed to restore the right order. This message is reinforced in the last stanza of their song (439–41) where the Chorus tell that the sanctity of oaths has gone and shame (*aidōs*) fled to heaven. The implication is that revenge is needed to restore the power of the oath, which Jason has violated, and to return shame to its erstwhile position as a force for human morality (cf. Hesiod, *Works and Days* 180–201).

Medea's next encounter, with Jason, wins sympathy for her by showing Jason as a selfish and insensitive social climber and cad (446–626). As soon as he comes on stage, Jason blames Medea for her exile, berating her for her fierce temper and refusal quietly to accept his marriage arrangements. His expectations of more accommodating behaviour from her reflect his total lack of understanding of what he has done. So does his rejoinder to her indictment of him, in which she reminds him – and the outer audience – that she abandoned her father and had Pelias murdered by his own daughters for his sake, lets it be known that he violated the sacred oath he made when he married her, and points out that he has left her alone with nowhere to turn – even though she had two children by him, thereby fulfilling her obligations as a wife. In his reply, Jason tries to slough off his obligation of gratitude to Medea, claiming that Medea did not help him of her own accord but was forced to do so by Aphrodite, who made her fall in love with him; and, that in any case, she got back more than she gave: she lives now among Greeks and not barbarians. And she is famous amongst them. He extols his upcoming marriage as a sensible means of ensuring a good standard of living for himself, Medea, and their children, who, he claims, would have grown up on the same footing as the children of his new wife. This claim is spurious.

Stepmothers were notorious in the tragedies for mistreating their stepchildren (e.g. Euripides, *Alcestis* 313–14) – an assumption reinforced by the irritation with which Jason's bride later receives his young sons (1145–9). The weight that should be given to Jason's rebuttal is indicated by the Chorus' observations that, although he marshalled his arguments skilfully, 'I think you have betrayed your wife and acted unjustly' (578).

The first movement ends with the visit of Aegeus, the king of Athens, from whom Medea obtains a firm pledge to provide her with refuge and protection when she goes into exile. She obtains this pledge with her usual craft: by enlisting his sympathy for her plight, while hiding from him her violent intentions. The visit sets the stage for the upcoming vengeance by providing Medea with the safe exit she needs to do the deed, and by providing the outer audience with yet another affirmation, by a generous and moral ruler, that Jason and Creon behaved very badly towards Medea (695–707).

Up until this point in the play, the Chorus are solidly on Medea's side and keep her victimization firmly in the audience's awareness. They pronounce that Jason has betrayed her (205–7, 578), reiterate the sufferings she will endure in exile (357–63), and recite the sacrifices she has made for Jason and her loss of her husband and marriage (432–8). By not letting the audience forget Medea's sufferings, the Chorus, and Euripides, make sure that the audience continue to sympathize with Medea even as less commendable aspects of her character reveal themselves and the violence of her intentions becomes increasingly clear. Up until this point, the play has thus fostered the audience's belief that Medea's revenge is imperative, the right and just thing to do, and, in so doing, has made them complicit in it.

The perspective shifts radically in lines 764–1316. Up until Aegeus' exit, the revenge remains largely abstract. Although Medea tells that she will turn her victims into corpses and that she will use poison to kill Jason's bride, the details remain vague. The audience could become caught up in the rightness of the revenge, because they didn't see it in all its terrible details. In the second part of the play, the revenge is brutally concrete and graphic. In keeping with the dramatic conventions discouraging the showing of violence on stage, its fearsome brutality is conveyed in the characters' words.

The shift begins with the long speech, in which Medea reveals her plans in their entirety (764–810). In the first part of the speech, she tells of the agonizing death she plans for Jason's bride; in the second part, she reveals her intention to kill her children. Her murder of her children is not integral to the myth. Scholars debate whether it was introduced by Euripides or by the tragic poet Neophron.[5] But even if Euripides did not introduce it, he chose to make it the culmination of Medea's scheme. Why? Why did he not stop with her murder of Jason's bride and her father?

In her long justification for killing her children, Medea emphasizes her unwillingness to be laughed at by her enemies (797). To the modern Western reader, this is a barely comprehensible motive for any violent act, to say nothing of killing one's own children. For Medea, however, it is a compelling motive, which she had stated earlier (398, 404–5) and repeats subsequently (1049–50, 1354–7, 1362). It would also have resonated with Euripides' audience. The abhorrence of being laughed at was anchored in Homeric values, which, though undergoing reconsideration at the time, were still held in esteem when the play was produced. In this value system, being mocked was tantamount to being dishonoured.

In her speech, Medea presents killing the children as the only way she can ensure that neither she nor they will suffer the dishonour of being laughed at. She presents it as essential to completing her revenge and, to the Chorus a few lines later, as 'what will hurt my husband most' (817). If she does not do it, she implies, she will be viewed as weak and pliable: 'Let no-one under-rate me, think me weak, a woman pliable and tamed, but rather know me to be otherwise, a terrifying scourge to lash my enemies, a gentle balm for family and friends' (807–9). It is the way, she goes on to say, to 'live a life of greatest glory' (810). Although Medea decides to kill the children only after her meeting with Aegeus brings home the great importance of children to a man, their murder becomes in the play the logical culmination of the principle of returning harm for harm, the means by which the individual wins respect. By adding infanticide to Medea's retaliation, Euripides thus takes the logic of revenge to its extremity, forcing the audience to see the full implications of their conviction that revenge is the right response to an affront.

Yet infanticide is a horrific deed. Children are innocent and vulnerable and should be protected. It is even worse when the killer is the parent. For the first time in the play, the Chorus withdraw their support of Medea's vengeance, urging her to abide by 'the laws of men' and 'not do' this thing (811–13). Their phrasing recalls their earlier branding of Jason's conduct as an inversion of the laws of nature. Now it is Medea, whom they present as violating a basic law, thereby suggesting that she is no better than those who victimize her. In their next song (824–65), they go on to tell her she will be polluted (850) by killing her children and once again beg her not to do so. The audience, for their part, do not need the Chorus' signal to recoil in horror as Medea unfolds her plan or to cringe as she remains adamant in face of the Chorus' pleadings (811–18).

The knowledge that Medea is planning to kill her children leads to a shift in perspective both on her and on the rightness of vengeance. To be sure, the play continues to depict Medea as a human and suffering figure. The Chorus express pity for her in the same breath as they tell that she will murder her children (996–7). In what is known as her 'great monologue' before the deed (1021–80), Medea's planned infanticide is presented as a wrenching decision which will cause her tremendous pain and deprivation. Medea, the human mother, is painfully aware that in depriving Jason of his children, she too will suffer: she will not see them grow up or wed, she will not have them to care for her in her old age or to perform her burial rites. These thoughts, along with the realization of how much she will miss the children – the sweetness of their smiles, the brightness of their eyes – almost bring her to renounce her plans (1048). In the end, though, her abhorrence of being laughed at and her fear that she will be seen as weak if she does not exact the maximum punishment, overcome her motherly feelings (1049–50) and she decides to go ahead with the infanticide. In its depiction of Medea's agonized inner conflict, the play refuses to present her as a monster from whom the audience – who, too, hold honour a core value – can readily distance themselves.

At the same time, with Medea's announcement of her plans to kill her children, the Nurse's dark forebodings in the prologue become imminent, and background becomes foreground. The Nurse had spoken of Medea's inordinate rage. Now Medea herself admits, at the end of the speech in which she struggles with conflicting impulses: 'but my wrath overbears my calculation, wrath that brings mortal men their gravest hurt' (1079–80).[6] By foregrounding her anger, the play points to the destructive passion which overrides all other emotions and drives Medea's vengeance, any vengeance, at least as much as her fear of being laughed at.

There is also a reappraisal of Medea's guile. In the scene in which Medea persuades Jason to enable her to send their children to his bride with the 'peace offering' of the deadly robe (866–975), her guile may be seen as considerably more sinister than it had been in the earlier scene with Creon. Much as she had tricked Creon, Medea tricks Jason into abetting her revenge by telling him what he wants to hear. She pretends to regret her previous anger and declares that she now sees the wisdom of his new marriage and the foolishness of her initial rejection of it. But now that the audience have heard her plans for her children, will they still judge her deceit as a legitimate instrument used by a wronged and powerless woman to obtain justice? Or will they see it as hard-hearted, immoral behaviour towards her innocent and vulnerable boys?

Most of all, the dramatization of her vengeance prevents the audience from being as sanguine about it as they had been in the first part of the play. Since violence was not usually shown on stage in the ancient Greek tragedies, the dramatization is effected verbally. It begins with the Messenger's detailed and vivid description of the deaths of Jason's bride and her father. For the first time in the play, Jason's bride is described at some length. The Messenger begins by telling how she is irritated with the children but greedy for their gift. He describes her donning the robe and golden crown, arranging her hair and admiring herself in the mirror, and walking about the room overjoyed with the gift. The description is not a flattering one. It shows her as vain and self-absorbed. But it also gives her a dimension, which she had not previously had, and makes her visible to the mind's eye, which she had not previously been. Thus, when the Messenger goes on to relate the details of her excruciating death, we see the revenge not as an abstract act done to an unknown person, but as a concrete act of horrendous violence inflicted on a human being with her own personality. Against this background, the detailed description of the poison taking its effect – the colour of her face changing, her staggering backwards, running with trembling legs, her falling onto a chair, her blinking and groaning, the fire devouring her hair and skin, her futile efforts to tear off the garments, her falling to the ground, the oozing of her blood intermingled with the fire, and the melting of the flesh from her bones – is truly appalling. The horror is further accentuated by the shrieking of her servant who witnessed the event and the terror that those present feel of touching her corpse. The Messenger continues with a description of the death of Creon, who had been summoned to the aid of his daughter. He, too, becomes a person with whom one can sympathize. He is shown not as the exiling ruler, but as a loving father who throws himself on his daughter's corpse, eager to die along with her. Although at the end of the description the Chorus state that Jason deserved the evils that befell him, they voice pity for the 'poor princess, poor Creon's child' (1233–5),[7] who, they imply, did not deserve the horrible death, that was meted out to her. By humanizing Medea's victims, the Messenger's speech and the hair-raising account of their deaths make the audience rethink the rightness of revenge.

Medea's murder of her children is dramatized in a less graphic and more succinct manner. Yet it is also presented so as to arouse the maximum horror. It is preceded by Medea's statement of her intention to kill her children by her own hand, her injunction to herself to arm her heart in steel, and her entrance into the house, where they are staying. While Medea is in the house, the Chorus pray, to no avail, to Earth and Helios to prevent her from killing her own flesh and blood and sing of her cruel and bloody mind and of the price of spilling kindred blood. It is then, at the end of the song, that a cry is heard from inside the house. The audience hear one child asking what he can do to escape his mother's hands and the other answering that he cannot tell him. The Chorus consider going inside to defend the children from murder, but do not. One of the children poignantly cries out for help, which will not come. The cry presages their ending, trapped by their mother's sword. With the children's deaths, the Chorus cease to express any sympathy whatsoever.

Instead they censure Medea for her hard-heartedness in planning to kill with her own hand 'the children you gave birth to' (1280–1).[8] The audience cannot but concur.

By the end of the second section, the view of revenge as right and necessary has been eroded. In its place, we are asked to consider whether the destruction wrought by Medea was really fitting. It may be appropriate that Jason is left alive to suffer the ruin of his house and the isolation and desolation that come with it. As Burnett points out,[9] these are much the same deprivations that his abandonment of Medea and his complicity in her exile caused her. But the children certainly did not deserve to die. And did Creon's vain and silly daughter deserve the excruciating death she suffered? And what about Creon? For all the wrong he had done to Medea, he had also shown her some kindness in allowing her to stay in Corinth for an extra day. Should his kindness have been repaid by such brutal harm? These questions remain unanswered. Instead of bringing closure, the last part of the play, the *exodos* (1293–419), is profoundly unsettling.

It begins with Jason's breathless arrival to try to save his children from the wrath of Creon's relatives, only to learn that Medea has killed them. For the first time in the play, Jason is not presented in an entirely negative light, but shown caring about his children and depicted as the victim of Medea's violence.

Also for the first time in the play, Medea is shown not only, or primarily, as a human woman but as the supernatural descendant of a god. She emerges in a chariot on the *mēchanē* (a sort of a crane which could hoist an actor, an object, or both up to a raised structure atop the stage-building). She is shown with the corpses of her children aloft on the winged chariot of her grandfather Helios, ready to ride across the skies to Athens. Helios, the Titan god of oaths, had not responded to the Chorus' earlier plea to prevent Medea murdering her children, but now makes his chariot available to rescue her from certain punishment in Corinth.[10] His assistance implies his approval of the vengeance in all its horror and lends divine endorsement to the revenge.

But does the play endorse it? In Helios' chariot, Medea is shown in her divine, non-human aspect riding above the audience. If we interpret her position figuratively, the scene shows her riding above human cares and regrets and underscores the role of the non-human in her revenge. By extension, it suggests that revenge of the sort she commits is inhuman, in the sense of lacking in the softer feelings and compassion that human beings are supposed to possess. Moreover, there is something galling in seeing Medea riding high, beyond punishment, even by her own conscience. Although she had earlier predicted a sad and lonely future for herself, the play closes with her in the ascendancy. Even if one does not support the principle of harming those who harmed one, seeing murder and infanticide go unpunished goes against our most fundamental notions of justice.

The scene also shows Medea in her human aspect, in an unbecoming and somewhat comic domestic squabble, trading stichomythic accusations with Jason, she from on high, he from stage level, as to who is at fault for her infanticide. In their exchange of words, both she and Jason show themselves deficient. Medea reveals no more understanding of the heinousness of her infanticide than she had before she committed it. She reiterates her refusal to be laughed at and points out, yet again, Jason's lack of gratitude and violation of his oath. She will not allow him to bury the children, as he requests, or even to kiss them a final goodbye. Justifying her refusal of his request to bury them, she informs him that she plans to bury the children in Hera's temple and to establish an annual feast and sacrifice. But do these gestures ameliorate her blood-guilt or compensate the children for their premature deaths? Jason, too, shows no more understanding of the wrong he had done than he had earlier in the play. He hypocritically blames Medea for the violence she had committed in her love for him and again wrongly accuses her of acting out of sexual jealousy.

At the same time, the appearance of Medea above stage in Helios' carriage squabbling with Jason below completes the reversal between victim and perpetrator that was begun with Jason's arrival on the scene as a distraught father. It is now he, not Medea, who is shown as the suffering victim as he reels from the murder of their children and she sits aloft and unreachable with their corpses. Our sympathies shift accordingly.

The Choral statement at the end settles nothing. The same lines with an additional first line appear at the end of *Alcestis, Andromache,* and *Helen.* The assumption is that the lines have been added either by actors or book-editors. If they are genuine, they are so generic that they have little significance.[11]

Five hundred years later, the Roman writer Seneca wrote a very different *Medea.* This is not the place for a full discussion of his play or for a detailed comparison with Euripides' treatment of the myth. A few salient points, however, may shed light on Euripides' achievement. Most of the scenes in Seneca's *Medea* have parallels to the Euripidean version and appear in similar order. But the dynamic and characterization are worlds apart and reflect totally different conceptualizations and purposes.

Seneca draws his Medea as the embodiment of evil and his Jason as an honourable and sensible man, who leaves his 'untamed' foreign wife for a virtuous Greek woman. In the very first scene, he shows Medea as an enraged and savage figure, not a grieving one. Without preamble, Seneca shows Medea working herself into a demonic and bloodthirsty frenzy, as she prays to the gods in their vicious and infernal aspects to help her accomplish a vengeance of extraordinary evil and brutality. She rages for over fifty-five lines before the Chorus raise their voices to sing in celebration of Jason's upcoming marriage and divorce. Everything in the play justifies the Chorus' view.

Seneca endows his Medea with a complex of qualities that make her the embodiment of evil. These include wildness and savagery; criminality, bestiality, and madness; and the sinister magical powers of a witch. These qualities are repeatedly referred to, separately and in combination: by Jason and the Chorus, the Nurse, and Medea herself, who revels in the bloody criminal acts she had committed to save Jason and the Argonauts (e.g. 563–4) and proudly terms her planned revenge 'a crime' (*scelus*, 1016).

These qualities are referred to throughout the play and dramatized in the fourth and fifth acts. The fourth act demonstrates her magical powers at length. Seneca first has the Nurse describe, in grisly detail, Medea preparing the poisonous potion, in which she will dip the robe for Creusa, Jason's bride. Then he brings Medea on stage, so that the audience can watch her doing it. He shows her summoning the gods of death and shades from the otherworld (740) and then calling on Hecate (770), a goddess associated with magic and witchcraft. What Seneca seems to be saying is that a human mother would not kill her children. Only an evil witch would.

The fifth act not only shows Medea killing her children on stage, but taking sadistic pleasure in it. In his protracted presentation, Seneca shows Medea drawing a sword and killing one child first, then, interrupted by the arrival of Jason and his men, contemplating her deed and conversing with Jason before killing the second child. After her murder of the first child, we hear her triumphing in the return of her former power, acknowledging her pleasure in the boy's murder, and, quite dreadfully, regretting that the murder was deficient in retributive power because Jason had not witnessed it with his own eyes (982–94)! To rectify the omission, she kills her second child in full view of her horrified husband, glorying in her crime and sadistically urging herself to 'Relish a leisurely crime, anguish, do not hurry' (1016–17)[12] before pulling the sword.

Both Euripides' and Seneca's plays produce in the audience a sense of horror and revulsion at the extremity to which Medea brings her vengeance. Unlike its Euripidean model, however, Seneca's play does not allow the audience to identify with Medea. From the very first, she is presented as being as different as possible from the good people of the audience, as 'not us'. The audience was invited to observe her from a distance, as a barbaric foreigner and supernatural witch, with whom they had nothing in common. At one and the same time, they were thus allowed to enjoy the sensation of horror that her conduct evoked, and to judge and condemn her conduct as something totally outside their own ken. In contrast, by leading his audience to identify with Medea, Euripides' more human and sympathetic depiction of her compelled them – and us – to acknowledge as their own the anger and violence, the desire to harm those who harm us, that we all possess.

Notes

1 Burnett (1998), xvi.
2 MacDowell (1978), 86–9.
3 Roisman (1999), 1–122.
4 Kovacs (1994).
5 Mastronarde (2002), 52–64.
6 Kovacs (1994).
7 Some editors regard these lines unauthentic; see Mastronarde (2002).
8 Kovacs (1994).
9 Burnett (1973), 14–15.
10 Cf. Burnett (1998), 221–4.
11 Mastronarde (2002).
12 Hine (2000).

Medea: Feminism or Misogyny?

Douglas Cairns

Marriage

Marital dysfunction looms large in Euripides' *Medea*. The plot involves no fewer than five marriages that fail to achieve their proper outcome. Most obviously, there is the marriage of Medea and Jason. Then there is the one between Jason and Creon's daughter. But we also hear about the marriages of Medea's and Jason's children that will not now take place (1025–36), as well as the one between Medea and Aegeus, alluded to at lines 1384–5 and present in the audience's mind during the Aegeus scene, especially in the allusions to the conception of Theseus at Trozen (679–88) and in Medea's (as it will turn out) unnecessary promise to end Aegeus' childlessness (716–18). The audience know that Medea will become Theseus' wicked stepmother, putting the continuation of yet another family line in danger. Here we shall concentrate on the two main marriages, those of Medea and Jason, and Jason and 'Glauce' (the daughter of Creon).

The marriage between Medea and Jason exhibits many of the regular features of an Athenian marriage, but in extreme form. Marriage in Athens was viri- or patrilocal: the husband brings a stranger into his or his father's *oikos* (household). In this case, the stranger in question is an anomalous, clever barbarian sorceress. *Medea* thus dramatizes in a particularly striking way a more widespread Athenian sense of the bride as an intruder, a potential 'enemy within'. Similarly, in the Athenian conception of marriage, in moving to a new *oikos*, the bride has to 'betray' her father, leaving behind the family she was born into (her 'natal family'). Medea has done this in a spectacular way: she formed an arrangement with Jason on her own, without her father's permission, eloped, and left her father's house far behind. She can never return, especially because she murdered her brother in the course of her escape. In this, she is in a sense a mirror image of Sophocles' Antigone. Where Antigone says that she would never have done what she did for a (replaceable) husband or child, but only for a brother (*Antigone* 905–15), and gives up the chance of marriage out of loyalty to her natal family, Medea chooses a husband at the cost of her brother's life, and thus puts conjugal family before natal.

Medea's marriage is dysfunctional from the outset. In lines 21–3 and 495–8 she claims that Jason has broken oaths or pledges solemnized by *dexiôsis*, the clasping of right hands, a ritualized gesture appropriate at the stage of betrothal (*enguê*). At Athens, however, *enguê*, sealed by *dexiôsis*, is not a contract between man and wife, but between the bride's male guardian or *kurios* and the bridegroom. Medea has subverted this process from the start. After this inauspicious beginning, Medea has regrets. Again, this replicates a popular conception of the feelings of an ordinary Athenian wife, albeit – in Medea's case – writ large. Medea repeatedly voices her regret at doing what all wives had to do, abandoning their natal family (166–7, 255–8, 328, 502–3, 800–1). She laments her own situation by picking up on a feature that is not unique to that situation, but common to all wives.

She makes these points, of course, only after the marriage has broken down. Her references to her father's house and to her homeland make the point that her marriage has been problematic from the beginning and serve to underline her regret. But the fact that she cannot, unlike a wife in normal circumstances, return to her father's *oikos* also stresses the enormity of Jason's betrayal. And although their marriage was anomalous and problematic from the start, its ultimate breakdown is Jason's responsibility. According to the Nurse in the prologue, Medea 'bent her will to Jason's' in everything she did (13). This, she observes, is as it should be in a marriage. But (as the Nurse goes on to emphasize) Jason has betrayed Medea and formed a new marriage; and for this he is condemned throughout the play – not only by Medea, but also by the Nurse, the Tutor, the Chorus, and (most importantly) the impartial Athenian king, Aegeus (17–18, 82–4, 116, 157–8, 410–13, 439–40, 577–8, 690–707, 1231–2).

Thus Medea's marriage with Jason and Jason's marriage with Creon's daughter overlap; the end of the one is the beginning of the other, and thus that beginning too is problematic and inauspicious. The extent of marital breakdown is emphasized by Medea's early laments and by the sympathy of the Nurse and the Chorus, especially during the Chorus' entrance song, in which they respond to the cries of Medea within the house (144–59):

Medea   (*Screaming*) The fire from heaven's shooting through my head! Why should I go on living? I wish that I could find some peace in death, some solace sloughing off this sordid hateful life!

Chorus   Did you hear? O Zeus and earth and sunlight, did you hear the scream, so eerie, terrifying? Did you hear the poor lost bride? / O,

Medea, in your madness, what lust is this for death's cruel stony bed?
She will hasten her own end, her death. / Don't speak of that! If your
own husband worshipped a new woman and her sex, you too would
know what she is suffering. Don't let it be a mortal wound! Zeus himself
will join with you to bring you justice. No! Don't grieve unnaturally, too
much, don't weep too much for him, your husband!

Medea wants to die, and the Chorus describe her wish as 'lust' 'for death's
cruel stony bed'. This is the familiar tragic motif of the 'marriage of death': one
marriage being ruined, Medea has a bride's passion for a new marriage bed,
in death. Medea is here explicitly a 'poor lost bride'. In her next utterance,
Medea uses the same Greek word (*numphê*) with reference to Jason's new
marriage (163–4):

> I wish that I could see him and his bride and his whole house torn up by
> their roots, for daring so to wrong me in my innocence!

Jason is implicated in two marriages, with two brides. The result will be
disaster in both cases.

The purpose (*telos*) of marriage in classical Athens was the production of
children and the continuation of the *oikos* that this ensured. A formula of
betrothal, 'I give you this woman for the ploughing of legitimate children',
recurs in the comedies of Menander (e.g. *Dyskolos/The Grouch* 842–3).
Medea's marriage fails utterly to achieve its purpose: the children whose
existence is its *raison d'être* are killed, and Jason's *oikos* is wiped out. This is
precisely Medea's aim in punishing him (794–6):

> And when I've turned all Jason's life upon its head, I shall leave Corinth
> and so endure my exile as the killer of my children, whom I love more
> than the world, the perpetrator of a deed of all deeds most unholy.

Jason's 'life' is, in the original Greek, his *domos*, his 'house'; but not just in
the physical sense. Jason's household, old and new, is to be extinguished,
precisely the opposite of the normal *telos* of marriage. Jason acknowledges
Medea's success: her murder of their children has left him 'bereft, destroyed'
(1326). He goes on to comment on the fatal outcome of their marriage
(1336–8):

> You were my wife. You bore my sons. And now, because of nothing more
> than sexual jealousy, you've killed them.

Compare 1347–50:

> All I have left now is to mourn the spirit of my own destruction – my bride, so young, so innocent, is there for me no longer, and my sons I brought up with such care – I'll never speak to them or see them in this life again. All that I had is gone.

Jason will not even be permitted a role in his own sons' burial (1377–81, 1410–14). And this is not all (1395–6):

> **Jason** Yes, I shall go. My sons are lost forever.
>
> **Medea** Your grief will grow as you grow old into great old age.

To the Athenian way of thinking, children should bury their parents, not the parents their children. Jason is denied even the opportunity to bury his sons, and, because Medea has destroyed his household, the contract between the generations – that parents care for children and children reciprocate by caring for aged parents, a contract that depends on and instantiates the continuity of the family – has broken down. Jason will have no one to care for him in old age, no one to see to his burial, no one to keep his memory alive as part of his family's household cult. Marriage is supposed to ensure all these things; for Jason, Medea has made sure that it will not.

But this affects her too (1021–37):

> Oh, my children! My children! This is your city and your home! When you no longer have your poor sad mother with you, you will stay here for all the rest of time without me. And I must go, a fugitive, an exile, to a strange land although I'll never have my joy of you or see your happiness, I'll never share your wedding day, never meet your bride or decorate the bridal chamber for you, never raise the blazing marriage torch in sacred ritual.
>
> I cannot weaken, and therein lies my tragedy. It was for something different that I brought you up. It was for something different I went through all the work and all the grind, the twisting agonies of birth-pangs just to bring forth sons to die. I had such hopes: I would grow old and you'd be there for me, and when I died you'd fold the death-shroud round for me and I would be the envy of the world. But as it is, all my sweet dreams are turned to dust. You see, I shall be lonely and alone without you, and so I shall drag out my life in bitterness and pain.

Medea will not see her sons' weddings, will not perform the tasks of preparing the bridal bed, of holding the torch as they bring home their brides. Bearing children was Medea's purpose in life; those children were born to marry and have more children. In killing her own children, Medea negates the purpose of her marriage; thus 'the twisting agonies of [her] birth-pangs' were in vain. Not only, however, will the children fail to achieve the *telos* of marriage; Medea too will be without care in old age, will not, as would be normal, receive funeral rites from her own children. The failure of Medea's marriage undoes all the sociocultural benefits that a successful marriage should bring.

The marriage of Jason to Creon's daughter and especially its newness are a central theme throughout the play. In these references to the new marriage, the girl is regularly referred to as *numphê*, bride. We have to assume that the wedding took place very recently indeed – or in fact, since an Athenian wedding was a process that was drawn out over several days, perhaps we are supposed to imagine that the wedding is actually still in progress. This is suggested by several passages that we shall look at below.

However that may be, marriage ritual is central to the fate of Creon's daughter. Medea's initial thoughts of vengeance give us an early indication. Having received a day's reprieve from Creon, she looks for ways of turning her three enemies – Creon, Jason, and Jason's bride – to corpses (374–5). These are the three parties to the marriage as a transaction between two households: the father who gives the bride away, the bridegroom who receives her, and the bride herself. Among the options Medea contemplates are the following (378–80):

> Perhaps I shall engulf their bridal home in fire or stalk in silence to their room, where they have spread their soft warm bedding, and so plunge a knife as sharp as any razor in their liver.

The methods of vengeance she considers are focused on marriage and pervert the process of marriage. The bride proceeds from her father's house to her new husband's house by torchlight; the bridegroom's mother awaits her arrival, torch in hand. The marriage will ultimately be consummated in the 'soft warm bedding' of the bridal chamber. The acts of torching the bridal chamber, or penetrating both partners with a sword, parody these normative features of the ritual. Medea's intentions are summed up at 399–400:

> I shall make their wedding-song a bitter song of lamentation, and their marriage desolate as my own exile.

She repeats the sentiment at the end of her set-piece debate (*agôn*) with Jason (625–6):

Go! Bed her! And maybe, if my words find favour with the gods, in marrying her you'll lose all chance you ever had of marriage.

The original Greek here stresses the newness of the wedding and Jason's current role as bridegroom. ('Bed her!' translates a verb that might be taken as something like 'play the bridegroom'.) The Greek also makes explicit the conflation of wedding and funeral ritual: Jason will 'celebrate a wedding of a sort that will produce lamentation' (626); the wedding songs (as Medea makes clear also at 399–400) will turn to funeral laments.

Medea's aim, then, is to turn Jason's new marriage – a new beginning, something hopeful, to be celebrated, and potentially fruitful – into its opposite, something to be lamented, a perversion or travesty of itself. And this is precisely what she does (784–9):

I shall send my sons with wedding-gifts for the new bride – a gauzy dress, a coronet of gold, an intercession, as it were, to ward off banishment. And if she takes these pretty trifles, swathes her skin in them, then she and any who has contact with her will choke out their lives in twisting agony. Such is the venom I shall smear upon my gifts.

Gifts, then as now, are an important part of the wedding. Athenian vases depict them being sent along with the bride in the procession from her father's to her new husband's house; but there was also a custom of bringing gifts to the newly-weds' house on the morning after their first night together. This is the stage of the wedding process that Medea's gifts evoke. But the gifts themselves, the robe and the coronet, are also the kind of thing the bride might wear during the wedding itself.

Medea's plan advances with the return of Jason at lines 866ff. She tells him that she has repented, come to her senses. She was wrong, she says (886–8):

I should have shared the planning, come to give my blessing at the marriage, yes, waited in attendance at your marriage bed, acted as a go-between to please you.

Medea here imagines herself playing the role of *numpheutria* (roughly 'bridesmaid'), a role normally taken on by the mother or a relative of the bride, who is often depicted on vases as present in the marital bedchamber to encourage the bride and ensure that all goes well. For wife number one to play this role for wife number two represents an extreme and heavily ironic departure from the ritual norm, much like Clytemnestra's welcoming of

Cassandra as though she were the bridegroom's mother in Aeschylus' *Agamemnon*.

Medea's desire to pervert the course of Jason's wedding is apparent also at the point at which she has the gifts brought out (950–8):

> Bring me the bridal gifts to dress her in. She will enjoy this happiness not once, no, but ten thousand times. Not only has good fortune given her the best of men in you as husband, but she has inherited the bridal gifts that Helios, the Sun-God, father of my father, once bequeathed to his descendants.
>
> *(to Sons)* Take the dowry in your hands. Take it. Give it to the princess, to the blessed bride. She will not think them insignificant, the wedding gifts she gets from me.

Medea's wish that the bride should 'enjoy this happiness not once ... but ten thousand times' is a perversion of a traditional speech-genre known as *makarismos*; the 'blessed bride' translates the adjective *makaria*. Medea is drawing on formulas of congratulation and praise; but her words imply the opposite. The word that she uses for 'gifts' in line 956 is *phernai*, a technical term for the bride's trousseau, personal possessions which she would bring from her old home to her new home. So in one sense, Medea is now representing herself as the mother of the bride, sending the bride to her new house with prized heirlooms. But these items are Medea's *own* heirlooms, handed down from her grandfather, Helios. There is a suggestion, perhaps, that Medea's trousseau has become the new bride's (just as Medea's husband has become her husband); but this is a trousseau that will undo the wedding.

In the ode that follows, the Chorus imagine the bride wearing Medea's gifts (978–89):

> The bride-girl will accept the coronet of gold, and with it her own death-pangs and destruction. And on her glowing golden hair with her own hands she'll place the wedding-veil of death.
>
> The beauty of the shimmering dress, taboo in its perfection, the golden-twining coronet will so seduce her and she'll hug them to her. And so she'll wrap her body in her bridal shroud all ready for her marriage-rites with death. The snare gapes open for the final dance of death and she will fall, for there is no escape, poor girl, from her destruction.

The scene is precisely that of a wedding, but one that becomes a marriage of death. Earlier, Medea had contemplated such a marriage for herself, but she will now inflict it on Creon's daughter.

The Tutor reports that the 'bride, the princess, happily accepted the gifts from [the children's] hands' (1003–4). The Messenger then reports the whole story. The boys entered the palace and 'went on through towards the bridal rooms' (1137). On seeing them, the bride veils her face (translated as 'the blood drained from her face', 1147) – a gesture suggesting anger, but also alluding to an important performative element of the Athenian wedding. She then puts on the coronet and the robe, and is consumed by flames – she becomes the torch at her own wedding. Creon embraces her and is killed too (1156–220). Creon sticks to his daughter; they 'wrestle' (1214: 'wrestling' is a common Greek metaphor for sex). The perverted marriage is concluded by a consummation of sorts, the wrestling of father and daughter. 'They're lying there now in death together – an old father and his child' (1220–1). A couple lie together: but father and daughter are now literally inseparable. The rite of passage from the father to the husband has not been completed.

Three households are thus destroyed: the one shared by Medea and Jason, that of Jason and his new bride, and Creon's. Jason loses the children he has and any hope of children from his new wife. For the Athenians, the incorporation of a woman, an outsider, in a new household was a process that had to be delicately negotiated, in life and in ritual. In this play, that process goes spectacularly wrong.

Medea and the 'ordinary woman'

The theme of marriage in *Medea*, then, is used, in a way typical of tragedy's dramatization of myth, to highlight (indeed to take to extremes) the risks felt to be inherent in ordinary ritual processes and social institutions. Marriage is an experience of ordinary Athenian women, and, as we have seen, Medea's status as an outsider and her 'betrayal' of her natal *oikos* represent the situation of the ordinary wife writ large. In this respect, Medea is both like and unlike the 'ordinary woman'. This proves to be a theme that is also relevant in other ways.

The situation of ordinary women is most relevant in Medea's first speech at lines 230–51:

> Of everything that lives, all creatures sentient, we women are most abject of them all. We must first with an exchange of money buy a husband, pass control of our own bodies even to his hands. And still there is an ordeal still more bitter yet to come. For in this getting of a husband is the greatest lottery there is – will he be cruel or good? There are no ways a woman can divorce and keep her honour, and she can't deny her husband.

So she comes to a strange house, a whole new set of rules and expectations
– and she needs to be clairvoyant for she's not learned this at home: how
best she should break in her husband. And if in this great undertaking
we succeed, so that our husband lives contentedly and does not fight
against the reins, our life is to be envied. But if we fail, we're better dead.
A man can leave the house and find some new distraction when he's had
enough, whenever he grows bored or irritated with the company at
home. But for us, necessity demands that we have eyes for just one man,
our husband. They speak about us, say how safe and sound our lives are
in our homes, while they go out to fight. How little these men know. I'd
rather stand my ground three times in battle, in the shield-line than
endure the agonies of child-birth once.

This general disquisition on women's lot in contemporary society, and the
sense of injustice that it conveys, is at the very least a sign that these issues
were 'in the air' in the 430s BC, that women themselves, at least, may have felt
that they had grounds for complaint, and that men knew the kind of
complaints women made or might make. We shall come back to this speech
in a moment.

Women and song: 'compensation for the female race'

The note of female rebellion that Medea sounds in the speech just quoted is
taken up in the theme of women and song which punctuates the play. First
the Nurse criticizes traditional (male) forms of song and poetry for their
inability to assuage grief and soothe pain (190–204):

You would not be mistaken if you said our ancestors were feeble-minded,
yes, not wise at all – they wrote their songs to sing at parties or at feasts
or banquets, charming tunes to tease the ear, but no-one found a
harmony, a gentle soft-stringed lullaby to soothe away the hates and
miseries of men, the seeds of death and dreadful accident that cause
whole households to come crashing down in total ruin. And yet to cure
such evils as these are with music – what profit that would bring to all
mankind. For when they've eaten well, when they're replete, relaxed,
what need have men for useless songs and taut-tuned melodies? The
very feeling of repletion that a good meal brings is joy enough!

The Nurse's complaint does not explicitly draw a contrast between men and
women, yet there is nonetheless an indirect opposition of male and female

concerns, first because the griefs that she has in mind are especially female, and because the context of song that she identifies is the *symposion*, the after-dinner drinking party from which respectable Athenian women were excluded. So already in this passage there is the beginning of a notion that men have had song to themselves for too long, and have not used it well.

This line of thought is carried forward in the first two stanzas of the first stasimon (410–30):

> The well-springs of the sacred streams suck back their waters, and all the universe, all Justice is turned upside-down. The male brain breeds deceit, and all the solemn promises of gods are crumbling. So now's the time that reputation too will turn and bring to womanhood, to me, respect and recognition. And so there'll come some compensation for the female race.
>
> The muses of dead dusty poets will cease their songs of woman's infidelity. For the god of inspiration, Lord Apollo, never did bestow the power to write the lyre-song in a woman's mind, else I would make reverberate a paean hymn against the whole male sex. The yawning years have much to say not just of men, but women too.

Male poets have been slandering women for their faithlessness, but now Jason has proved that it is men who are faithless, and the tide is going to turn; a women's song will redress the balance. Inspired by Medea's feminist rhetoric in the previous scene the Chorus sing (417–18) that there will 'come some compensation for the female race' – or, in the more traditional version, one that helps bring out the notions both of male-female competition and of the popular recognition of women's worth, 'honour is coming to the race of women'. The same theme recurs (albeit with considerably less optimism and confidence) in the Chorus' chanted lines at 1081–9:

> I've often been involved in softer sophistries [*mythoi*] and in debate more subtle than a woman should. But women have their muse of inspiration, too, which brings them understanding. Not all, perhaps, but there are some (how could there not be) and you'd find them out, I think, among the many. For womankind is not devoid of inspiration.

As the Nurse wished, they go on to sing (or, in this case, chant) of female concerns, the pain of bearing and raising children (1090–115).

The same old song

Some (for example, Bernard Knox) have argued that the song which redresses women's wrongs and helps bring honour to the race of women is *Medea* itself. But this is unlikely. First, Medea's feminist rhetoric in her opening speech is not to be taken in isolation from its context. Medea does indeed stand up for ordinary women in her words at lines 230–51 (quoted earlier), but she does so in order to get the Chorus on her side. Their very next song, in which they are enthused by Medea's project of punishing Jason's infidelity and see this as a way of striking a blow for all womankind, shows that she has been successful. Elsewhere in the play, when Medea appropriates the model of the 'ordinary woman', she does so for her own, manipulative, insincere ends – as when she presents herself as too weak to harm Creon (307–8, 314–15), and especially in her second scene with Jason, when she feigns repentance over her earlier and typically feminine 'foolishness', affirms her 'respect' for Jason's masculine intelligence (872–93), and uses her genuine tears at the prospect of losing her children to add plausibility to her assumption of the passive, subordinate, and weakly emotional woman's role (902–5, 925, 927–8, 930–1).

But Medea is no ordinary woman. She is a non-Greek, from the faraway, eastern kingdom of Colchis. Her grandfather is the god, Helios. She is a sorceress (395–7, 789, 806). Out of love for Jason, she has killed not only Pelias, Jason's enemy (9, 486–7, 504, 734), but her own brother (167, 1334–5). Throughout the play (as interpreters never fail to point out) she appropriates and magnifies male, heroic values, demanding violent revenge when insulted and regarding it as unbearable to be mocked by her enemies. Medea follows her general reflections on women's position in society with these words (252–8):

> But the situation's not the same for you and me. You have your city here, your fathers' homes. You have life's luxuries, companionship and friends. But I have no-one. *I* have no city and my husband treats me shamefully. He took me from my home as plunder to a strange land and, in the face of all I'm suffering, I can't weigh anchor and sail safe home to my mother or my brother or my family.

Jason *did* treat Medea shamefully – as we saw, all those who express an opinion, not only Medea's supporters, but also the impartial Aegeus, agree on this. But the reason why Medea cannot return to her father's house, as an ordinary woman might do on divorce, is that she betrayed her father to his enemy. That betrayal included the murder of her brother, the devastation of her father's hopes for the continuation of his family line. Medea has just lamented this fact in lines 166–7 ('My father and my city! It was so shamefully I slunk from you, my brother's murderess!'). The situation is indeed not the same for Medea as it is for the women of the Chorus. This conclusion is there for an audience, and especially for a predominantly male Athenian audience, to draw, when, having secured the Chorus's support by playing on their sense of female solidarity, Medea makes it clear that their silence is one of the instruments she requires if she is to implement a plan of vengeance (259–63).

Yet precisely in her difference from the ordinary woman, Medea is, in a sense, a type of womanhood: she takes to extremes characteristics traditionally seen as feminine. She is every Athenian's worst nightmare of what a woman might be and might do. Thus even in her attempt to present herself to the Chorus as an ordinary woman there is an element of stereotyping (the common prejudice of women's allegedly typical use of *dolos*, guile, to get their way). The guile that Medea uses in getting the Chorus on her side will serve her well in the encounter with Creon that follows, her manipulation of Aegeus and Jason, and ultimately in the murder of Creon and his daughter.

It is striking that Medea ends her great speech to the Chorus with the following words (263–6):

> For in all else, a woman is consumed by fear, no mettle when it comes to facing force or steel. But when she has been slighted in her marriage and her sex, there is no force more murderous.

We should compare this perspective with the famous lines, often quoted out of context, that conclude the purely general part of her speech (248–51):

> They speak about us, say how safe and sound our lives are in our homes, while they go out to fight. How little these men know. I'd rather stand my ground three times in battle, in the shield-line, than endure the agonies of child-birth once.

If those lines emphasize women's physical courage and a strength of character that is vastly underestimated by men, lines 263–6 return to the stereotype of their weakness as warriors. Perhaps, one might say, the later passage is ironic or sarcastic. But in fact both passages construct female lives, female emotions, and female courage from male perspectives. Childbirth is no doubt excruciatingly painful; it is only very recently that the real risk of death that it carries has, at least in some societies, receded into the background. But the attitude of women to childbirth as an experience is surely very different from that of men to the prospect of killing or being killed in battle. If these lines pay a tribute to women's courage, they do so from a male point of view.

Also stereotypical is Medea's emphasis on sex, especially on the intensity of women's sexual jealousy. Ultimately, it is for sex that Medea betrays her father, kills her brother, kills Pelias, kills Creon and his daughter, and kills her own children. She herself laments the power of *erôs* ('The lusts of men are such a crushing evil', 330; the Greek *brotoi* here refers not only to males, but to all human beings); the Chorus sing that she 'sailed out from [her] father's home, [her] heart mad, mind irrational' (432–4); Jason several times accuses her of being motivated by nothing but sexual passion (526–31, 549–73, 913, 1338). And in this he appears to be correct: this view is endorsed by the Chorus ('A woman's sexuality can bring many pains; it has already reaped its swathe of suffering for men', 1290–2) and by Medea herself – Jason could not 'humiliate her bed' and get away with it (1354). Compare lines 1367–9:

Jason   And so you thought your jealousies could justify such slaughter? [Literally: 'So you thought it right to kill them for the sake of sex?']

Medea   Do you think that a woman cares so little for a husband's infidelity? [Literally: 'Do you think this is a small hurt for a woman?']

Jason   A woman who is rational would, yes! [Literally: 'For a modest (*sôphrôn*) woman, yes.'] For you, though, everything that's done you think is done to hurt you.

Modesty, *sôphrosynê* (also sometimes translated as 'self-control'), is the woman's virtue *par excellence*, precisely because of the alleged danger of women's giving in to excessive appetites, especially *erôs*. Medea thus embodies – and exults in – the stereotype of the 'bad', insatiable woman. Medea's anger (conventionally a feminine as well as a barbarian trait), and especially her failure (despite her attempts, in her monologue at 1040–80) to overcome passion with reason, speak to the same deficiency. We might contrast the Chorus (much closer to an approximation of the ordinary woman than Medea herself, despite her great speech) who pray (in the second stasimon, 627–44) that *sôphrosynê* should enfold them, that they might be spared the ravages of excessive *erôs*:

When Lust comes, swooping down too heavily on men, it saps good reputation, saps morality. Yet if Desire, if Aphrodite, comes with due propriety, there is no other god more gratifying. And so I pray you, mistress, lady, never turn your golden bow on me and launch at me your arrows, inescapable, smeared with the poisoned balm of longing, no, but rather let chaste modesty [*sôphrosynê*] enfold me, which is, of all the gifts the gods bestow, most beautiful. I would that Aphrodite, that Desire, in all her awesome terrifying power, does not unleash on me contentious argument or strife, whose appetite knows no abatement. May she not craze *my* very soul with longing for another's bed, but rather, with unerring mind, may she preside in equitable judgement over all the marriages of womankind, honouring those women's beds where harmony prevails.

With Medea's own endorsement of evaluations offered not only by Jason, but also by the sympathetic women of the Chorus, it appears that misogynist Athenian stereotypes regarding the nature of women are vindicated by the play's end. There are plenty of earlier indications of the same. As we saw above, for example, Medea concludes her 'feminist' manifesto with a reference to the 'murderous force' of a woman when 'slighted in her marriage and her sex' (265–6). After her victory over Creon, and having restated her determination to take revenge, she once again casts her motives in the same light (407–9):

I am a woman, and although we women are so useless when it comes to good, yet as the architects of every ill, there is none more accomplished.

She returns to the same theme in her later manipulation of Jason (889–90):

But we women are as women are – I shall not slander us. But just because we're women does not mean we must inevitably act badly or strive to outdo one another in our foolishness.

It does not seem to me that a play in which women make these generalizations about themselves is designed to upset such prejudices. Of course, these statements could be presented – and on the modern stage probably would be – as an ironic appropriation of misogynist stereotypes, enlisting them in the cause of a feminine backlash. Perhaps there were even some enlightened souls in the theatre of Dionysus in 431 BC, who took them in that sense. But there must, surely, have been a substantial element of the audience for whom such views were simply an accepted element of their conventional world-view. In conventional Athenian terms, Medea represents men's worst fears of what women may be capable.

If Medea has what are regarded as typical feminine traits in abundance and to an extreme degree, by end of play she is, in effect, more than just a woman, but rather some form of female *daimôn* (in the chariot of her grandfather, Helios, 1321; in her prophecy of future cult, like a *dea ex machina*, 1382–8) – or, as Jason prefers to phrase it, a monster, like Scylla, or a lioness

(1342–3, 1406–7; cf. Medea at 1358). Euripides' *Medea* does not subvert Athenian male stereotypes; it revels in them. Far from questioning the lot of women in Athenian society, it suggests that chaos and destruction would result should women ever act like men, demand equality, and throw off the constraints that their society places on them.

Note on further reading

For an excellent introduction to the play, its issues, and its interpretation, see Allan (2002). See also Scodel (2010), 120–32. For some background on constructions of the female in fifth-century Athens, see Gould (1980), 38–59; Just (1989). On the Athenian wedding, see Oakley and Sinos (1993). On tragedy's treatment of the theme of marriage in general, see Seaford (1987). And for further discussion of the main issues raised in this chapter, see especially Knox (1977); Flory (1978); Visser (1986); McDermott (1989); the articles by March, Seaford, and Williamson in Powell (1990); Rabinowitz (1994), 125–54; and Rehm (1994), 97–109.

11

Divine and Human in Euripides' *Medea*

Edith Hall

At the climax of Euripides' *Medea*, the voices of the Colchian sorceress' two young boys, inside their house with their mother, are heard screaming for help from backstage. But then they fall silent. Jason arrives at his former residence in Corinth and demands that the doors be opened. Like Jason and the chorus, we have every reason to believe Medea is inside, with the slaughtered children. We actually saw her enter the house just a few minutes previously, stating unambiguously in her last speech that she was going to kill them, with a sword, without further delay. Our experience of Greek tragedy leads us to expect that the doors will open, and on the wheeled platform called the *ekkyklema*, or 'rolling-out machine', a terrible tableau will come into view – Medea, covered in blood, bestriding the corpses of her little ones with a gore-streaked weapon in her hands. As Jason bangs at the doors, physically trying to force them open, our eyes are therefore concentrated on the level of the entrance represented by the staging. We expect the house to open and reveal the scene of carnage inside. Yet nothing happens on this level of view: instead, it is only on the upper periphery of our vision that the swinging stage crane at first comes to our attention, with Medea and the two little corpses visible within.

In Greek tragedy, ordinary mortals do not pass from the interior of houses to the sky without using doors and without our noticing it. Nor do they travel by the supernatural means represented by the machine for the gods. We now know that Medea, for all her plausible emotional anguish and ability to talk in an astonishingly frank and accessible way to ordinary Corinthian women, is superhuman. Aristotle, who explained tragedy entirely in terms of human ethics and psychology rather than theology, sensed that this '*ex machina*' scene was completely anomalous if Medea is understood to be an ordinary mortal woman; he therefore objected to the 'inorganic' and 'improbable' ending of the play (*Poetics*, 15, 1454b):

> The denouements of plots ought to arise just from the imitation of character, and not from a contrivance, a *deus ex machina*, as in *Medea*.

The contrivance should be used instead for things outside the play, either
all that happened beforehand that a human being could not know, or all
that happens later and needs foretelling and reporting, for we attribute
omniscience to the gods.

Aristotle is quite explicit that the sort of omniscience which Medea seems to
possess at the end of the play, when she can predict the moment and manner
of Jason's death, belongs not to humans but to gods.

After the final, vitriolic quarrel between Medea in the chariot and Jason
on the earth, the murderous heroine nevertheless flies off, as the vindictive
Aphrodite disappears from the stage in *Hippolytus* and Dionysus vanishes at
the end of *Bacchae*. Her crime, like a god's action against a mortal, will remain
unpunished, and she gloats over her possession of the precious corpses. The
chorus are stunned: this is how they conclude their day outside that tragic
household in Corinth (1415–19):

Zeus on Olympus dispenses many things.
Gods often contradict our fondest expectations.
What we anticipate does not come to pass.
What we don't expect some god finds a way to make happen.

They are trying to make sense of the horrifying events they have witnessed,
from a religious point of view. They need to assume that unseen, supernatural
factors or agents, such as gods, have been at work – factors beyond
the material, physical world. This is the realm of the unseen and the divine
which the Greeks called 'beyond the physical' – 'metaphysical'. And this
chorus are thoroughly metaphysically *confused*. They are not even sure
exactly which god has brought about the events that have just taken place,
and insist that they had no way of anticipating the tragedy at all. 'Gods often
contradict our fondest expectations.' The Corinthian women's metaphysical
incomprehension is important and not atypical of tragedy, a genre in which
bafflement is a characteristic philosophical attitude of both staged sufferer
and watching spectator.[1] We, too, are fundamentally perplexed, even
bewildered, by what happens to Medea and Jason's sons. Can the gods really
have intended the terrible deaths that have just occurred to take place? If so,
why? Indeed, all the characters in the play, except for Medea, are left either
dead or bemused.

Medea is one of the most adapted and performed of all ancient dramas.
It has been turned into operas, dance theatre, novels and films as well as
new plays. It has proved to be one of the most readily transferable of all the
Greek dramas to different religious and cultural contexts. There have been

Roman Catholic Medeas, Protestant Medeas, Jewish Medeas, Australian aboriginal Medeas, Japanese Buddhist/Shinto Medeas, Hindu Medeas, Confucian and Dialectical Materialist Medeas.[2] *Medea* is a tragedy that can speak to every community within the global village, and through performances and adaptations has already spoken to more of them, probably, than any other ancient Greek play, except Sophocles' *Oedipus* and *Antigone*. There are several reasons why it has proved so endlessly enduring. They include its focus on conflict between the sexes, its staging of dialogues between individuals of different ethnicity, and its psychological exploration of the ambivalent feelings that children can arouse in a mother. It is also, importantly, an extraordinary exploration of the mind of a murderer, in the process of working herself up to kill another human, which raises timeless legal questions about premeditation, provocation and diminished responsibility.[3] But a neglected reason why *Medea* is still so powerful is that it asks more metaphysical questions than it answers, even though its theology throughout is basically that of Olympian polytheism. The play leaves problematically *open* the question of the true religious or cosmic purpose of the events it has portrayed.

This inherent metaphysical openness has, in turn, allowed the play to be rewritten and performed in infinite different cultural and religious contexts without ever losing its basic intellectual power. Medea's children continue to scream for help as they die backstage, with the community powerless to help them. Jason's irresponsibility and selfishness continue to be repaid by the disproportionate punishment of multiple bereavements. A completely innocent teenage girl, Creon's daughter, continues to die in agony because she is marrying the man her father has approved. Medea herself, however mysterious she turns out to be, continues to lose her beloved children because her anger is too great to contain. Two entire families – Medea's and the Corinthian royal family – continue to be destroyed, by a terrifying female figure who claims to be implementing the will of the gods, and seems to be unaccountable. Human helplessness in the face of arbitrary and dreadful suffering never received a more compelling dramatization.

An enquiry into the metaphysics of the tragedy and their instrumentality in its cultural stamina needs to look, first, at how the characters in the play themselves explain in religious terms what they are doing and suffering. The most prominent god in the play by far is the supreme ruler of gods and men, Olympian Zeus himself. Zeus supervised the implementation of the rules which constituted Greek popular ethics, and in this capacity was worshipped in a similar way all over the Greek world, by both men and women. His primary assistants in this awesome task were his one-time consort or daughter, Themis (whose name means 'The Right [way of doing things]' or 'Natural

Law'), and his daughter, Dikē ('Justice'). The 'rules', which Zeus oversaw, regulated human relationships at every level. They forbade incest, kin-killing, harming suppliants, hosts or guests, failure to bury the dead and perjury. Sometimes they were called 'the unwritten laws' or the 'laws of all the Greeks'. Traditionally-minded Greeks believed that, if they committed any of these crimes, then Zeus might blast them with a thunderbolt or exact retribution another way, often with the assistance of Themis or Dikē. In *Medea* the theology of the play as understood by the nurse, the chorus, and Medea, is on one level, and at the opening of the play, remarkably simple: Jason has broken his marriage vows, the promises he swore to Medea, and has therefore made himself vulnerable as a perjurer to the 'Justice of Zeus'. There was even a special title for Zeus in his capacity as superintendent of oaths, and that was Zeus *Horkios*. The theology of the play is very traditional, and the key divinity is Zeus in his capacity as *Horkios*, along with his designated partner in oath-protection, Themis, and the elemental gods Earth and Sun, by whom oaths were conventionally sworn and who were named as witnesses to them.

The nurse says that Medea is calling on 'Themis, who hears our prayers, and Zeus, who guards the promises men swear' (168–70). The chorus intuitively feel that a woman whose husband has broken his oaths will be protected by Zeus (158–9), and state that Medea calls on Themis (208–10):

Daughter of Zeus, goddess of the oaths,
Which carried her across the ocean
To Hellas, through the dark briny sea.

Indeed, when Medea gloats at the stricken father of her children from the safety of her chariot, she reaffirms that 'Father Zeus' knows what has really passed between them (1352–3), and asks what god would listen to 'a man who doesn't keep his promises, a man who deceives and lies to strangers?' (1391–2).[4]

The play, then, in one sense, is a simple parable of perjury punished. Yet its theology also involves cults that were specifically associated with Corinth and its surrounding areas. Jason owes his safety, he claims, solely to the patronage of the goddess Aphrodite (527). Aphrodite and her son, Eros, are of course thematically relevant to the play, because Medea originally abandoned her homeland and took to crime in order to follow the man with whom she had fallen hopelessly in love. But it will have been just as relevant to Euripides' audience that Aphrodite was also the most important god at Corinth, and the chorus of Corinthian women sing an ode to her (627–41). The temple of Aphrodite at Corinth stood high on the rocky 'Acrocorinth', the hill which towered over the city. By the time of Pindar (that is, before Euripides), there were many maidens serving the goddess in the temple, and the city was famous for its prostitutes, who may have plied their trade in direct connection with Aphrodite's cult. Corinth, which had a steamy reputation, was the perfect setting for a tragedy about sexual jealousy.

Even more significantly, at the end of the play Medea says she is flying off to Athens via the cult centre of Hera Akraia, across the Corinthian gulf at Perachora (one of the wealthiest sanctuaries ever to have been excavated in Greece). She will bury the boys and thereby found a Corinthian ritual (1378–83), which will atone in perpetuity for their deaths. The Doric temple of Hera Akraia, which can still be visited, was ancient and spectacularly adorned with marble tiles; everyone in Euripides' audience will have known of it. Moreover, the large number of votive objects that have been found there by archaeologists (amulets worn by pregnant women, and figurines) show that it was visited by individuals anxious about the health of babies and young children.[5] The killing of Medea's children was therefore presented by the tragedy as the 'charter' or 'foundation' myth for a specific set of cult practices in the Corinthian area. Greek myth and religion often exhibit this 'dialectical' tendency, where opposites are united in the same figures: seers like Teiresias are blind, and children, who have been destroyed, are here somehow to protect other children from destruction.

All over the Greek world, Hera was the deity who represented women's social status as respected wives. Hera was worshipped as Hera *Nympheuomene* (Hera the Bride), Hera *Chera* (Hera the Widow), but also as Hera *Teleia*, Hera the Fulfilled or Fulfiller, the goddess who helped women finalize their marriages satisfactorily with the production of a healthy son. She is, in addition, the angry wife of Zeus, permanently disgruntled at his infidelities. In both capacities – Hera *Teleia* and Hera humiliated by her husband's straying – she is a figure who offers a parallel to Medea in a less specifically Corinthian way. But a discussion of the religion in this play is not complete without Medea's special relationships with two other gods, on the first of whom she calls when no men are in earshot (395–8):

By Hecate, the goddess
I worship more than all the others,
The one I choose to help me in this work,
Who lives with me deep inside my home,
These people won't bring pain into my heart
And laugh about it . . .

It was as a result of this passage that Hecate came to dominate ancient literature's scenes of female witchcraft. Greek lyric poets had already presented her as the dark daughter of Night, the bearer of flaming torches, with some special association with sexual desire implied by making her an attendant of Aphrodite. In art, she is often associated with the huntress Artemis, but in an underworld form, followed by the triple-headed hound of Hell, Cerberus, rather than the hunting dogs who attend Artemis in sunlit glades. But Medea's statement, that Hecate is her favourite goddess, fed the ancient literary imagination. By the time of the third book of *Argonautica*, Apollonius' epic on the Argonauts two centuries later, Medea is imagined to have been a full-time priestess serving in the temple of Hecate in Colchis by the Black Sea; Hecate has taught her how to use magical herbs, which can put out fire, stop rivers in full flow and change the movements of the stars and moon. But Euripides' portrayal of Medea in 431 BC was exploiting the *real* anxieties of Athenian men, who feared women with expertise in lotions, potions and incantations. This is shown by the evidence relating to the real-life fourth-century trial of a woman named Theoris, who was executed, along with her whole family, for the use of 'drugs and incantations'.[6] A speech by the sophist Antiphon survives from the fifth century, in which a young man accuses his stepmother of murdering his father with poison, and the speaker is clearly able to exploit a strong social stereotype associating female guile with pharmaceutical expertise.

After invoking Hecate, the goddess 'deep inside her home', Medea continues her crucial self-address like this (401–6):

> So come, Medea,
> call on all those things you know so well,
> as you plan this and set it up. Let the work,
> this deadly business, start. It's a test of wills.
> You see what you have to put up with.
> You must not let Jason's marriage make you
> a laughing stock among Corinthians,
> compatriots of Sisyphus, for you
> trace your family from a noble father
> and from Helios, the Sun. So get to work.

Medea's other special relationship is with her grandfather Helios, who, indeed, lends her the chariot in which she can escape at the end of the play. The Sun is also invoked by Aegeus, when he swears his oath to Medea, as it is by many other oath-takers in Greek tragedy, and this reflects standard practice; the regular divinities invoked in oaths, as we have noted, were Zeus, the Earth and the Sun.

Helios is actually a rather difficult god to grasp, at least as early in antiquity as this, when in most places in Greece he does not seem to have been particularly important, and it is not yet clear that he has been firmly identified with Apollo. It is from much later antiquity that his connection with Corinth is implied by the eleven slabs with mask-like heads of Helios which have been excavated in the Corinthian Odeum; these may actually have decorated the *scaenae frons* (facing of the stage building). Helios had a major cult in rather few Greek communities, the most important, of course, being on Rhodes, where a spectacular sacrifice took place: a team of four horses and a chariot were made to crash into the sea. The myth of Phaethon – which Euripides himself staged in a famous tragedy – may be related to this ritual.[7] An Athenian audience in 431 BC will have been reminded of the Helios on the newly completed east Parthenon pediments (now in the British Museum), riding with his team of horses from the waves. But Helios was not very significant in Athenian religion in Euripides' day, and the epigraphic evidence for Helios being honoured in cult there, even in a minor role, does not occur until the early fourth century (IG II, 2 4962). Helios seems to have been associated with the growth of crops, and was connected with the festival of Thargelia, held in May, when the first cereals and fruits were ripe. Passages in Plato imply that those Athenians who paid the Sun/Helios special respect, in the fifth century at least, were regarded as rather avant-garde and odd, if not actually outlandish and barbarian. After all, in Aristophanes' *Peace* (421 BC) we are told that Helios and Selene (the Moon) are betraying Hellas to the barbarians (406ff.) and the reason the hero Trygaeus gives is that 'we sacrifice to the Olympians, but barbarians sacrifice to *them*'.

Medea, therefore, has rather offbeat divine associates in Hecate and Helios. She is not exactly a goddess, but neither is she susceptible to most of the constraints of mortality – she can physically escape what, for a mortal woman, would now be certain death at the hands of Jason and the Corinthians, and she can fly in a supernatural vehicle; what is more, there is no known ancient tradition, in any Greek or Roman author, that she ever died. 'Witch' is far too weak a term for her; she sees herself as the agent of Zeus' justice, and, as some sort of demigod, she never reveals exactly what goes on when she is communing with Hecate and Helios. No wonder the chorus, and the audience, end the play so baffled.

The play, therefore, is paradoxically both traditional and extremely peculiar in its metaphysics. It offers a relatively simple explanation of the role of the major gods in the action: Jason is punished by Zeus *Horkios*, through Medea, for perjury; Corinth is the kind of place where sex becomes an issue, especially in the case of a man already patronized by Aphrodite; the events are a theological explanation for the origins of rituals at the cult of Hera Akraia. But Medea herself destabilizes this simple explanation. At first one of Euripides' apparently most accessible heroines, who speaks in ways that can seem astonishingly direct and immediate even today, she turns out to have been completely unknowable all along. She has not been playing the game of life according to the ethical rules understood or decipherable by humans at all.

Perhaps the most important theological moment in the play occurs at the point where Medea makes up her mind to kill the children. After the scene with Aegeus, she calls out, triumphantly (764–6):

> Oh Zeus, and Justice, child of Zeus,
> and flaming Helios – now, *my friends*,
> we'll triumph over all my enemies.

Medea, astonishingly, counts amongst her 'friends' and allies not only Helios and Justice, but the top Olympian god, Zeus himself. The chorus hear this strange note that she strikes, and respond in what are the most telling lines, perhaps, in the whole play (811–13):

> Since you've shared your plans with me, I urge you not to do this.
> I want to help you, holding to the standards of *human* law.

The chorus are, in fact, articulating a view consonant with the contemporary agnostic political theorist and philosopher, Protagoras, who insisted that humans had only their own powers of observation and reasoning to rely on in looking for explanations of events and phenomena. He famously said:

> About the gods, I am not able to know whether they exist or do not exist, nor what they are like in form; for the factors preventing knowledge are many: the obscurity of the subject, and the shortness of human life.[8]

The chorus are insisting, quite rightly, that *human* law does not sanction the murder of children in punishment of oath-breaking husbands. Medea, on the other hand, instantiates the philosophical principle underlying the whole play – that human reason is *not* a sufficient resource for ensuring happiness, since life is uncontrollable, disaster is unavoidable, the principles driving the universe are inscrutable, and suffering is indiscriminate and unfair. Most people who attend a production of *Medea* today do not think very hard about the role of the gods, if they think about them at all. But they still feel just as powerfully the philosophical bewilderment that Medea's role arouses. This is surely an important explanation for the translatability of the tragedy into every cultural and religious tradition that has performed it in the global village.

In the European Renaissance, the Euripidean Greek *Medea* was rediscovered, and began to be read alongside the Senecan version, which was more accessible because it was in the more widely understood Latin language. Seneca had reacted to the metaphysical bafflement which Medea inspired, in all who watched her on stage or heard about her in epic poetry, by making her summon the help of what feels at the time like half the divinities in the pantheon. This is his Medea's opening imprecation (1–12):

> You, gods of wedlock and you,
> Juno Lucina of the wedding bed,
> And you, Minerva, who taught Tiphys
> To conquer seas in his new craft,
> And you, cruel ruler of the deep Ocean,
> and Titan, who shares out daylight to the world,
> and you, triple-bodied Hecate, whose shining countenance
> ratifies the silent rites of the mysteries,
> and whichever of the gods Jason swore his oaths to me by –
> gods to whom Medea may appeal more lawfully than he did –
> and Chaos of eternal Night, realms remote from the gods, Unhallowed
>   Ghosts
> and Lord of the kingdom of despair, with your Queen, abducted by
>   force . . .

Some of these gods are culturally 'translated' into their Roman avatars from the Euripidean Medea's own speeches – thus Hera becomes Juno Lucina, Helios becomes Titan and Hecate remains Hecate. But Seneca's Medea adds and names other gods altogether. They include 'gods of wedlock' (presumably Hymen), Minerva (because she helped make the *Argo* and supported its helmsman), Ocean, Night, the ghosts of the unburied, Pluto and Proserpina. Seneca's Medea then explicitly summons to her side the 'Furies who avenge crime, Furies with loose unkempt hair, writhing with snakes, and clutching the smoking torches in your gory hands' (13–15). If they compared Euripides' heroine with Seneca's, and her liberally invoked divine assistance, new dramatists attempting a play about Medea must have felt even more confused. They will have been further perturbed by the newly philosophical tone of Seneca's Jason. Seneca, being a Stoic, was not fully satisfied with such a god-centred explanation of Medea's crime, either: something closer to his own philosophical position on her crimes may underlie the final lines of the play, in which Jason tells Medea to be gone to the furthest regions of the universe as understood in the physics as well as the metaphysics of the Stoic and Epicurean schools of philosophy: 'Travel on, then, through the lofty spaces of high heaven and bear witness, where you ride, that there are no gods!' (1026–7). If the Roman dramatist could so drastically amplify, supplement and rewrite the religious and philosophical dimension of Medea's story, no wonder much later playwrights felt that they had every right to make it comprehensible to their own, very different, audiences.

By the eighteenth century, Euripides' play, as well as Seneca's, had become increasingly familiar through translation into modern languages and adaptation for performance. Christianized neoclassical Medeas were the eighteenth-century norm in spoken theatre. The horror of the intentional child-killing needed to be ameliorated for an audience with strong ideals of femininity and equally strong Christian beliefs. One way of making Medea acceptable was to allow her exculpating fits of madness in which she committed her murders, as Agave in *Bacchae* is deranged when she kills her son Pentheus, or Heracles is psychotically deluded when he commits triple filicide in *Heracles Mainomenos*. In Richard Glover's *Medea*, performed in London at Drury Lane in 1767, for example, a good deal of emphasis was given to Medea's temporary madness or 'phrenzy'. Another strategy was to bestow an altruistic motivation upon Medea, for example, that the Corinthians would kill them by a much worse death if she did not kill them quickly herself. This was the expedient selected by Ernest Legouvé for his popular *Médée*, much performed after its 1857 premiere in Paris.[9] In more recent times, adaptors and theatre directors have adopted several different strategies for dealing with the play's pagan religion. The first strategy has been wholesale *deletion* – many adaptations and stagings of *Medea* simply omit many of the references to the gods, certainly to the more obscure figures such as Themis and Dikē. The specific references to Zeus and Hera often become rephrased as vague reference to 'god' or 'gods' or 'heaven', adaptable to almost any cultural context. More importantly, very few productions suggest in the final scene that Medea is perhaps not a human, after all.

Since the early twentieth century, the chief strategy used to make the religion in *Medea* comprehensible to theatre audiences has, however, been allegory. 'The gods' have been made to stand for something else, for another force of immense destructive potential, which is not fully comprehended or controllable by humans, any more than the chorus of Euripides' *Medea* understand her or can control her actions, when she claims that 'Zeus and Justice' are her allies. One of the first productions to allegorize the chariot scene was also the first in a translation (rather than adaptation) into the English language. This production, directed by Harley Granville-Barker in

London in 1907, was very important in cultural history because of its connection with the movement for women's equality in the United Kingdom.[10]

The translation was by the Oxford Greek scholar Gilbert Murray, who had supported the women's suffrage movement since 1889. Murray and Barker may have been influenced by the success of Max Reinhardt's Berlin production of *Medea*, in a translation by the famous German classicist Ulrich von Wilamowitz-Moellendorff, in 1904. But the political climate also made *Medea* a significant choice. In 1906 the movement for women's suffrage had been inaugurated, and in 1907 the first mass arrests of suffragettes shocked the public: no fewer than sixty-five served sentences in Holloway Prison. Support for the movement grew rapidly, inspiring Barker to produce the first of the whole series of suffrage plays, which flourished on the commercial stage, *Votes for Women*, by the Ibsen-influenced Elizabeth Robins. This impassioned piece staged a suffragette meeting in Trafalgar Square. October 1907 saw the staging at the Royal Court of Mrs W. J. Clifford's dramatic examination of the effects of divorce on women, *Hamilton's Second Marriage*. But it also witnessed the actress Edyth Olive, in the title role of Euripides' *Medea*, emerging from her house in Corinth and lecturing her audience on the injustices suffered by women at the hands of men.

Yet this 1907 suffragette Medea was no divinity. Reviewers remarked on how surprisingly 'human' Medea was, and complimented Olive on winning the audience's sympathy. In a seminal study of Euripides, published in 1913, Gilbert Murray writes about Euripides thus:

> To us he seems an aggressive champion of women; more aggressive, and certainly far more appreciative, than Plato. Songs and speeches from the Medea are recited today at suffragist meetings.[11]

Murray's book has proved perhaps the most influential interpretation of Euripides of all time. But Murray's translation, Harley Granville-Barker's production and Edyth Olive's acting combined to present the theatrical *machina* as a *metaphor*. It symbolized something very real – the scale of the consequences of a man hurting a very *human* woman. Although his translation was fairly conservative – even archaizing – in style and idiom, and kept almost all of the references to specific divinities, in the 'Introduction' Murray saw the ancient gods, and Medea especially, as designed to be read allegorically:

> The truth is that in this play Medea herself is the *dea ex machina*. The woman whom Jason and Creon intended simply to crush has been transformed by her injuries from an individual human being into a sort

of living Curse. She is inspired with superhuman force. Her wrongs and her hate fill all the sky. And the judgment pronounced on Jason comes not from any disinterested or peace-making God, but from his own victim transfigured into a devil.

Medea is a hate-filled woman, transformed by her injuries into something almost superhuman – a human victim of male irresponsibility and cruelty transformed by injustice into a daemonic negative force of almost cosmic potency.

Gilbert Murray himself regarded Medea's child-killing as realistic: 'Euripides had apparently observed how common it is, when a woman's mind is deranged by suffering, that her madness takes the form of child-murder.'[12] The prominent suffragette Sylvia Pankhurst recalled how the great stirring of social conscience in 1906 had led to economically privileged women noticing the hardships of women in the lower classes. The focus was on a number of tragic cases of poor women, 'which in other days might have passed unnoticed', but were now used to underline women's inferior status:

> Daisy Lord, the young servant sentenced to death for infanticide; Margaret Murphy, the flower-seller, who, after incredible hardships, attempted to poison herself and her ailing youngest child . . . Julia Decies, committed to seven years' penal servitude for throwing vitriol at the man who had betrayed and deserted her; Sarah Savage, imprisoned on the charge of cruelty to her children for whom she had done all that her miserable poverty would permit. By reprieve petitions, by propaganda speeches and articles, the names and the stories of these unfortunates were torn from their obscurity, to be branded upon the history of the women's movement of their day.[13]

The dismal crimes of these modern Medeas – infanticide, violence against their husbands, child abuse – were now seen as caused by their social status. Even intentional child-murder by women was now being seen as connected with male irresponsibility: like Daisy Lord and Margaret Murphy, Medea could now kill her children with premeditation and be given, at least in the progressive theatre, a sympathetic hearing.

Many productions of *Medea* have followed this seminal theatrical event by 'allegorizing' Medea's wrath and superhuman power as the potential reaction of women suffering under a patriarchal social system. This was especially the case in the late 1970s and 1980s, when the Feminist and Women's Rights movements were at the top of the political and cultural agenda, at least in Western Europe and the USA. But in more recent productions, the divine element has often also been 'allegorized' in a psychological way, as representing Medea's disturbed psyche. This was certainly the case, for example, in Deborah Warner's production, starring Fiona Shaw, which was such a commercial hit in both London and New York in 2000–1. There was no sign of any god from the machine; Medea clearly had a mental breakdown, and ended the play in a bizarre dialogue with Jason, washing the blood from her body. Similarly, the 2006 *Medea* at the Deutsches Theater in Berlin, directed by Barbara Frey and starring Nina Hoss, was a psychological interpretation, although the damage to Medea's psyche was clearly caused in part by sexism. Medea spent most of the play confined inside a box-like house that represented both her dismal apartment and her inner mental world. Disturbing images and sounds were experienced by her and the audience, which seemed to represent the fluctuating pictures and sensations in her disturbed consciousness, while hands and other objects protruded inwards from the walls, when her subconscious or conscious violent impulses were threatening to overwhelm her.

But there has been another way in which the divine element has been understood over the last half-century, and that is more to do with post-colonialism than with either feminism or psychoanalysis. Medea's revenge has very frequently been 'allegorized' as the violence of an oppressed people or ethnic group against their long-term imperial masters. This is an interesting development, because before World War II, Medea's religion was often represented precisely as a retrograde, primitive, barbaric belief system, in contrast with what was presented as the more enlightened, Western, Christianized religion practised by Jason and his countrymen. This pattern can be seen, for example, in the Russian verse tragedy *Georgian Night* of the 1820s by A. Griboedov, where the Medea figure was a superstitious pagan Georgian serf-class mother, taking revenge on her owner with the aid of the *Ali*, malicious female spirits of Georgian paganism. Griboedov almost wilfully ignored the actual official Christian status of Georgia in this presentation of the mother as an atavistic Asiatic barbarian.[14]

As Betine Van Zyl Smit explores in her chapter for this volume, Henri-Rene's Lenormand's rewriting of *Medea* as *Asie* in 1931 similarly substituted a Christian religious framework by contrasting his Medea-figure's 'heathen' religion with the Christianity practised by her errant husband's culture. The Indo-Chinese Princess Katha Naham Moun's children have been educated in the Christian faith by French missionaries, and this has alienated them from her. De Mezzana (Jason) tells his significantly blonde European Creusa (Aimée) that his marriage was scarcely valid as it was performed to the sound of tom-toms in the presence of tribal demons.[15] Only a year later, Maxwell Anderson's *The Wingless Victory* (1932) staged a North American marrying a

Malay wife, Aparre. He comes from strict Puritan family and Creusa's name could not be more Christian – 'Faith'. But Aparre comes to realize that she must carry out the fate that her old religion *dictates* must befall the children of someone who elopes from her Malaysian culture with an alien, and that fate is death.[16]

In the era of European empires, such an interpretation of Medea's religion as inherently inferior but extremely frightening was frequent. But over the last few decades, the gods, in whom Medea believes, have often been used in anti-colonial and anti-racist productions to symbolize the original, pre-colonial identity and culture of people who have subsequently been subjugated, oppressed, deracinated and transplanted, and therefore as a potentially liberating force. Medea's escape in the machine can become, in such productions, a metaphor for the acquisition of political independence, but with a warning: alongside liberation comes the threat of terrible, violent reprisals against the colonizing power. This was the way in which the religious element in the play was used, for example, in a South African production directed by Mark Fleishman and Jenny Reznek at the Arena Theatre, Cape Town, in 1994.[17] The different cultural and religious backgrounds of the people of South Africa were suggested by the use different languages including Xhosa and Zulu, as well as English and Afrikaans. The production was 'a timely reminder to South Africans rejoicing in their new freedom that a meeting of different cultures must be managed in a transparently fair and equitable way if disaster is to be avoided';[18] Medea's superhuman quality therefore embodied the potential for catastrophic anarchy to break out in post-apartheid South Africa.

Ethnic and racial resistance are often more or less commensurate, as in racially divided South Africa, with class identity, and it is the threat of class warfare that is the final way in which I want to suggest that Medea's divinity has been allegorized in recent decades. In Latin America, for example, Medea's religion has been a symbol of the suppressed African origins and identity of a large proportion of the population, whose ancestors arrived as slaves in South America centuries ago. A play by Chico Buarque de Hollanda and Paolo Pontes (1985), entitled *Gota d'Água* (*Drop of Water*), relocated the story of Medea to Brazil, and involved the Afro-Brazilian spiritist religions, that date from the arrival of African slaves to Brazil in the sixteenth century. They ultimately derive from Yoruba, the West African religion, but have syncretically assimilated Amerindian and Roman Catholic elements. The most significant one, and the one in which their Medea figure is an expert, is called Umbanda. Since the 1930s, Umbanda's adherents have been closely identified with the poor urban working class and underclass in Brazil. They worship a range of spirits (*orixás*) intermittently identified with Christian saints – Ogum, for example, is St George.[19] The Umbanda religion uses much magical discourse and many spells. The play *Gota d'Água* pits Creonte's atheist, sceptical, capitalistic rhetoric against the Medea figure's magical language, and she wins. He is scornful of her religion and it thus becomes a crucial factor. But the reason is not that the playwrights are believers – more that the magic becomes a metaphor for potential ethnic and class resistance.

The Brazilian version of *Medea* devised by de Hollanda and Pontes is one where Medea's ancient religion represents the anger and potential revenge of people oppressed not only by institutionalized racism, that goes back centuries, but by their abject position in the economic and social systems. It is not the spirits of Umbanda who unleash their terrible violence, through the superhuman Medea, but the wrath of people humiliated and kept in poverty. The transmission of this kind of interpretation all over the planet, to Africa, India and Australia as well as Brazil, is partly a result of the influential film *Medea* of 1969, directed by Pier Paolo Pasolini and starring Maria Callas. This film uses Medea's religion in a fascinating way, implying that the sacrifice of the children is an ancient practice endorsed according to her own culture in cases of desertion by a husband. Pasolini is certainly influenced here by anti-colonialism and its defence of the rights of all peoples to religious self-determination. But it is even more important that he himself saw the religion in *Medea* as a symbol of what was fundamentally a *political* issue: he saw no difference, he said, between the fundamental Marxist argument underlying his film *The Gospel According to St Matthew* (1964) and his *Medea*:

> In reality a director always makes the same film, at least for a long period of his life, just as a poet always writes the same poem. These are variations, even profound ones, on a single theme. And the theme, as always in my films, is a type of ideal and ever unresolved relationship between the poor and the common world, let's say the sub-proletariat, and the educated, middle-class, historical world. This time I have dealt directly and explicitly with this theme. Medea is the heroine of a sub-proletarian world, an archaic and religious world. Jason is instead the hero of a rational, lay, modern world. And their love represents the conflict between these two hemispheres. It's an old polemic of mine: the centre of the petit bourgeois civilisation is reason, while everything that is irrational, for example art, challenges bourgeois reason.[20]

Medea worships, and in some ways actually is herself representative of, the 'archaic' and 'religious' gods, that are also the 'sub-proletariat'. Jason represents the 'reason', on which the bourgeois ruling class pride themselves, and with which they have dominated the world. These two groups are in perpetual conflict. Here Medea becomes not only the force that can challenge the ruling class, but a metaphor herself for Art, the 'irrational' medium, which can nevertheless challenge the bourgeoisie's hegemony.

What a long way we have come from the bafflement of the women in Euripides' play, when they realise that Medea is somehow working the will of heaven! The blinding, elemental force of the Euripidean Medea, aloft in her fiery chariot, was, for believers in Olympian religion, a symbol of the terrible things that Fate can deal out to humans who have broken any of the fundamental taboos. In later eras, Medea's existential status as a quasi-god or demi-god has usually been replaced: her strength has sometimes been interpreted as the workings of a character suffering from psychosis, but equally often as a social or political force – the anger of oppressed women, ethnic groups and social underclasses. But, when we approach Euripides' play, it always needs to be remembered, that it is the awesome, unknowable religious element, the metaphysical power embodied in the mysterious figure of Medea, which ultimately underlies all these interpretations.[21]

Notes

1 Buxton (1988) 41–51.
2 For discussions of some of them, see Hall, Macintosh and Taplin (2000), Rubino (2000), Bätzner, Dreyer and Fischer-Lichte (2010), Biglieri (2005), Lorenzi (2008), Eichelmann (2010), Yixu (2009), Adriani (2006), Nissim and Preda (2006), Behrendt (2007). Unusual adaptations of *Medea* are discussed in several of the essays in both Hall, Macintosh and Wrigley (2004), and Hall and Harrop (2010).
3 Hall (2010b) Ch. 4.
4 Kovacs (1993) 45–70.
5 Baumbach (2004); Johnston (1997) 44–70.
6 See the speech *Against Aristogeiton*, attributed to Demosthenes (25.79–80), and Collins (2001) 477–93.
7 Burkert (1987) 175.
8 Protagoras Fragment 1 Diels-Kranz.
9 See Hall, Macintosh and Taplin (2000); Hall and Macintosh (2005) Ch. 14.
10 See Hall (1999) 42–77.
11 Murray (1913) 32.
12 Murray (1906) 94.
13 Pankhurst (1931) 225–6.
14 See Layton (1992) 195–213.
15 See Macintosh (2005) 65–77.
16 See Belli (1967) 226–39.

17 Well analysed by Yvonne Banning (1999) 42–8.
18 See the review of this production by Betine Van Zyl Smit, available online at www.didaskalia.net/issues/vol1no5/vanzyl.html.
19 See DiPuccio (1990) 1–10.
20 See www.filmfestival.gr/tributes/2003-2004/cinemythology/uk/film36.html, a translation of passages from Pasolini's *Le regole di un'illusione* (Rome, 1991).
21 A shorter and rather different version of part of this article, with less emphasis on the ancient religious and cultic elements, was first delivered as a lecture in Berlin at the Schaubühne am Lehniner Platz in 2009, and published in German as 'Medea als Mysterium im Global Village' in Bätzner, Dreyer and Fischer-Lichte (2010). I am very grateful for helpful suggestions made at that time by Bernd Seidensticker and Erika Fischer-Lichte.

12

Black Medeas

Betine Van Zyl Smit

Euripides' *Medea* is one of the ancient Greek tragedies which has been produced and adapted most often in the modern world. The reasons for the widespread and continued interest in this play must lie in the complexity of the character of the protagonist, which allows different aspects of her persona to be brought to the fore according to the period and place of the production and the intention of the producer or author. The mythical Medea is a helper-maiden, passionate lover, loving parent, enchantress/witch, abandoned wife, foreigner/outsider and infanticidal mother. All of these aspects have been elaborated in different treatments of the Medea myth since Euripides' *Medea* was produced at the Great Dionysia in Athens in March, 431 BC. Such was the impact of this brilliant dramatization that it underlies all later adaptations of the myth.

Medea is a woman who has given up her country because of her love for Jason, the Greek hero. She is a mother who loves her children. She has the courage of a male hero and stands up for herself when she is wronged. She is an outsider in Greece, but has won the friendship of Greek women. All these aspects make her believable as a human character in spite of her magic powers. It is precisely because she is credible as a wife and mother that the form of her revenge is so shocking. Yet, although she has supernatural powers, she cannot win back her husband, Jason, and she is a foreigner, who is politically at the mercy of powerful men. In an attempt to explain the heinousness of Medea's revenge, her murder of her own children, Euripides' Jason ascribes her act to her sexual jealousy and also to her belonging to a different culture. She is not a Greek. A Greek woman would never commit such an act. That Medea is a barbarian must be a factor.

In the modern world Medea's revenge has been interpreted in a far more sympathetic light. Feminist readings of *Medea* since the early twentieth century see her action as the result of abuse and domination by men. Coupled with an understanding of Medea's plight as a woman, some authors have developed the themes of exploitation to include her cultural background, so that the heroine is not only of a different, and inferior, culture, but of a different and despised race. Basing their interpretation of the treatment of Medea on modern attitudes to people of a different race, many dramatists depicted her not only as non-Greek, but as non-white. This is achieved by transferring the action of the play to a world where the Greeks become representatives of the first world and Medea, the barbarian, epitomizes the oppressed and colonized, usually a darker-skinned race.

One of the earliest dramatic treatments of the myth in which race is an important factor is the *Medea* of the German author and dramatist, Hans Henny Jahnn, first produced in 1926. Jahnn was deliberately addressing the racist attitudes of his contemporaries. He explained the reasons for his decision to adapt the tragedy so radically:

> What barbarians represented for the Greeks, Negroes, Malays and Chinese are for us modern Europeans. One of the most shameless traits of Europeans is the lack of respect for individual representatives of non-white races. I could make the whole of the marriage problem of Medea and Jason clear only by bringing the woman on stage as a negress.

Jahnn's Medea is an old and ugly black woman, while Jason, through Medea's magic, has been 'blessed' with everlasting youth and beauty. Medea singles out 'negress' and 'barbarian' as two of the terms with which Jason reviles her. In addition to injecting the strong racial element into the tragedy, Jahnn also heightens sexual tensions by increasing the age of the sons so that one of them becomes a rival for the hand of Creon's daughter. Creon himself hates foreigners and is a rabid racist. He rules out the marriage of his daughter to a 'half-negro' and lauds Jason as the most handsome, pure Greek, hero. Creon's contempt for people of dark skin is so intense that he regards them as lower than animals. He explicitly threatens Medea that if she and her sons do not leave, they, as negroes and barbarians, will be killed like wild beasts.

Jahnn's reimagining of the Medea myth scandalized his contemporaries and was not a success in production. The play was, however, more successfully produced several times in post-war Germany. In his prose writings Jahnn made it clear that he saw the acceptance of the mingling of the races as fundamental for the peaceful coexistence of humanity in the modern world. That the sons of Jason and Medea are killed thus takes on a pessimistic dimension and implies the difficulty of realizing this ideal of racial harmony. Critics have interpreted Jahnn's subtext as suggesting that the Black or African Medea is also a representative of non-Aryans in the Germany of his time, in other words, Jews and gypsies. In this reading, Jahnn's *Medea* can thus be seen as a prophetic text warning of the dangers implicit in the application of the ruler's (Creon's) policy of racial purity and the catastrophic consequences it could have.

Many other modern dramatic versions of the Medea myth present the adventure of Jason and Medea as a fable about colonialism and imperialism, in which colour prejudice and cultural conflict play a considerable role. This chapter will discuss the 'Black' Medeas of Henri Lenormand's *Asie* (1931), Maxwell Anderson's *The Wingless Victory* (1936), Jean Anouilh's *Médée* (1946), Jim Magnuson's *African Medea* (1968) and Guy Butler's *Demea* (1990). Some of these playwrights have chosen to transpose the Greek drama to a new cultural environment in order to make the message to their audience more explicit. Thus the remoteness of ancient Greece makes way for the worlds more familiar to the French, American and South African audiences respectively of Lenormand, Anderson and Butler. This process inevitably entails certain problems. By changing the title of the play and the names of the characters, the three dramatists were constrained to delineate new backgrounds for their plays. Anouilh and Magnuson, on the other hand, by preserving the names of Medea and Jason, immediately linked their plays to the rich mythical tradition of the Medea legend. Its various elements become the background of their plays and they are able to select and alter aspects of the story to suit their themes and characterization.

Henri Lenormand's *Asie* was first produced in Paris in 1931 at a time when many French playwrights, such as Jean Cocteau, Jean Giraudoux and André Gide, were reworking Greek tragedies and myths to engage with contemporary problems. Lenormand transferred the action of the play to the French colonial world in the period following the First World War. He preserved the traditional core roles under new names. The Medea role is assumed by an Asian princess, Katha Naham Moun, who has an Ayah as a confidante and child minder. The roles of Creon and his daughter are taken by a French colonial administrator, de Listrac, and his daughter Aimée, while Jason is transformed into an adventurer-turned-entrepreneur, called de Mezzana. The parts of the children are expanded while the action takes place over a number of weeks in different locations.

At the start of the play, de Mezzana, who has married the princess of the kingdom of Sibang, is on his way back to France. On board the same ship are de Listrac and his daughter. There is much emphasis on how out of place Katha Naham Moun is in the French world. Her spoken French is atrocious and she chews betel nuts. The conflict between her world and Europe is concentrated in the position of the children who have been renamed by the Christian missionaries at the school they attended. The struggle for the souls of the children is represented on de Mezzana's side also by his enthusiasm for technology, while the princess prefers that they should believe in the primitive forces of demons. The future of the children thus encapsulates the future of the relationship between France and Asia. On the one side is European civilization, Christianity, technological progress and exploitation of overseas possessions, and on the other the way of life and beliefs of the indigenous peoples. Similarly the two women, Aimée and Katha Naham Moun, represent these opposing poles. As they approach France, de Mezzana sees the attractions of having a wife who is part of this civilized world.

The decision that de Mezzana is to marry Aimée and that the princess is to be repatriated is facilitated by de Listrac's new position as Prefect of Marseille. He thus holds power over the rights to domicile of foreigners, in effect the Creon role. The outline follows that of the ancient tragedy, but with new elements in the characterization derived from the new environment. Thus de Mezzana becomes overtly racist. He wants Katha Naham Moun to return to her country, where she will be happier with a man of her race. He is now marrying a woman of his race. He will atone for his past mistake by devoting himself to bringing up his mixed-race sons in the best and most modern way possible, according to civilized standards. Lenormand made some changes to the plot required for verisimilitude in the European world. Thus Aimée and her father are not killed. The killing of the children is depicted in a very different way. The princess' motives are not only revenge for her treatment, but have the positive aim of saving them from the racial prejudice they would suffer in France and preventing them from losing contact with the gods of their ancestors. The deaths are presented on stage as euthanasia. The children fall asleep and die in their sleep as they have been poisoned by mango jelly. Katha Naham Moun then opens the window to the rising sun and jumps to her death. The play ends as the Ayah looks after her mistress, not down to the earth where she lies, but up at the sky.

This is clearly a far more sympathetic depiction of the Medea figure, but the conclusion of the play offers little faith in humanity. The representative of Asia has been crushed after having been exploited and then cast aside. The lives of the two boys who were the living product of a union between Asia and Europe have been extinguished. Lenormand chose to emphasize a particular aspect of the relationship between Medea and Jason. In the process Katha Naham Moun becomes more than a barbarian; she represents a whole continent of underdeveloped and scorned people. Conversely, it is the whole of France and the civilized world that must be held accountable for the injustice she suffers.

The dominant theme of *Asie* of the dangers of racial intolerance is also that of an almost contemporary American adaptation of Euripides' *Medea*. The play is again set in a new world, this time in a different period, and the characters have again been given names to fit in with their new environment.

The Wingless Victory by the socially and politically engaged dramatist Maxwell Anderson was first staged in 1936. Anderson set his play in Salem, a town in New England, at the beginning of the nineteenth century. The distance in time thus gave it some of the perspective lent by using myth. Salem was notorious as a result of the trials for witchcraft there in the late seventeenth century. It would also provide the setting for Arthur Miller's *The Crucible*, in which the witch-hunts provide parallels for the smelling out of communists in the McCarthy era of the 1950s.

Like Lenormand, Anderson makes use of the outline of Euripides' tragedy, but prefaces it with various scenes which provide background information and establish the mood of the play. The picture is created of a narrow-minded, loveless, Christian community, who collectively represent the Creon figure: the Rev Phineas McQuestion, his mother and the elders of the church. News is brought of Phineas' brother Nathaniel, the Jason character, who has returned, after an absence of seven years, as the owner of a five-mast ship laden with spices. He has acquired not only wealth, but a Black wife and two children. This poses a dilemma for his family and the Puritan community, as they are racially prejudiced, but desperately in need of Nathaniel's money, as they are facing financial ruin.

It is against this tense background that the Medea character, the dark princess, Oparre, enters. Significantly she is admitted through the kitchen door, thus pointing up the general attitude in Salem that anyone who is not White is a menial and a servant. In spite of this cold treatment, Oparre expresses her determination to make a new life for herself and her family in the orderly society. Anderson shows the couple as devoted to one another at their arrival in Salem, but in the second act, six months later, unbearable pressures are clearly taking their toll. In spite of Nathaniel's financial support of the community, his family are treated as slaves and he is summoned to give a bond for them. Oparre has tried to fit into the community by dressing like them, but realizes that she will never be accepted. Her longing for a neutral country, where they could be safe, cannot be realized, as their money has been tied up in Salem. The Rev Phineas finds out about possible criminal conduct in the acquisition of the ship and uses that knowledge to blackmail his brother into agreeing to send Oparre back to her country. This Jason character thus does not abandon his wife for another woman, but surrenders to the forces of hatred and materialism. Oparre remains loyal and pleads with Nathaniel to return with her, even if they are penniless. But Nathaniel is not strong enough. He has been affected by the attitude of his family and the other Puritans and now even feels some of the racial prejudice himself.

The resolution of the drama takes a similar path to that of *Asie*. Oparre herself takes poison, that she has brought from the East, and also gives some to the children (daughters in this play), and rocks them to sleep. As she kneels and prays to her god, she is interrupted by Nathaniel, who has repented and realizes he cannot face life without her. Oparre, however, makes clear that his rejection of her has changed her attitude to life completely, but she dies confessing that she still loves Nathaniel and wants to free him by her death. For the first time we see a Jason who assumes responsibility for his wife's actions, which have led to the deaths of his children and, in this case, her own as well. The impact of the altered ending shifts responsibility for the tragic outcome to the intolerance of the Puritan community. Oparre must be one of the purest and noblest Medea figures to have been imagined. In many ways she is almost the antithesis of the traditional conception. She lacks the force of the typical Medea figure, who is fired by hatred and the thirst for revenge. Anderson's goal with this reinterpretation was to warn against the disastrous effects of racial prejudice, bigotry and materialism, and he thus created a community, who represent all that is bad, while the Medea figure incarnates the ideals of unconditional love and selflessness.

This tame Black Medea is exceptional, as most of the modern adaptations do preserve something of the steely quality of the ancient Medea. This is evident in the French adaptation by Jean Anouilh, which was published in 1946, but first performed in 1953. Anouilh had already produced two other plays based on Greek models, notably *Antigone*, which was staged in Paris during the German occupation and presented the theme of resistance to unjust rule under the camouflage of Greek myth. Anouilh's *Médée* is heavily indebted to Seneca's *Medea*. Like Seneca he omits Aegeus, and the children are to be allowed to stay with Jason. A technical innovation by Anouilh is the omission of a chorus, but the most striking aspect of the French play is the reinterpretation of the relationship between Médée and Jason. Jason's new marriage is not the root cause of the rupture of their relationship, but the final symptom of an unbearable tension that has been building up between them for years. Médée's outsider status is indicated by making her a gypsy, squatting in a caravan outside the town. Her hatred for Jason is vividly depicted, but this is the other side of her fierce love for him which is part of their intense sexual relationship. Anouilh does not elaborate on the effect of his Medea figure being a gypsy. It is part of her wild nature. She is shown as always craving action, always ready for a new adventure, but Jason is tired of a life of adventure and wants a settled life. Thus Anouilh's Black Medea is not the victim of oppression because of her colour, but her dark skin marks her as different to the settled, bourgeois community and expresses her restlessness and inability to settle in an orderly society. This Medea also kills herself along with the children, by setting fire to the caravan when they are all inside. Ironically, although she thinks that this mode of death will make her an indelible part of Jason, he is shown at the end of the play as getting on with civic duties. In this way Anouilh moves the spotlight from Médée, and Jason becomes the hero, an everyman whose positive approach to the problems of human existence leaves the audience with a feeling of relative optimism.

The title, *African Medea*, indicates that Jim Magnuson's adaptation involves the Third World. That an American playwright chose in 1968 to set his Medea play in Africa raises several questions. Why not set it in the USA where there is a huge Black population engaged in the struggle for civil rights, or why not set it in a country where the USA has significant involvement, such as Vietnam? The answer must be that by choosing nineteenth-century Portuguese colonial Africa, Magnuson was ensuring that the message of the play would become more general and not be considered as confined to the specific American problems of the moment.

Magnuson follows the outline of Euripides' tragedy closely, but has made changes to the characters in keeping with the new location. Medea is a princess of the Bono, a distant tribe in Africa. Her Nurse is an old slave woman. Jason is a Portuguese adventurer, slave-trader and dealer in ivory, while the Creon role is transformed to that of Barretto, the Portuguese governor of the city. His daughter, Cecilia, is not a *dramatis persona*. The Tutor of the two boys, who have small speaking parts, is an old Black man, while Adago, the king of another African country, has the role of Aegeus. The chorus consists of 'poorly dressed African women'. A soldier plays the role of the Euripidean messenger, while a blind beggar, a character invented by Magnuson, represents certain elements of the native population.

The opening scene already indicates general disharmony between Black and White, between indigenous Africans and Portuguese overlords. The Black beggar's words are ominous: 'Awake, masters, for you are in Africa! ... Your many kindnesses to us – slavery, death, disease, are soon to be repaid. The time is near.' (p. 155). Thus the conflict between Medea and Jason is played out against the background of strife, which adds an extra dimension to their own struggle. The religious element in their conflict is again highlighted: Jason is free to marry the blonde daughter of the governor, because his marriage to Medea was not a Christian one. Medea, on the other hand, calls on the Sun goddess, Nyame, to help her avenge her wrongs. Medea refuses the sympathetic solidarity of the chorus. They have accepted their position as slaves and have thus become accomplices of the oppressors.

This play also touches on the difficult position for the children as they are 'mulatto'. That makes their future uncertain, as they belong to neither the Black nor the White world. In addition, Medea, in her hatred for Jason and all who have betrayed her, also has a revulsion for the whiteness in the children.

Magnuson enhances the significance of the Golden Fleece. Its holiness is emphasized throughout and Medea displays the bodies of her sons against the Fleece when she has killed them. She refuses to leave the children's corpses but will take them with her. She is able to leave safely, as her magic power protects her against bullets, and she is surrounded by poisonous snakes.

Magnuson's creation of a background of racial and political unrest in the city lends even more urgency to the execution of Medea's vengeance. The creation of the Black beggar, who voices the feelings of those who do not accept the colonial dispensation, adds to the racial tension. The last words of the chorus, however, effectively convey the utter chaos and despair caused by the completion of the dramatic action: 'We watched helpless as violence raced violence, as evil mated evil' (p. 190). There is no hope for ordinary people left behind in the strife-torn city now deprived of its governor, while Medea's future is also uncertain. Magnuson's conclusion is unequivocal: wrongs or injustices repaid in kind will provide no lasting solution. The beggar's dream of a violent overthrowing of the local order is contrasted with Medea's goal of reaching 'a land of hope where [she] could be safe and free' (p. 173). Both these ideals are shown to be unrealistic. Moreover, the terms in which Medea's utopia is described, 'a land where men have died to win their liberty, and freedom stretches as far as the mountain's horizon' (p. 174), evoke the popular image of the USA. The implication of the chorus' final words is that Medea will not reach that land – that it may, in fact, not exist. Thus Magnuson's play ultimately points to the impossibility of achieving freedom and justice by unjust means. This lesson would apply to the goals of the Civil Rights movement in the USA, which was at its height at the time of the play's first performance, and also to the war being waged in Vietnam. Medea as a Black freedom fighter is thus shown up as flawed because of the violence of her means.

Another Black Medea who symbolizes the struggle for equal rights for those suffering discrimination as a result of imperialism is Demea, the protagonist of the South African poet Guy Butler's reworking of Euripides' *Medea* to highlight the injustices of the apartheid regime in South Africa. Butler transfers the action of the play to the late 1820s on the Eastern Cape frontier where the British settlers and the indigenous Xhosa tribes met, often in war. Butler changes the names of the characters without obliterating their link with the Greek originals. Thus the protagonists become by anagram, Demea, a Black princess, and Captain Jonas Barker, a British officer in the Peninsular wars, who, since 1815, has been an adventurer-trader in Southern Africa. Butler explicitly states that he was prompted to create his play by his interpretation of Euripides' *Medea* and his concern for the situation in contemporary South Africa:

> I was particularly struck by the *Medea* of Euripides, which dealt with an issue much on my mind: racial and cultural prejudice … In writing *Demea*, I have turned the *Medea* into a political allegory of the South African situation as I saw it, at the height of the idealistic Verwoerdian mania.

Butler wrote his play in the 1950s, but it could only be published and performed in 1990, when the political situation in the country had changed and the legislative framework that upheld apartheid was being dismantled.

Further changes to the details of the Greek tragedy in order to fit in with the new context are that Jonas and Kroon, an older White Afrikaner, are both leaders of *treks* (groups of people who left the Cape Colony during the nineteenth century). Jonas' group is multiracial, but Kroon, the Creon figure, leads a pure White *trek*. When the play opens, Jonas has become disillusioned with the prospects of a mixed community and has decided to disband his *trek*, to abandon his wife Demea and their sons, to marry Kroon's daughter and to join his party. This sets the stage for the revenge of the Medea figure. Butler makes use of South African history to flesh out the details. His Aegeus figure is Agaan, a tribal chief, who conspires with Demea to enlist the support of Black allies to attack Kroon's *trek* on the day when the wedding of Jonas and Kroon's daughter is celebrated. They will kill the Boers and also Demea's children, who will be sent with a gift to Kroon. Butler substitutes this ploy, which has historical precedents in South Africa (notably the ambush and slaughter of Piet Retief and his Voortrekkers at the kraal of Dingaan, chief of the Zulus, in 1838) for the magic robe and tiara in the Greek drama and for the killing of the children at their mother's hands. As in *Asie* and *The Wingless Victory*, the Medea figure kills her children not only to punish her unfaithful husband, but to spare them the humiliation of suffering from racial prejudice. However, Butler sharpens the conflict between White and Black insofar as Demea is not isolated, but enjoys the support of Agaan and his allies. Before Demea takes leave of her sons, she changes from Western clothes, that she calls 'slave's clothes', into her tribal dress. This indicates her total rejection of the 'White' world and identification with her own people. Some interpretations have seen this allegory as aimed especially at the betrayal of Black South Africa (Demea) by the English (Jonas), who makes common cause with the racist Kroon. However, the outcome of the play, the disastrous consequences of the betrayal of trust between White and Black, has wider and more permanent significance.

These examples of adaptations of Euripides' play illustrate how modern authors have elaborated Medea's status as an outsider in the Greek world to find equivalents in the modern world and thus broach themes important in the new contexts. There are also examples of performances where directors have been less explicit in transferring the play to the modern world, but have indicated the relevance of the themes of racial prejudice and colonial exploitation simply by casting a Black actress as Medea. Kevin Wetmore in his *Black Dionysus*, that deals with the reception of Greek tragedy by black Americans, mentions that in 1936 the black actress, Rose McClendon, was set to take on the Medea role in a version of *Medea*, which was not 'Africanized' in any other way.

Much has been written on the performance and adaptation of the Medea story over the centuries. Some versions emphasize her role as a murdering mother and attempt to provide a psychological explanation; some emphasize her position as a woman. This chapter has shown how the modern world has tried to deal with her depiction as a non-Greek in the ancient play and that, for many modern playwrights, the solution has been to make her non-white.

Euripides' *Medea*

Translated by David Stuttard

Dramatis Personae

In order of appearance:

Nurse	member of Jason and Medea's (former) household
Tutor	member of Jason and Medea's (former) household with responsibility for educating the children
Sons	Jason and Medea's two sons
Chorus	of (fifteen) Corinthian women
Medea	Colchian princess, brought by Jason to Greece
Creon	king of Corinth
Jason	prince of Iolcus, hero of voyage of the *Argo*, taker of the Golden Fleece, faithless husband of Medea
Aegeus	king of Athens
Messenger	member of Jason and Medea's (former) household

The action takes place outside (perhaps in a courtyard of) the royal palace of Creon in Corinth. Although the play is set in an heroic kingly age, some eight centuries or more before the date of its first production, it imagines its social context as containing elements of fifth-century democratic Athens.

Euripides' *Medea* was first performed at the City Dionysia in Athens in Elaphebolion (March/April) 431 BC as part of a tetralogy, which also contained the now lost plays, *Philoctetes, Dictys* and (the satyr play) *Reapers*. The tetralogy was awarded third prize.

No stage directions appear in the received texts. The only real direction in this translation concerns the *ex machina* ending, where the appearance of Medea on high is of importance. Other minor directions are, in fact, translations of phrases in the text; for example, 'sobbing' can translate the Greek, '*ió*' or '*ió moi moi*', and 'screaming' the Greek, '*aiai*'.

Prologue

Nurse   Oh, how I wish that ship, the *Argo*'d never spread its sails and soared between the Clashing Rocks, slate-grey Symplegades, to Colchis and our home. I wish they'd never felled the pine-trees in the hidden glens of Pelion, or made them oars for heroes' hands, that they might come as raiders for the Golden Fleece – all for the sake of just one man, Pelias.

For then my mistress, my Medea, never would have sailed to Greece and to the towers that ringed Iolcus, her mind askew, her heart crazed, captivated by her lust for Jason. She'd never have beguiled Pelias' daughters, then, to kill their father, never come to live here in this land of Corinth with her husband and her sons.

Oh, yes! In everything she does, she bends her will to Jason's, makes his happiness her chief concern. Well, it's the best way for a woman to ensure security – not to argue with her man.

But now all's turned to hatred. Love has sickened and turned sour. You see, he has betrayed his own sons and my mistress, too. Yes, Jason's getting married. A royal wedding. Yes! He's marrying the daughter of this country's king, King Creon.

And poor Medea, so humiliated, scorned, keeps crying out on the oaths they swore, keeps calling up their promises, her trust and her fidelity, so total and so absolute, keeps calling on the gods to witness Jason's treatment of her in return. She won't get up. She will not eat. She's even harming herself physically. Deliberately. And she dissolves all time itself in tears. And since she learned of how her husband's wronged her, she has not raised her eyes or lifted her head up from the ground.

Her friends try talking to her, but she's like a stone, a rolling sea-wave, unresponsive. She only turns her ghost-white face away and groans for her dear father and her home, her native land, all she betrayed to come away with Jason, who has now humiliated and dishonoured her. And in her suffering she knows, poor woman, just how sweet a thing it is never to leave your native land.

She takes no pleasure now in seeing her sons. No. She resents them. I'm frightened that she may be plotting some new terrifying revenge. Her mind is dangerous. She won't put up with such outrageous treatment. Yes. I know her, and she frightens me.

I hope she doesn't take a dagger, razor-sharp, and creep inside his house in silence, find his bed, and skewer his liver, kill his new bride, kill the king, and so bring greater tragedy upon us. Yes. She is awesome, frightening. No-one who crosses her will come out of it easily, unscarred, victorious.

But here are her sons now. They've been out at their sports, their running. They don't know anything about their mother's troubles. Young minds like theirs are free from worries!

Tutor You've been in my mistress' possession as her house-slave for a long time now. What are you doing out here, alone, just loitering by the gates, while she's all by herself, distraught with all her worries? Why? Does Medea *want* to be left alone?

Nurse You're a respected and experienced old man. Well! Jason's chosen you to look after his sons! The troubles, that befall our masters, fall hard on faithful slaves. And they distress us. I was getting so upset. I had this overwhelming urge to come out here and tell the very earth and heaven of all my lady's suffering.

Tutor So the poor thing's not stopped crying yet?

Nurse I wish I was you sometimes! This trouble's just begun. It's nowhere near being over yet.

Tutor With all respect (she *is* my mistress), but she doesn't understand. She has no inkling of the latest blow she'll have to bear.

Nurse What is it? Tell me. Don't keep it from me!

Tutor Nothing! No! Forget I spoke.

Nurse By all that's holy! Don't keep a secret from a fellow slave! I won't tell anyone! I'll keep quiet if I have to!

Tutor I heard someone talking – oh! he didn't know I was listening! I was going to play backgammon, where the old men sit around the sacred waters of Peirene. This man said King Creon means to exile these boys here with their mother from the land of Corinth. But if the rumour's true or not, I do not know.

Nurse Jason has his quarrels with their mother, I know that – but will he let his *sons* be treated in that way?

Tutor Old ties and old relationships have given way to new. Jason is no friend to this household.

Nurse Then we are lost completely – if this new disaster's added to the old. The situation as it was before was bleak enough.

Tutor Wait! Listen to me! Now's not the time to tell our mistress. No! Stay calm. Say nothing.

Nurse My children! Do you hear how your father treats you? I wish he was dead! No! He *is* my master. But he's proved so cruel and thankless to his family and friends.

Tutor He's human. Who'd not do the same? You must have realized by now that everyone cares for themselves more than for their family and friends – some for good reason, others looking to the main chance – and that is why another woman's bed has made their father cease to love his children.

Nurse Go on, children – into the house. It'll be alright.

(To Tutor) Do what you can to keep them away from her. Don't take them to their mother in her present mood. I saw her just a little while ago, staring at them full of hate, smouldering like a bull, as if *they* were to blame. I know well enough her fury will not cease until she's found some victim, swooped and made her kill. I hope her gaze falls on her enemies and not her family and friends.

Medea *(Sobbing)* Poor lost Medea! The sorrows! The misery! I wish I were dead!

Nurse My boys, my darlings, that's what I meant! Your mother lashes her heart, lashes her anger. Hurry, quickly – go inside the house! And don't let your mother see you! Don't go near her! Be on guard against her savage temper and her single-minded all-consuming hatred. Go now – as quickly as you can – inside!

I know this shouting's just a prelude, which her fury will soon fan like some small cloud, that boils and bellies till it breaks in thunder. Her anger's bursting. She can't be stopped. Her very spirit has been battered by such suffering – what will she do?

Medea *(Screaming)* Look what they've done to me! Look what *he's* done to me! Misery! Pain! Oh! I curse you, my children! Yes! I wish that you would die with my hatred, your mother's, you and your father! And let all the household crash down to ruin!

Nurse Oh, my mistress, so ill-used and yet so cruel! What have your boys to do with the sins of their father? Why do you hate them? My poor, poor children! I am so worried something will happen to you.

Those who hold power have savage, terrifying tempers. Perhaps it is because they get their way so much and are so rarely checked their moods, their angers swing so harshly. I think it's better to lead your life from day to day with those of your own status. As far as I'm concerned, I'd rather have just what I need and grow old gracefully.

Parodos

Chorus I heard a voice! I heard her screaming! Poor Medea, so far from her homeland! Has her anger not subsided yet? No! Tell me, old woman! In the inner courtyard with its double gates, I heard her screaming. This house's troubles trouble *me*. Tell me, dear lady! Tell me what has happened!

Nurse Our house exists no longer. It is already rubble. A royal bedding's got him now, and she, my mistress, in her chamber dissolves her life in tears, and not one of her friends or all her household can comfort her in anything we say.

Medea *(Screaming)* The fire from heaven's shooting through my head! Why should I go on living? I wish that I could find some peace in death, some solace from this hateful life!

Chorus Did you hear? O Zeus and earth and sunlight, did you hear the scream, so eerie, terrifying? Did you hear the poor lost bride?

O, Medea, in your madness, what lust is this for death's cruel stony bed? She will hasten her own end, her death.

Don't speak of that! If your own husband worshipped a new woman and her sex, you'd know what she is suffering. Don't let it be a mortal wound! Zeus himself will join with you to bring you justice. No! Don't grieve unnaturally, too much, don't weep too much for him, your husband!

Medea O, Themis, mighty, everlasting, and you, my Lady, Artemis, see how I suffer, bound, united by such mighty oaths to him, my husband, cursed and damned. I wish that I could see him and his bride and his whole house torn up by their roots, for daring so to wrong me in my innocence! My father and my city! I left you in such shame, my brother's murderess!

Nurse Do you hear what she says, how she calls on Themis, the Protectress of Promises, and Zeus, whom all men hold the guardian of oaths? My lady's anger is so great – she won't recover quickly.

Chorus   If only she would come where we could see her, let us talk to her and answer all she says in all her stubbornness. If only she would put aside this passion which has gripped her mind, this seething anger deep inside her heart. I wish that I could always show my care to friends and family. Go in to her and bring her out. Dear lady, if you dare, go! Hurry now before she does some harm to those inside. Her grief is so distressing!

Nurse   Yes, I shall go. But I fear that I shall not persuade my mistress. It is a heavy task you lay upon me, but I shall do it. And yet, whenever any of us tries to talk to her or comes within her sight, she glares at us, her house-slaves, like a bull or baneful lioness protecting new-born cubs.

You would not be mistaken if you said our ancestors were feeble-minded, yes, not wise at all – they wrote their songs to sing at parties or at feasts or banquets, charming tunes to tease the ear, but no-one found a harmony, a gentle soft-stringed lullaby to soothe away the hates and miseries of men, the seeds of death and dreadful accident that cause whole households to come crashing down in total ruin. And yet to cure evils such as these with music – what profit that would bring to all mankind! For when they've eaten well, when they're replete, relaxed, what need have men for useless songs and taut-tuned melodies? The very feeling of repletion that a good meal brings is joy enough!

Chorus   I heard her screaming, weeping uncontrolled, and groaning, crying in her distress and calling on the man who has betrayed her bed, her faithless husband. And in the midst of all her sufferings and such injustice, she is crying to the gods, to Themis, child of Zeus, protectress of oaths, who brought here beyond the seas to Greece, slicing through the dark night waves, toward the heaving narrows, which unlock the vast Black Sea.

Episode 1

Medea   Women of Corinth, I have come outside because I don't wish you to blame me. I know that there are many who are haughty and aloof, some plainly so, because we see them, others who acquire bad reputation just because they stay inside and do not mix, because they're quiet. There is no Justice in the eyes of men, who hate another just from seeing him, unprovoked, before they've taken proper time to get to know his inner heart. A foreigner should do his best to fit in to a city, and I can't condone a citizen who through insensitivity brings bitterness and misery to fellow townfolks' lives. But I . . .

This business is so sudden, unexpected, crashing down on me and it's broken my heart. It is all over for me. Life has no more happiness. My dear friends, I just want to die. You see, my husband was the world to me, how well he knows it! And now he's proved himself to be the worst of men.

Of everything that lives, all creatures sentient, we women are most abject of them all. We must first with an exchange of money buy a husband, pass control of our own bodies to his hands. And yet there is an ordeal still more bitter yet to come. For in this getting of a husband is the greatest lottery of all – will he be cruel or good? There are no ways a woman can divorce and keep her honour, and she can't deny her husband. So she comes to a strange house, a whole new set of rules and expectations – and she needs to be clairvoyant, for she's not learned this at home: how best she should break in her husband. And if in this great undertaking we succeed, so that our husband lives contentedly and does not fight against the reins, our life is to be envied. But if we fail, we're better dead. A man can leave the house and find some new distraction when he's had enough, whenever he grows bored or irritated with the company at home. But for us, necessity demands that we have eyes for just one man, our husband. They speak about us, say how safe and sound our lives are in our homes, while they go out to fight. How little these men know. I'd rather stand my ground three times in battle, in the shield-line, than endure the agonies of child-birth once.

But the situation's not the same for you and me. You have your city here, your fathers' homes. You have life's luxuries, companionship and friends. But I have no-one. I have no city, and my husband treats me shamefully. He took me from my home as plunder to a strange land and, in the face of all I'm suffering, I can't weigh anchor and sail safe home to my mother or my brother or my family.

So I would ask this one request of you: if I can find some way, some scheme by which I might exact some justice on my husband in return for all the wrongs he's done to me – keep quiet. For in all else, a woman is consumed by fear, no mettle when it comes to facing force or steel. But when she has been slighted in her marriage and her sex, there is no force more murderous.

Chorus   I shall keep quiet. Medea, you are right to seek vengeance on your husband. Faced with such treatment, grief is natural. But I see King Creon coming with news of fresh decisions.

Creon   You, Medea, with your black looks and your bile against your husband – I give you this command: to go away, out of this land in exile, and take your two sons with you. Don't put it off. I am your judge in this, and there is no appeal. I shall not leave or go back inside until I cast you out beyond the boundaries of my land.

Medea *(Gasping)* I am lost completely! My enemies are spreading my sails full to catch the storm winds of destruction and there is no safe haven I can moor to ride my ruin. Creon, my persecutor, still I'll ask you this: *why* will you banish me?

Creon Because I fear you. That is my reason – I've no need to hide it. I am afraid of the harm you might do to my daughter. So many things conspire to make me fear. You are a clever woman, skilled in evil arts, and now you are no longer welcome in your husband's bed, and so you have been wounded. I hear you're making threats – that's what they're telling me. You're threatening me, Jason and his bride. And so, before you carry out your threats, I shall ensure our safety. It is better for me to have you hate me now than weaken, lady, and then later, in the face of tragedy, regret.

Medea This is not the first time, Creon, no, it happens *all* the time that men's perceptions of me injure me and work great harm against me. No man who's wise himself should have his children taught to be too clever. It's just another useless trick, and earns the bitter envy of their fellow citizens. For if you offer fools a new philosophy, they mock you as a useless imbecile. And if you seem to have some subtle understanding stronger than those the city think are wise, they make you an outcast and a thing of scorn. This is the treatment I myself have known. Yes, I am clever, and, though my cleverness is not unusual, I'm either hated with cold jealousy or else I'm shunned.

And so you fear me. Yet you've suffered nothing at my hands that jars with justice. Do not fear me. It's not my nature to do any harm to royalty. What have you done to wrong me? You've merely wed your daughter to the man of your own choice. For me, I hate my husband, yes, but you, I think, have been throughout a gentleman. And now I bear no grudge against you. No, I wish you well. Make your marriage, and I wish them every happiness. But let me live here in this land. And though I've been ill-used, I shall keep quiet. Those who are stronger than I am have beaten me.

Creon Your words have brought some comfort, yet I still fear your ill will, and so I trust you even less now than I did before. A woman, sharp with anger, or a man the same, is easier to guard against than one who's quiet and clever. So get out now, and go, as quickly as you can, and no more words. My mind's made up. You have no arguments to let you stay. I know you hate me.

Medea   No! By your pity! By your daughter, newly-married!

Creon   You're wasting words. You won't persuade me. Ever.

Medea   Have you no pity, no reverence for my prayers?

Creon   I love my family more than I do you.

Medea   My fatherland, my home, the memories I have!

Creon   Next to my children, my own land's dearer to me than anything.

Medea   Man's lusts can bring such evil!

Creon   Well that, I think, depends upon the circumstances.

Medea   Zeus! I pray your eye of Justice fixes Jason, architect of all my sufferings, for ever.

Creon   You empty, foolish woman, go! And don't give me the trouble of expelling you.

Medea   The troubles that we have already are enough. We need no more.

Creon   My men will use force if they have to.

Medea   No! No! No need for that! No, Creon! No – I beg you, though …

Creon   I think you mean more trouble, lady.

Medea   No, I shall go. That is not why I'm supplicating you.

Creon   So why do you resist? Why will you not just go?

Medea   Let me stay this one last day and put my thoughts in order, think where to go and find some new beginning for my boys since their own father takes no interest in his children. Take pity on them. You are a father. You have children. My concerns are not for me, what I will do if we should go; my tears are all for them, their tragedy.

Creon   Though I'm a king, it's not my nature to abuse my power, and often in the past my sense of fairness has not served me well. And now – although I can see clearly, lady, that it's a mistake – yet, nonetheless, it shall be as you ask.

But I give you this warning. If Helios, the sun-god, rises with tomorrow's dawn and sees you and your sons still here, within the boundaries of this land, you die. There. I have spoken, and it will be so. So now, if you must stay, stay for this one last day. You'll not do anything so terrible that I need fear you.

Chorus   Poor lady! Your troubles are so bleak. Where will you turn? Who now will take you in, what house, what land, to be your saviour in the face of all your suffering? Some god has sent you out, all rudderless, upon the great sea-swell of sorrows, poor Medea.

Medea   My situation's fraught with troubles on all sides. There's no denying it. But don't think the game is over yet. There are still conflicts, trials ahead for this new bride and groom, and no small troubles for their family. Do you think that I would ever fawn and flatter him like that, unless I had some plan in mind to bring me profit? I never could have brought myself to *speak* to him; I never would have touched him. But he has come to such a state of 'empty foolishness' that, though he could have exiled me this moment and destroyed my plans, he's let me stay this one day in which I'll turn three enemies to corpses: Creon and his daughter and my husband.

Dear friends! I hold the secret of so many paths to lead them to their deaths! I do not know which first to try. Perhaps I shall engulf their bridal home in fire or stalk in silence to their room, where they have spread their soft warm bedding, and so plunge a knife as sharp as any razor in their liver – no! This one thought gives me pause: if they should take me stalking through their house, ravelling my plots against them, *I* shall die, and, dying, give my enemies a cause for gloating laughter. The strongest way's the most direct, the way in which I am by nature most experienced – to poison them.

Well so, then, they are dead. What city will receive me then, what guest-friend offer me asylum in his land, safe haven with his family, and so protect and shield me? No-one. Then I shall wait a little time and, if some man should come to me, some tower of safety, then I shall carry through my murder silently, seductively, but, if things should conspire to exile me before I can work out some subtle way, I shall myself take up a knife and, even if it means that I must die, I'll steel myself to walk upon the path to brutish violence, and kill them.

For by my mistress, black force of darkness, goddess Hecate, whom I revere above all others, my accomplice and my ally both, who has her dwelling in the shifting shadows of my hearth, there is no man alive or woman either, who will wound my heart and live to take their pleasure of it. But I shall make their wedding-song a bitter song of lamentation, and their marriage desolate as my own exile.

So now, Medea, put nothing by of all your knowledge, all your spells, all your contriving. Go on to the abyss and to the horror. Now is the very test and touchstone of your courage. Do you see how they have treated you? You have no need of this, to be the butt of jokes for Jason's treacherous marriage, sordid, Sisyphean, you who are the daughter of a brave and noble king, grand-daughter to the sun-god, Helios. You have your knowledge, yes – and more: I am a woman, and although we women are so useless when it comes to good, yet as the architects of every ill, there is none more accomplished.

Stasimon 1

Chorus   The well-springs of the sacred streams suck back their waters, and all the universe, all Justice is turned upside-down. The male brain breeds deceit, and all the solemn promises of gods are crumbling. So now's the time that reputation too will turn and bring to womanhood, to me, respect and recognition. And so there'll come some compensation for the female race.

The muses of dead dusty poets will cease their songs of woman's infidelity. For the god of inspiration, Lord Apollo, never did bestow the power to write the lyre-song in a woman's mind, else I would make reverberate a paean hymn against the whole male sex. The yawning years have much to say not just of men, but women too.

But you, Medea, sailed out from your father's home, your heart mad, mind irrational, and burst the barrier of double rocks, the very ocean's boundary. And so you live here in a strange land all unhonoured, husbandless, the ties of sex that bound him to your bed all gone, and they are driving you, a fugitive, to exile.

The sanctity of oaths exists no longer, and from vastness of all Greece, respect is gone, soaring through the limpid air, abandoning mankind. And in your father's house, poor woman, you can find no anchorage to ride the sea-swell of your sorrows, now that another princess has your home and with a smile of triumph tenses her taut body in your bed.

Episode 2

Jason   This is not the first time – no, I've seen it often – your temper leading to such unbelievable disasters! You could have stayed here in this land, this house, if you had just borne lightly the resolutions of those who have more power than you. But as it is, because of empty words, you're to be exiled. Now, as for me, this is no matter. You can keep on saying for ever how

Jason is 'the worst of men'. But consider yourself lucky, in the light of all you've said against the royal family, to have escaped with exile.

I wanted you to stay – I tried to turn aside their anger as they raged against you. But you could not stop behaving stupidly or speaking disrespectfully or cruelly of the king. And so you're to be exiled.

But even so, despite all this, I've not abandoned you. I've come to you now as a friend – I've given it much thought. I don't want you and my children to have need of money or of anything, my lady, in your exile. Exile itself brings with it ills enough. There, you see – even if you hate me, I should never manage to think ill of you.

Medea You – 'worst of men'! That *is* the only name that I can call you now! You coward, you have come to me? You've come, my mortal enemy? Oh, this is more than mere bravado on your part or manly posturing! This is the greatest sickness that a man can have – a total lack of shame. And yet you have achieved *some* good by coming here. For I have things to say to you, harsh things, harsh words, the saying of which will cleanse my mind and bring you pain and sorrow as you hear them.

I'll take as my beginning *our* beginning, too. I saved you, well your ship-mates on the *Argo* know, who sailed with you from Greece – I saved you then, when you were sent to yoke the bulls, whose breath was fire, and sow the field of death. And I killed the dragon, which was coiled around the Golden Fleece, tight in a stranglehold, its guardian, unsleeping, and so I lifted high for you the beacon of salvation. And I betrayed my father and my very home and came with you back to Iolcus and Pelias' land, so eager, so naive, uncalculating, killed Pelias – such a painful death at his own daughters' hands – and devastated utterly his house.

You let me do all this for you and then, you worst of men, betrayed me for another woman's bed, *though we had children*. Oh yes, if you'd been childless still, I might have pardoned you for lusting after this new bedding, but as it is you have betrayed your oaths, and so I wonder: do you think the gods have no more power, no more authority, or do you think a new morality's laid down for modern man, since you know all too well your perjury, now you have broken all the oaths you ever made me!

This is my hand you held so often! These are my knees you clung to in an empty sordid lie, and so built up such hopes that turned to ashes!

But come – I shall ask your advice, as if you were my friend still, enter on some make-believe, perhaps, that you still wish me well. Why not? My questions will but show your shame the more. Where can I turn to now? My father's house, which I betrayed for you – can I go home to my own country? Or to the poor grief-stricken daughters of Pelias? Yes, they would welcome me into their house with open arms – their father's murderess.

You see, that's how things are. My family, my friends – *you* – hate me, and those I never should have harmed think me their mortal enemy for all I did to please you. Oh yes, yes, because of all I did, you've made me envied by so many women throughout Greece! O, what a wondrous, faithful husband in my misery I have in you, if I am to be driven out in exile, cut off from all friends, from all family, and all alone with my poor lonely sons. This is a pretty taunt to tell a bride-groom on his wedding night, how his own sons and I, who saved him, wander through the streets as beggars.

Zeus, why have you given men clear evidence to tell true gold from false, when there's no mark, no, nothing physical to show a worthless man?

Chorus   Such anger's terrifying and hard to remedy, when bitter hatred crashes cruel on those, who most should love.

Jason   It seems I must produce a reasoned speech and, like a helmsman of a ship, in whom men trust, run up the ragged tatters of my slapping sails and make my dash for shelter from the ceaseless storm-burst of your tiresome tongue – my lady!

But me – since you build up the reasons I should feel some gratitude to you too much – I think that it was Aphrodite, Lust, alone of gods or mortal men who saved me, when I sailed out on my quest to find the Golden Fleece. You have a subtle mind, it's true – but there's nothing positive to gain from cataloguing how raw Lust, how Eros bent you to his will with arrows you could not resist, so you would save my skin. I'll not set out too vividly each little detail. For, whatever service you provided me, the end result is fair. For, you achieved more than you gave, in terms of benefit, from saving me, as I shall show.

To begin with, you are living here in Greece instead of in your own land with uncivilized barbarians, and so you know the benefits of Justice and a life that's led within the framework of the law, not at the mercy of some cruel capricious overlord. Now all Greeks think of you as wise and hold you in some honour. But if you'd lived out at the very limits of the earth, no-one would have heard of you at all. Now, as for me, I'd take no pleasure from a house that groaned with gold, or if I had the power to sing more sweetly than an Orpheus, if my achievements and my fame went all unrecognized.

That's all I have to say to you about my quest, my struggles. It was *you*, after all, who raised the issue.

But all these accusations, that you've made against me and my marriage with the princess – I shall show you first how rational, how thoughtful I have been, how great a friend and ally both to you and to my sons – no! no! stay where you are! When I came from Iolcus here, so weighted down by all the troubles, inescapable, that clung to me, well, what solution could I find more fortunate that that, an exile and a fugitive, I should become the husband of the daughter of a king? I know it's this that wounds you, but it was not because I loathe your bed, or that I had been struck with longing for a new young bride, or that I had some sudden urge to breed as many children as I could – those that I have are quite enough for me; I cannot fault them – but so that we (and this is my prime motivation), so that *we* could live well, not always have to worry about poverty (and I know well how poverty drives all your friends away), and so that I could bring my own sons up in my own house as they deserve, and in begetting brothers for them set them on an equal footing with the sons I've had by you, so that in making this alliance between both our families, we should be happy.

And in the end, what need have you of children?

But me – it is to my advantage that I give some benefit to my existing children through those other children I intend to have. So was that such a crass solution? You would yourself agree if only your bruised sexuality would let you. No, but you women all have come to such a pass, that you think satisfaction in your bed is everything, but if you have some terrible disaster with your sexuality, you think that everything that's good and honest is against you. Mankind should beget children from some other source and then there'd be no need at all for women. And so, I think the cause of every ill there is for men would be removed.

Chorus Jason, you have set your case out well, but, even if my words now will offend you, I think you have betrayed your wife and acted quite unjustly.

Medea I must be very different from my fellow men. You see, to me a man who can speak cleverly but is in fact corrupt deserves the greatest punishment there is. For, in his arrogance of eloquence, he cloaks his crimes in robes of seeming virtue and, in his overbearing confidence, he'll stop at nothing. Yet there are limits on his cleverness – yes, even yours. You see, one word can fell you. If you were a kind and noble man, you should have talked to me, persuaded me to let you make this marriage, and not, no!, not concealed it from your family.

Jason Oh yes, I think that you'd have made a pretty speech to help me woo her if I'd told you of my marriage plans, as even now you cannot bring yourself to put aside your fury.

Medea That was not why! No! Your barbarian bed-mate growing old did not provide you with sufficient glamour and prestige.

Jason Get this clear now: it is not because of the girl that I am making this royal marriage – as I am – but, as I said just now, because I wish to save *you*, because I wish to father royal sons who'll share my children's blood-line and so will be the bulwark, the insurance for our family.

Medea I don't *want* a life of luxury if it involves such pain, I don't want wealth if it involves such torture to my mind.

Jason Do you not realize how much more clever, more sophisticated you would seem if you'd but change your attitude? I wish that you'd not always think that what is for the best is for the worst, or that your situation is unbearable when you are in fact fortunate.

Medea You are so arrogant! You have a way out and a future. Me – I'm about to be dispatched alone to exile.

Jason The choice was yours. You are alone responsible.

Medea What did I do then, marry *you* and betray *you*?

Jason You unleashed cruel and godless curses at the royal family.

Medea And for *your* household too I am become, I think, a cruel and vengeful fury.

Jason I can't discuss these matters with you any longer. But if you need some help from me with money for the boys or for your exile, tell me. I'm ready to be generous. I'll send a letter introducing you to some acquaintances, who'd be of use to you. You are a fool, my lady, to refuse. If you but laid aside your anger, you would get more profit from it.

Medea We have no need of your acquaintances, and we would not take anything from you, so give us nothing. There's no pleasure to be had in gifts from the mean-minded.

Jason Well then, I call the gods to witness how I tried to help you and my sons in every way I could. You take no joy in what is good for you, but turn your back on friends and family from self-willed stubbornness. And so you make things worse.

Medea He's gone. He's seized with longing for his newly-bedded girl; he doesn't want to waste time here with us. Go! Bed her! And maybe, if my words find favour with the gods, in marrying her you'll lose all chance you ever had of marriage.

Stasimon 2

Chorus When Lust comes, swooping down too heavily on men, it saps good reputation, saps morality. Yet if Desire, if Aphrodite, comes with due propriety, there is no other god more gratifying. And so I pray you, mistress, Lady, never turn your golden bow on me and launch at me your arrows, inescapable, smeared with the poisoned balm of longing, no, but rather let chaste modesty enfold me, which is, of all the gifts the gods bestow, most beautiful.

I would that Aphrodite, that Desire, in all her awesome terrifying power, does not unleash on me contentious argument or strife, whose appetite knows no abatement. May she not craze *my* very soul with longing for another's bed, but rather, with unerring mind, may she preside in equitable judgement over all the marriages of womankind, honouring those women's beds where harmony prevails.

O my fatherland, my home! I would that I might never lose *my* city and so know that yawning life of helplessness, that cannot be endured – of all the sorrows in the world, most pitiable. No! I would sooner die and put an end to all the long days of my life, for there is no grief greater than to lose your native land.

Yes. We can see it. I have no need to show the proof of it at second hand. For you are suffering the most appalling of all fates, and there was no friend, no, no city, to show you any sympathy in all your suffering. May he die in abject misery, who shows no honour to his friends, his family, opening his heart to them in grace and kindness. May such a man as he is never be a friend to me nor one of my own family.

Episode 3

Aegeus Medea! Grace and kindness to you! There is no fairer greeting that I know with which first to address one's family and friends!

Medea Grace and kindness to you, too, Aegeus, son of clever Pandion! Why have you come to see me here? Where have you come from?

Aegeus   I'm on my way from Delphi and the ancient oracle of Phoebus.

Medea   The very centre of the earth, where god's true voice is heard! Why were you there?

Aegeus   I went to ask how I might manage to beget children.

Medea   By all the gods! You have no children, then?

Aegeus   Some spirit has seen to it that I should be childless.

Medea   You have a wife, though? You're not celibate?!

Aegeus   I have a wife, yes – I am married.

Medea   And what did Phoebus tell you about children?

Aegeus   His words were too sophisticated for a mortal man to understand.

Medea   Is it allowed for *me* to know the god's reply?

Aegeus   Most certainly. A clever mind like yours is what I need.

Medea   What did he say? Tell me, if it's right for me to hear.

Aegeus   He said that I should not unstop the wine-skin's neck . . .

Medea   Until you do what? Till you come where?

Aegeus   . . . until I come back home to my ancestral hearth.

Medea   So why have you sailed to Corinth? What do you want?

Aegeus   There is a man – the King of Trozden, Pittheus . . .

Medea   The son of Pelops – yes, they say he is a holy man . . .

Aegeus   I wish to meet with him and to consult with him about the oracle.

Medea   Yes, rightly. He's a wise man and experienced in matters of this sort.

Aegeus   And more – of all my guest-friends and war-allies he's the closest.

Medea   Then may good fortune smile on you and may you get what you desire . . .

Aegeus   But you – you're crying!

Medea   Aegeus, I have the worst of husbands.

Aegeus   What are you saying? Tell me more plainly what is troubling you.

Medea   Jason has betrayed me, though I've done him no harm.

Aegeus   What has he done? Tell me more clearly!

Medea   He's taken a new woman in my place to be the mistress of his house.

Aegeus   How has he had the face to act so shamefully?

Medea   I'll tell you plainly: our former family and friends dishonour us.

Aegeus   Is it his desire for this other woman makes him so, or has your marriage soured?

Medea   His great desire. He shows no loyalty to friends or family.

Aegeus   Then let him go, if he's as heartless as you say.

Medea   His heart's set on a marriage with the royal family.

Aegeus   Who is the girl's father, then? Tell me everything.

Medea   Creon, King of Corinth.

Aegeus   Yes, you have every reason – more than any woman should – to grieve, my lady.

Medea   Yes. I am completely lost. You see, besides all this I am being exiled.

Aegeus   Who's doing this? It's unthinkable!

Medea   Creon's bundling me off his land to exile.

Aegeus   And Jason lets him? Surely *he's* not happy about this?

Medea   He has said nothing. He wishes to be strong.

I beg you by your beard, your knees – I supplicate you – take pity on me; pity me in all my helplessness, my sorrow! Look at me now, abandoned, exiled! Let me come and live with *you* in Athens, in your house, and so may the gods grant that your longing to have children reach fulfillment and that you yourself may end your days in richness and in blessing! You don't know what you have found now you've found me. No! I shall put an end to your being childless. Yes – thanks to me you will beget a household full of children! I am familiar with certain drugs and medicines . . .

Aegeus   Lady, there are many reasons I am well disposed to grant this favour, that you ask – first there's the gods, and then the promise I'll have children. For in that matter, I'm completely at a loss.

But this is how things are: I am a just man, and if you can get to Athens I shall do all in my power to grant you sanctuary and protection. But I must tell you this now, lady, at the start: I am unwilling to convey you out of Corinth, but if you come by your own doing to my house, then you can stay there safe from all aggression, for I shall not give you up to any man. But you must leave this land yourself by your own doing. I would be blameless in my dealings with my guest-friends.

Medea   So be it. But now swear an oath ...

Aegeus   What is it worries you so much? Do you not trust me?

Medea   I trust you. But the family of Pelias, yes, and Creon, too, all hate me. And if you were bound tight to me by oaths, you would not give me up to them, as they tried to abduct me from your land, but if we reached some understanding in words only and not sacred oaths before the gods, I would be vulnerable and by no means on an equal footing, if it came to terms. For I am powerless, whereas they have wealth and all the trappings of a king.

Aegeus   You have weighed your future carefully and given it close thought. And if you want to do this, I will not refuse. You see, this offers me the best security of all, since, if I'm called upon to do so, I can use the oath to justify myself before your enemies, while you gain more security. Tell me the gods by whom you'd have me swear.

Medea   Swear by the sacred soil of Earth, and by my father's father, Helios, the Sun, and swear by all the tribe of gods ...

Aegeus   What would you have me swear to do, what not to do? Say now!

Medea   ... that you yourself will never drive me out in exile from your land, and if another man, an enemy, should try to take me, you yourself, while you still live, will never willingly abandon me.

Aegeus   I swear now by the sacred floor of Earth and by the light of Helios, the Sun, and all the gods: I shall abide by all that you have said.

Medea   It is enough. But if you don't abide by what you've sworn, what would you suffer then?

Aegeus   The punishment that waits for all, who break the bonds of piety.

Medea   Go on your way now, and good fortune with you. All is well. And I shall come to you in Athens in all speed, when I have done what I shall do, when I've achieved my purpose.

Chorus May Hermes, son of Maia, Lord of all Journeyings, be with you. And may you soon achieve all you desire. You are a good and noble man, Aegeus. So I consider you.

Medea O Zeus, and Justice, child of Zeus, and light of Helios the Sun! Look how we are become now beautiful in victory against our enemies, and how we are already on our way! For there is hope now, that I shall exact some justice over those I hate. For where before I pitched and laboured like a storm-soaked ship, he has appeared to me like some safe haven now for all my calculations, and so I'll bind the stern-rope fast to shore and come to Athens and the safety of her city and her citadel.

And now, to you, I shall reveal my calculations and their stark truth all unprettified. I'll send a house-slave to request of Jason that he comes to me, and, when he does, I'll speak to him with soft, seductive words, assure him that I think he's acted for the best, convince him that I realize that all my suffering is for the best. But I shall beg him to allow my sons to stay – not so that I might leave them in a hostile country with their enemies, but so that with their help and through deception and deceit, I'll kill the daughter of the king.

For, I shall send my sons with wedding-gifts for the new bride – a gauzy dress, a coronet of gold, an intercession, as it were, to ward off banishment. And if she takes these pretty trifles, swathes her skin in them, then she and any who has contact with her will choke out their lives in twisting agony. Such is the venom I shall smear upon my gifts.

Enough of that. What I must do next breaks my heart. For I must kill my sons. No-one will stop me. And when I've turned all Jason's life upon its head, I shall leave Corinth and so endure my exile as the killer of my children, whom I love more than the world, the perpetrator of a deed of all deeds most unholy. My friends, I can't endure being laughed at by my enemies. So let whatever happen. What can it profit me to live? I have no homeland and no home, no place to turn in all my sufferings. I forfeited them long ago, when I went from my father's house, seduced by sweet words whispered by a Greek, who soon will suffer retribution for my sake and for the gods. For, from this time he'll never see our sons alive, nor will he ever father children by his newly-bedded bride. Necessity has settled cruel on her, that she must die in cruel agony through my sweet venom. Let no-one under-rate me, think me weak, a woman pliable and tamed, but rather know me to be otherwise, a terrifying scourge to lash my enemies, a gentle balm for family and friends. For it is thus that in this life we earn the most respect.

Chorus   Since you have taken us into your confidence, and as I want to help you and uphold the laws of men, I tell you – do not do it.

Medea   It can't be otherwise. Yet it is understandable for you to speak like this. You have not suffered cruelly as I have.

Chorus   But will you bring yourself to kill your children, lady?

Medea   Yes. That is what will hurt my husband most.

Chorus   And so you would become the most unhappy woman of us all.

Medea   Enough of that. There's no use now in talk. No. Go inside and bring me Jason. Whenever matters call for great discretion, I can trust in you. Now, if you wish your mistress well, and more – if you're a woman – you will not say a word to anyone of my decision.

Stasimon 3

Chorus   Since time began, the citizens of Athens have been rich indeed, the children of the blessed gods, dwellers in a holy land that's whole and pure. And so they grew strong in the shining light of wisdom, stepping lightly in the clear pellucid air, where once they say that golden-headed Harmony gave birth to the nine sacred Muses – and the clear-flowing waters of Cephisus nurtures them.

And so they say that Aphrodite, goddess of Desire, drinks deep of the Cephisus, sailing in her barge to Athens, fanned by breezes scented in the honeyed air, and on her hair her retinue of Lusts, which bring sweet knowledge in their train, sweet loveliness, scatter flowers, seductive in the soothing scent of garlands twined with blushing damask rose.

And so I ask, how will the city welcome you, Medea? How will Cephisus with his sacred streams, how will the very soil of Athens learn to love you, stained by the blood-guilt of your sacrilege, your own sons' murderess. Think of it, raising your own arm to stab your sons. Think of their blood and what you do. Don't kill your sons, we're begging you! We're falling at your feet!

How can you have such icy thoughts, how can you feel such cold determination in your hand, your heart to see this terrifying cruelty to its fulfillment? How can you look on your own sons and not dissolve in tears? How can you kill them? Your sons will fall before you, begging, supplicating, and you will not be able then to steel your heart and soak your hands in their lifeblood.

Episode 4

Jason You sent for me. I've come. You see, although you hold me in such hatred, I won't fail you. No, I'll listen to whatever new request you have of me, my lady.

Medea Jason, I ask you to forgive all that I said before. It's only fair that you should bear my violent swings of temper, since once we shared so much affection, you and I. I've gone through all your arguments and I've rebuked myself: 'For shame! What am I doing, ranting so, abusing those who wish me well, thinking that the king's against me, and my husband too, who is in fact so thoughtful to me and so sympathetic, making royal alliances through marriage, fathering new brothers for my sons? Can't I forget my anger, since in truth I am not suffering – the gods, in fact, are treating me so well. Do I not have my sons still? Did I not know when we came here that we were friendless migrants?'

I thought all these things over in my mind, and understood how foolish I had been and just what little grounds I had for anger. Now I respect you, and I see how rational you've been in marrying a second bride, and how irrational I am. I should have shared the planning, come to give my blessing at the marriage, yes, waited in attendance at your marriage bed, acted as a go-between to please you.

But we women are as women are – I shall not slander us. But just because we're women doesn't mean we must inevitably act badly or strive to outdo one another in our foolishness. So, I concede. And I admit that what I thought before was wrong. But now I've reached a better understanding of the situation.

Children! Children! Come out here! Come outside! Speak to your father. Say goodbye to him with me; and with your mother now be reconciled for all our former hatred towards those we loved. For we are bound together once again. Our anger is all over. Take his hand . . .

(Groans) I was thinking of the suffering that lies ahead, unseen. My children, will you always stretch your arms out to me just like this all your life long? How quick to weep I am, so full of fear. After so long I've put away my quarrel with your father, and now look, see! I've made your little face all wet with tears.

Chorus   Tears wet my eyes now, too. I wish no greater sufferings were added to those we suffer now.

Jason   Lady – I respect all that you've said just now, and I forgive you for the way that you behaved before. It's natural for women to be angry with their husband, when he takes another wife. But now, albeit late, you've recognized the weakness of your argument and your response as a result is much more sensible. Yes, this is how a woman who is rational *should* act.

My sons, your father has your interests at heart, and with the gods' help everything will turn out well. You see, I think, with your new brothers, that you'll be the greatest men in Corinth. Yes! Grow up strong – your father and all those who love the gods will do the rest. I long to see you big and strong, come to the full strength of your manhood, masters over all my enemies.

(to Medea) Why are you crying? Why so pale? Why have you turned your back on us – are you not glad to hear my words?

Medea   No reason. I was thinking of my sons.

Jason   Well, do not worry. I shall arrange all well for them.

Medea   No, I'll not worry. I do not doubt what you have said. As for my tears – it is a woman's nature.

Jason   Why so much crying for your sons? You go too far.

Medea   I gave them life. And when you prayed just now for our sons lives, I felt compassion that it might be so.

But as for what you came to hear me say, some I have said; the rest I shall say now. Since the royal family has decided to exile me from Corinth, this course seems better to me too – I recognize this now – that I should not live here in Corinth in your way, or in the way of the royal family. You see, they'd think I was not well disposed to your new household. And so, I'll take myself away in exile. But our sons – ask Creon not to exile them, that they may be brought up by your own hand.

Jason   I don't know if I can persuade him, but I must try.

Medea   Then tell your wife to ask him for you.

Jason   Yes, I shall do that. I think I can persuade *her*.

Medea   You will, if she's like other women. And I shall help you overcome the difficulties, too. I shall send her gifts, more beautiful than any other gifts the world has seen – I know well what to give her – a gauzy dress, yes, and a coronet of gold. I'll give them to my sons to take to her.

(to Nurse) So, quickly as you can now, go. Bring me the bridal gifts to dress her in. She will enjoy this happiness not once, no, but ten thousand times. Not only has good fortune given her the best of men in you as husband, but she has inherited the bridal gifts that Helios, the sun-god, father of my father, once bequeathed to his descendents.

(to Sons) Take the dowry in your hands. Take it. Give it to the princess, to the blessed bride. She will not think them insignificant, the wedding gifts she gets from me.

Jason Why would you give these things away? Be sensible. Do you think the palace is in need of clothes, of gold? Keep them. Don't give them away. For I know well that, if my wife thinks anything of me at all, she'll listen to me more than gold.

Medea Please don't refuse. Words backed by gifts can sway even the gods, and among mortals gold has more power than ten thousand words. The power of the spirit world is focusing on her, and even now the gods cause everything to do with her to bloom, for she is young and royal. And if it would prevent my children's exile, I would exchange not money merely, but a soul.

And so, my children, go. Enter this rich palace, supplicate your father's newly-wedded wife, my mistress. Beg her not to send you out in exile from this land. This is the most important thing of all, that she accepts these gifts with her own hands. Go now, as quickly as you can. And may you bring your mother the good news of your success she so desires, how you have done all well.

Stasimon 4

Chorus I have no longer any hope left for the children's lives. No longer. For they are going to their slaughter even now. The bride-girl will accept the coronet of gold, and with it her own death-pangs and destruction. And on her glowing golden hair with her own hands she'll place the wedding-veil of death.

The beauty of the shimmering dress, taboo in its perfection, the golden-twining coronet will so seduce her and she'll hug them to her. And so she'll wrap her body in her bridal shroud, all ready for her marriage-rites with death. The snare gapes open for the final dance of death and she will fall, for there is no escape, poor girl, from her destruction.

And you, too, Jason, bridegroom of sorrows, standing proudly at the altar of the king, you do not know how you are leading your own sons to their destruction, and with them your own wife to face her bitter death.

Poor Jason, how your destiny has tricked you. But most of all, I mourn your suffering, your pain, Medea. Mother, in your misery, you will slaughter your own children out of vengeance for your marriage-bed, betrayed beyond all laws of justice, when your husband set up his home with his new bride.

Episode 5

Tutor   Mistress, I have news for you. Your children's banishment has been revoked. The bride, the princess, happily accepted the gifts from their hands. And so, peace and security have come to your children.

Medea   *(Sighs)*

Tutor   Why are you so anxious, so confused, now things have turned out well? Why are you not glad to hear my words?

Medea   *(Groans)*

Tutor   Your reactions are quite out of keeping with my words.

Medea   *(Groans)*

Tutor   Does my announcement have some implication I don't know? Was I wrong to think my news was good?

Medea   Your news is as it is. I am not angry with you.

Tutor   Why are you crying? Why won't you look at us?

Medea   Old man, there are many things that make me cry. You see, the gods and I, with all my cruel plots, have brought myself to this.

Tutor   Have hope. You will be saved from exile, too, by your sons and so will come to rest.

Medea   Before that day, I must bring others to their rest.

Tutor   Other women, too, have lost their sons. We mortals must endure our sufferings as best we can.

Medea   Yes, I shall do that. Go back inside and do whatever you must do to get things ready for my sons like any other day.

Oh, my children! My children! This is your city and your home! When you
no longer have your poor sad mother with you, you will stay here for all the
rest of time without me. And I must go, a fugitive, an exile, to a strange land
although I'll never have my joy of you or see your happiness, I'll never share
your wedding day, never meet your bride or decorate the bridal chamber for
you, never raise the blazing marriage torch in sacred ritual.

I cannot weaken, and therein lies my tragedy. It was for something different
that I brought you up. It was for something different I went through all the
work and all the grind, the twisting agonies of birth-pangs just to bring
forth sons to die. I had such hopes: I would grow old and you'd be there for
me, and when I died you'd fold the death-shroud round for me and I would
be the envy of the world. But as it is, all my sweet dreams are turned to dust.
You see, I shall be lonely and alone without you, and so I shall drag out my
life in bitterness and pain. You'll never watch your mother with your lovely
eyes again; no – life holds such a different path for you to follow.

My children! Why are looking at me? Your lovely eyes! Why are you
smiling? You'll never smile at me again. What am I going to do? Women!
When I look at them, my boys, their shining eyes – it breaks my heart!
I could not do it! All that I meant to do just now – forget it all. I'll take my
children with me when I go. Why, just to make their father suffer, must
I suffer twice the suffering I would inflict on him? I will not do it. I shall
forget all that I meant to do.

And yet – what has come over me? Do I want to hear their mocking
laughter always in my ears because I've let my enemies escape unpunished?
I must go through with it. Yes! I have acted badly. I let soft sentimental
arguments corrupt my mind. Children! Go inside!

If any here is barred by law or ritual from sharing in my sacrifice, let them
withdraw. My hand is resolute. I shall not weaken now.

No! No! My anger! No! Don't do this! Let them go! And we'll all live happily
in Athens.

No! No! By the stalking wraiths of Hades and the dead, I will not let it
happen that my enemies point mocking fingers at my sons and laugh in
hollow, boastful, arrogant derision.

What I would do is done already. There's no escape. The crown is on her
head already and the dress is even now destroying the bride, the princess.
I know – I see. But I am going on the saddest road of all, and yet the road
I send my children on is sadder still.

I want to talk to my sons! Children, give me your hands and let me kiss them. Say goodbye now to your mother. Your lovely hand! Your little mouth I love so dearly! Look at you! And your little faces, both so brave, so noble. Be happy where you'll be. What you had here – your father's put an end to everything. I love our hugs, our kisses, their silken skin, my sons' sweet breath against me. Go. Go! I cannot look at you as I once did. I am possessed by evil.

I have been told the evils I must do. My passion's stronger than my resolution, and this lust for vengeance is the well-spring from whose waters pour the greatest sufferings for man.

Anapaestic Interlude

Chorus   I've often been involved in softer sophistries and in debate more subtle than a woman should. But women have their muse of inspiration, too, which brings them understanding. Not all, perhaps, but there are some (how could there not be) and you'd find them out, I think, among the many. For womankind is not devoid of inspiration.

And I maintain that being childless, having no experience at all of children, brings more happiness than parenthood. The childless, through their inexperience, can speculate on whether children are a blessing or a curse, and yet are free from all the toil.

But those, who have the 'joy' of children growing up in their own homes – I see them worn inexorably down by worries: first how best to bring them up and how to make enough of an inheritance to leave them when they die. And then, how do they know if all this toil, this effort, is for children who are virtuous or bad?

One worry still remains to parents everywhere, the last of all: for even if they've found the means to bring them up, and if their children have grown big and strong, and if they've turned out virtuous, Death still is there to snatch the corpses of your children down to Hades and so turn your former happiness upon its head. Why, then, should we embrace this new anxiety of parenthood, when there already are so many others, that the gods bestow on men?

Episode 6

Medea   My friends! It seems like an eternity I have been waiting, listening, intent for any sign to tell what is to be. And now I see a servant, one of Jason's household, coming here. He's breathing hard. He speaks of horrors strange and new.

Messenger   Medea! All you have done! The cruel atrocities! Go! Go away! Use any means you can!

Medea   What have I done that I should run away?

Messenger   The girl, the princess is destroyed, and Creon too, her father, all through your venom!

Medea   You tell such an enchanting story, that I'll think of you for all the rest of time as my well-wisher and my friend.

Messenger   What are you saying? Are you thinking clearly, lady? Are you mad? The horror you've unleashed upon the royal house – how can you hear what you have done and smile and be not terrified?

Medea   There is much that I could say to justify what I have done. But take your time, my friend, and tell me how they died. You see, you'll give me twice the satisfaction if their death was hard, in twisting cruelty.

Messenger   Your two sons came in with their father and they went on through towards the bridal rooms. And we were glad – the house-slaves all had been distressed to see you suffer so. And so at once, there was much talk throughout the house, how you had put aside your former quarrel with your husband. They took your two boys' hands and kissed them, and they kissed their golden hair. And I myself was moved so by my happiness I followed the boys all the way inside the women's quarters.

She was there – our mistress, now that you are our mistress no longer – but at first she did not see your sons. Her eyes were searching only for her Jason. But then she saw them, and the blood drained from her face. She turned away, her fists clenched to her eyes, in indignation and revulsion that your sons had been brought in. Your husband went to her and tried to soothe her, comforted the child, and said: 'Will you not put away this anger with my friends and family? Will you not check your temper? Look at me. Will you not think of my friends and my family as yours, accept these gifts and ask your father to revoke my children's exile for my sake?'

And when she saw the beauty of your gifts, well, she could not resist. No. She agreed to everything her husband asked. And as soon as Jason and his sons had left her rooms, she took the dress, so shimmering, so fine, and wrapped it round her. And she set the golden crown upon her head and took a mirror in her hand and in its brightness bunched her curls and laughed to look upon the ghostly spectre of her face reflected there. She stood up from the chair she sat on, and she walked from room to room, treading softly, airily on milk-white feet, enraptured by your gifts; and many times she'd arch her back and gaze in admiration at her loveliness.

But then what we saw next – so horrible to see! You see, all colour drained from her; she staggered, stumbled, her limbs shaking uncontrolled; she would have fallen headlong on the ground, but somehow found a chair and sank down huddled in it.

One of her servants, an old woman, thought that it might be the anger of some god, of Pan, had settled on her and she raised the ritual wail to ward off evil. But then she saw the white saliva seeping from her mouth, she saw the girls' eyes twisting up, contorted, in their sockets and her bloodless skin. Her ritual wail became a scream that froze the soul. At once one of her servants ran to Creon's quarters, one to Jason to tell him of his bride, how she was suffering. The whole house thundered with the clattering of running feet.

It happened all so quickly, in the time a sprinter takes to run two lengths, and then her eyes, which had before been dull and lifeless, snapped into sudden focus and she groaned – a terrifying unearthly groan. You see, a double agony was pressing raw against her. The golden garland, which had sat so lightly on her head before, began to smoulder with a stream of fire, supernatural, corroding all it touched. The gauzy dress, which your own sons had given her, tore through her soft white skin. She staggered from the throne. She tried to run. Engulfed in fire, her hair, her head shook violently in spasms as she tried to tear away the crown. But still the golden chains clamped tight, and every movement of her head but fanned the fire the more. Exhausted by the pain, she fell, disfigured, features gone. Only a loving parent would have recognized her then. Her eyes were melting and her face had lost all form, and from her forehead gouts of blood and fire drenched down. And as the poison ate its acid way unseen, her very flesh, like glistening drops of resin, oozed from her bones.

It was so harrowing to see. We all were terrified to touch her corpse. What she had suffered stood as warning to us all.

But suddenly her father burst into her chamber. He did not know how she had suffered, and he fell down on his knees beside her corpse. And as he did so, he let out a groan. He hugged her to him, kissed her, talked to her: 'My poor dear child! Which of the gods so hated you to make you die like this? I am an old man, near to death; who has bereft me of my only child? Oh, how I wish that I could die with you, my child!'

When he had stopped, and tried his tears, he tried, so old, so frail, to stand. But he could not. The gauzy dress stuck to him fast like ivy to a laurel shoot. He wrestled desperately to stand, but as he struggled to his knees, her weight dragged leaden down and made him fall. And if he tried to free himself by force, he tore his flesh, so old, so dry, from off his bones. In time, the poor man sank, exhausted, to the ground and so gave up his soul. You see, the evil and the pain had broken him.

They're lying there now in death together – an old father and his child – a destiny to make the very world dissolve in tears.

(*To Medea*) But as for your affairs, Medea, you will yourself know how you best can ward off punishment. I shall not speak of that. But I have thought before and think it now, how human life is nothing but a shadow. For there's no man alive who can be truly free from cares. If he has gained great wealth, one man perhaps may seem more lucky than another but his cares are with him always.

Chorus   On this one day, I think, some spirit's clamped so many sorrows hard on Jason, but with justice. Our poor princess, poor Creon's child, what grief is ours for all your suffering! And even now you make your lonely journey down to Hades' house of death, your only crime: to marry Jason.

Medea   My friends, the die is cast. I must lose no time, but I must kill my children and so flee this land. For if I hesitate, I shall by my delay but turn my children over to another's hands to die more cruelly. Compulsion crowds them from all sides and they must die. Since it is so, then it is better I should kill them, for I gave them life. So, steel yourself, Medea. Why hesitate, when there is no escape from pain and cruel compulsion? My hand, my hand! Come, take the knife and trace that narrow line, which starts my future and yet ends their past. Do not shrink back! Do not think back on their sweet childhood, how you cradled them, your babies. No! For this one day forget they are your children. You will have all your life to mourn. And if you kill them, well, at least you loved them once. I am a woman and my destiny has overwhelmed me.

Stasimon 5

Chorus   You, Earth, and you, you golden shafts of sunlight, look! Look on this woman now, taboo, before she stains her hands in the black blood of her own children's slaughter! Your shimmering sunlight gave her birth, your blood flows in her veins, and terror comes to mortal men when the gods' blood is spilled. So, sunlight, Zeus-born, stop her! Stay her hand! Drive her away! She has become a Fury bent on blood, lashed to a vicious frenzy by the screaming wraiths of death.

Was it all empty, then, the loving care you gave them? And all the love that they returned, was that all nothing, too? Why did you ever cross the Clashing Rocks, slate-grey Symplegades, the boundary that separates the ordered world from chaos? How can your mind be so consumed by such a holocaust of hatred, such a lust for blood? When we spill the blood of our own blood, a terrifying miasma settles, seeping from the ground, and from the sky-gods comes the curse of their anathema.

(The children scream within)

Did you hear them scream? The children! Did you hear them? The woman is accursed!

Child A   What shall I do? Where can I flee my mother's hands?

Child B   I do not know, my dearest brother! We are lost!

Chorus   Shall I go inside? I should protect them!

Child A   Yes! By the gods, protect us!

Child B   The sword-snare closes tight!

Chorus   Medea! Your spirit must have been as hard as stone, as iron to grasp fate in your hands and kill your children! I've heard tell of one woman only, who in time past raised her hand to kill her sons, when Ino, maddened by the madness of the gods, was driven from her house by Hera, wife of Zeus, to wander far from home. She flung herself headlong into the salt-sea-swell because she'd killed her children in her cruelty. She stepped into the stomach-churning void from the high cliff and died to join in death with her two sons. So what should now seem strange or terrifying? A woman's sexuality can bring many pains; it has already reaped its swathe of suffering for men.

Exodos

Jason   Women, oh!, the horror and the cruelty of all she's done, Medea! Is she inside or has she fled? Yes, she must either hide below the very earth or soar on spreading wings into the vastness of the sky, if she is not to suffer retribution from the royal house. Or does she think that she can kill a king, a princess, and escape the direst punishment?

And yet my thoughts are not so much for her as for my children. Yes, Medea's fate lies in the hands of those, whose relatives she's killed, but I've come to save my children's lives, lest Creon's family carry out some grim atrocity in retribution for their mother's sacrilegious crime.

Chorus   Jason, you poor man! You do not know the depths of all the suffering you must endure. For if you did, you'd not have spoken so.

Jason   What then? Does she want to kill me too?

Chorus   Your sons are dead. Their mother killed them.

Jason   No! What will you say? It will destroy me, women!

Chorus   Accept it Jason – they are dead.

Jason   Where did she kill them? Out here? In the house?

Chorus   Open the doors and you will see them dead.

Jason   Unbar the doors, slaves, now! As quickly as you can! Unlock the bolts that I might see the horror of my children's death and take my vengeance on their murderess!

Medea   (*Appearing high above the palace in the fiery chariot of Helios, the sun-god, drawn by serpents. She holds torches in both hands. Her children's bodies lie at her feet.*)

Why are you straining at the doors? Why would you open them? What is it that you hope to find? The corpses of the dead? And me, who murdered them? Stop now! If you would speak to me, then speak! But you will never touch me. My father's father, Helios, the Sun, has given me his chariot, my tower and my defence against my enemies.

Jason   You! You! I hate you! Of any woman anywhere you've earned the greatest hatred of the gods and me and all mankind! You so endured to stab and stab again your sons, whom you yourself had borne, and so leave me bereft, destroyed! And now, you still can show your face before the sacred sun and earth, though you are guilty of the greatest sacrilege! Damnation take you!

I now see clearly, though I did not see it clearly then before, that when I brought you from your palace and your strange barbaric land to Greece and to my home, I brought in you a mighty evil, yes, a woman who'd betrayed her father and the very land that brought her up. The gods unleashed you on me as a demon to destroy me. You killed your brother at your hearth and so stepped on my ship, my *Argo*, in all its sacred innocence. And so it all began. You were my wife. You bore my sons. And now, because of nothing more than sexual jealousy, you've killed them. There was no woman ever in the whole of Greece who could have done such things, and yet I did not marry any Greek. I married you. I married hatred, spite, destruction – not a woman but a lioness unleashed and more inhuman than the sea-snakes circling Scylla. Why catalogue your countless crimes? You have no concept of remorse.

My curse goes with you! Yes, your life is sordid, you, your children's murderess! All I have left now is to mourn the spirit of my own destruction – my bride, so young, so innocent, is there for me no longer and my sons I brought up with such care – I'll never speak to them or see them in this life again. All that I had is gone.

Medea   I would construct a lengthy argument to meet your accusations, but Zeus, the Father, knows not only what I've done to you but what I've done *for* you as well. You were not to humiliate my marriage and my bed, while you yourself enjoyed a charmed life, ridiculing me with mocking laughter. Nor could the princess, no, nor Creon either, who'd arranged your marriage, banish me and go unpunished. So do what you will. Call me a lioness unleashed, if that gives you some pleasure. Think of me, if you like, as more inhuman than the sea-snakes circling Scylla. But I have done all I set out to do. My venom is implanted in your heart.

Jason   But they were your sons, too! Your loss, your grief's as great as mine!

Medea   Know this: you cannot ridicule me now, and that soothes all my pain.

Jason   My sons, your mother was so cruel.

Medea   My children, no, it was your father's weakness, that destroyed you!

Jason   It was not I, who killed them!

Medea   No, but it was your arrogance and your decision to take your new bride.

Jason   And so you thought your jealousies could justify such slaughter?

Medea   Do you think that a woman cares so little for a husband's infidelity?

Jason   A woman who is rational would, yes! For you, though, everything that's done, you think is done to hurt you.

Medea   Your sons are dead, and I have had my vengeance.

Jason   Yes, they are dead, and they will have *their* vengeance upon you!

Medea   The gods know who it was began this conflict.

Jason   Yes, and they know your mind and it repels them.

Medea   Hate all you will. The shrillness of your ranting merely fills me with contempt!

Jason   As I feel nothing but contempt when I hear you! Yes, I am glad to see you go!

Medea   Then I shall go. No more delay. I have no wish to stay now.

Jason   Wait! Let me bury them and carry out the rituals of death for my dead sons!

Medea   No. I shall bury them with my own hands. I'll take them to the sacred precinct of the goddess Hera on her headland where it overlooks the sea, and there, where none who hate them may dishonour them, I'll build their tomb. And for all future time in Corinth, in this land, I shall ordain a solemn festival and rites, an expiation for their death and for my sacrilege. And I shall go to Aegeus in Athens and there shall live with him. But you, as is a coward's due, will die all shabbily, struck on your head by a splinter of your ship, your *Argo*. So in the squalor of your death will die our marriage and our union.

Jason   The furies of your children's vengeance, yes, and blood-soaked Justice damn you!

Medea   There is no god or spirit hears you now, for you have broken solemn oaths and sullied all the sacred ties of friendship!

Jason   You cursed abomination! You have slaughtered your own sons!

Medea   Go back inside. Bury your wife.

Jason Yes, I shall go. My sons are lost forever.

Medea Your grief will grow as you grow old into great old age.

Jason My sons! I love my sons so much!

Medea Their mother loves them. You do not.

Jason And still you killed them.

Medea That they might break your heart.

Jason I wish so much that I could kiss my children one last time!

Medea Yes, there is so much that you would say, so many kisses, yet a moment since you'd drive them out in exile.

Jason By all the gods! Let me caress their soft skin one last time!

Medea It cannot be. There is no longer any use in words.

Jason Zeus! Hear how she rejects my prayers; see how I suffer at her hands! She is a savage lioness, a foul abomination! She has killed my sons!

But now, as best I can, though it can be but poorly, I must mourn all that has happened here, and call the gods to witness how you killed my sons and then denied me any right to lay their bodies out or bury them. I wish that I had never fathered sons to see them so destroyed, and you their murderer.

Chorus Zeus on Olympus watches over many things. The gods have many shapes and they appear most often when you don't expect them. What seems most likely does not come to pass. A god can find a way to do the unexpected. Such is what happened here.

Figure 4 Modern stage production of *Medea*, produced and performed by the Actors of Dionysus 2013 (© David Stuttard)

Figure 5 Tamsin Shasha as Medea in Actors of Dionysus' 2013 production at the Rose Theatre, Kingston.

Bibliography

Adkins, A. W. H., *Merit and Responsibility: A Study in Greek Values*, Oxford, 1960.

Adriani, E., *Medea: fortuna e metamorfosi di un archetipo*, Padua, 2006.

Allan, W., *Euripides Medea*, London, 2002.

Anderson, M., 'The Wingless Victory', in J. L. Sanderson and E. Zimmerman (eds) *Medea: Myth and Dramatic Form*, Boston, 1967.

Anouilh, J., 'Médée', in *Nouvelles Pièces Noires*, Paris, 1961.

Arnott, W. G., 'Off-Stage Cries and the Choral Presence: Some Challenges to Theatrical Convention in Euripides', in *Antichthon* 16, 1982.

Bakhtin, M. M. (trans. Hélène Iswolsky), *Rabelais and his World*, Indiana, 1984.

Bakola, E., *Cratinus and the Art of Comedy*, Oxford, 2010.

Banning, Y., 'Speaking Silences: Images of Cultural Difference and Gender in Fleishman and Reznek's *Medea*', in M. Blumberg and D. Walder, D. (eds) *South African Theatre As/And Intervention*, Amsterdam/Atlanta, 1999.

Bassi, K., *Acting Like Men: Gender, Drama and Nostalgia in Ancient Greece*, Ann Arbor, 1998.

Bätzner, E., Dreyer, M., Fischer-Lichte, E. and Schönhagen, A. (eds), *Medeamorphosen*, Berlin, 2010.

Baumbach, J. D., *The Significance of Votive Offerings in Selected Hera Sanctuaries*, Oxford, 2004.

Behrendt, L., *Contemporary Indigenous Plays*, Sydney, 2007.

Belli, A., 'Lenormand's *Asie* and Anderson's *The Wingless Victory*', *Comparative Literature* 19, 226–39, 1967.

Biglieri, A. A., *Medea: en la literatura española medieval*, La Plata, 2005.

Boedeker, D., 'Becoming Medea: Assimilation in Euripides', in J. J. Clauss and S.I. Johnston (eds) *Medea: Essays on Medea in Myth, Literature, Philosophy and Art*, Princeton, 1997.

Bond, G. W., 'Euripides' Parody of Aeschylus', *Hermathena* 118, 1974.

Bongie, E. B., 'Heroic Elements in the *Medea* of Euripides', *Transactions and Proceedings of the American Philological Association* 107, 1977.

Bowie, A. M., *Herodotus Histories 8*, Cambridge, 2007.

Burkert, W., *Greek Religion: Archaic and Classical*, Cambridge, 1987.

Burnett, A. P., 'Medea and the Tragedy of Revenge', *Classical Philology* 68, 1973.

Burnett, A. P., *Revenge in Attic and Later Tragedy*, Berkeley/London, 1998.

Butler, G., *Demea*, Cape Town, 1990.

Buxton, R., 'Bafflement in Greek Tragedy', *Métis* 3, 1988.

Carlson, M., 'The Haunted Stage: Recycling and Reception in the Theatre', *Theatre Survey* 35, 1994a.

Carlson, M., 'Invisible Presences – Performance Intertextuality', *Theatre Research International* 19, 1994b.

Cartledge, P. A., *The Greeks: A Portrait of Self and Others*, Oxford, 2002.

Cohen, B., 'Introduction', in B. Cohen (ed.) *Not the Classical Ideal: Athens and the Construction of the Other in Greek Art*, Leiden, 2000.

Collard, C., 'Philoctetes', in C. Collard, M. J. Cropp and J. Gibert (eds) *Euripides: Selected Fragmentary Plays*, Oxford, 2004.

Collard, C. and Cropp, M. J., *Euripides: Fragments*, Vols I–II, Cambridge, 2008.

Collard, C., Cropp, M. J. and Lee, K. H. (eds), *Euripides: Fragmentary Plays*, Vol. I, Warminster, 1995.

Collins, D., 'Theoris of Lemnos and the Criminalization of Magic in Fourth-Century Athens', *Classical Quarterly* 51, 477–93, 2001.

Csapo, E., 'The Men Who Built the Theatres' in P. Wilson (ed.) *The Greek Theatre and Festivals*, Oxford, 2007.

Davies, J. K., 'Athenian Citizenship: The Descent Group and its Alternatives', *Classical Journal* 73, 1978.

Diggle, J., *Euripidis Fabulae*, Vols I–III, Oxford, 1981–94.

DiPuccio, D., 'The Magic of Umbanda in *Gota d'água*', *Luso-Brazilian Review* 27, 1–10, 1990.

Dover, K.J., *Greek Popular Morality in the Time of Plato and Aristotle*, Oxford, 1974.

Easterling, P. E., 'The Infanticide in Euripides' *Medea*', *Yale Classical Studies* 25, 1977.

Easterling, P. E., *Sophocles Trachiniae*, Cambridge, 1982.

Easterling, P. E., 'Weeping, Witnessing, and the Tragic Audience: Response to Segal', in M. S. Silk (ed.) *Tragedy and the Tragic*, Oxford, 1996.

Easterling, P. E. (ed.), *The Cambridge Companion to Greek Tragedy*, Cambridge, 1997.

Eichelmann, S., *Der Mythos Medea: sein Weg durch das kulturelle Gedächtnis zu uns*, Marburg, 2010.

Faraone, C. A., 'Salvation and Female Heroics in the Parodos of Aristophanes' *Lysistrata*', *Journal of Hellenic Studies* 117, 1997.

Finglass, P. J., *Sophocles Ajax*, Cambridge, 2011.

Flory, S., 'Medea's Right Hand', *Transactions and Proceedings of the American Philological Association* 108, 1978.

Foley, H. P., 'Medea's Divided Self', *Classical Antiquity* 8, 1989.

Foley, H. P., 'Anodos Dramas, Euripides' *Alcestis* and *Helen*', in R. Hexter and D. Selden (eds) *Innovations of Antiquity*, London, 1992.

Foley, H. P., *Female Acts in Greek Tragedy*, Princeton, 2001.

Foley, H. P., *Reimagining Greek Tragedy on the American Stage*, Berkeley, 2012.

Gantz, T., *Early Greek Myth: A Guide to Literary and Artistic Sources*, Baltimore, 1996.

Garland, R., *The Greek Way of Death*, London, 1985.

Garland, R., *Daily Life in Ancient Greece*, Westport, 2009.

Geddie, P., 'Running Upstream: The Function of the Chorus in Euripides' *Medea*', *Hirundo* 3, 2004.

Goldhill, S., 'Representing Democracy: Women at the Great Dionysia', in
    R. Osborne and S. Hornblower (eds) *Ritual, Finance, Politics*, Oxford, 1994.
Gould, J., 'Law, Custom, and Myth: Aspects of the Social Position of Women in
    Classical Athens', *Journal of Hellenic Studies* 100, 1980.
Gould, J., 'Tragedy and Collective Experience', in M. S. Silk (ed.) *Tragedy and the
    Tragic: Greek Theatre and Beyond*, Oxford, 1996.
Gregory, J., 'Euripides as Social Critic', *Greece and Rome* 49(2), 2002.
Griffiths, E., *Medea*, London/New York, 2006.
Guthrie, W. K. C., *A History of Greek Philosophy*, Vols I–VI, Cambridge, 1962–81.
Hall, E., *Inventing the Barbarian: Greek Self-Definition through Tragedy*, Oxford,
    1989.
Hall, E., 'The Sociology of Athenian Tragedy', in P. E. Easterling (ed.) *The
    Cambridge Companion to Greek Tragedy*, Cambridge, 1997.
Hall, E., 'Medea and British Legislation Before the First World War', *Greece &
    Rome* 46, 1999.
Hall, E., *Greek Tragedy: Suffering Under the Sun*, Oxford, 2010a.
Hall, E., 'Medea and the Mind of the Murderer', in H. Bartel and A. Simon (eds)
    Unbinding Medea: Interdisciplinary Approaches to a Classical Myth, Oxford,
    2010b.
Hall, E. and Harrop, S. (eds), *Theorising Performance*, London, 2010.
Hall, E. and Macintosh, F., *Greek Tragedy and the British Theatre*, Oxford, 2005.
Hall, E., Macintosh, F. and Taplin, O., *Medea in Performance 1500–2000*, Oxford,
    2000.
Hall, E., Macintosh F. and Wrigley, A. (eds), *Dionysus since 69: Greek Tragedy at
    the Dawn of the Third Millennium*, Oxford, 2004.
Halleran, M. R., *Stagecraft in Euripides*, London/Sydney, 1985.
Hamilton, R., 'Cries Within the Tragic Skene', *American Journal of Philology* 108,
    1987.
Harrison, G. W. M. and Liapis, V. (eds), *Performance in Greek and Roman
    Theatre*, Leiden, 2013.
Hart, M. L. (ed.), *The Art of Ancient Greek Theater*, Los Angeles, 2010.
Harvey, F. D., 'Sick Humour: Aristophanic Parody of a Euripidean motif?',
    Mnemosyne 24, 1971.
Henderson, J., 'Women and the Athenian Dramatic Festivals', *Transactions of the
    American Philological Association* 121, 1991.
Hine, H. M., *Seneca: Medea*, Warminster, 2000.
Hourmouziades, N., *Production and Imagination in Euripides*, Athens, 1965.
Hutchinson, G. O., 'Euripides' Other "Hippolytus"', *Zeitschrift für Papyrologie
    und Epigraphik* 149, 2004.
Jahnn, H. H., *Medea*, Stuttgart, 1966.
Jebb, R.C., *Sophocles'* Trachiniae *with Introduction by B. Goward*, Bristol, 2004.
Johnston, S. I., 'Corinthian Medea and the cult of Hera Akraia', in J. J. Clauss and
    S. I. Johnston (eds) *Medea*, Princeton, 1997.
Jouan, F., *Euripide et les legendes des Chants Cypriens*, Paris, 1966.
Jouan, F. and van Looy, H., *Euripide: Les Fragments*, Vols I–IV, Paris, 1998–2003.

Just, R., *Women in Athenian Law and Life*, London, 1989.

Kannicht, R., *Tragicorum Graecorum Fragmenta (TrGF)*, Vol. V, 1–2: *Euripides*, Göttingen, 2004.

Karamanou, I., 'An Apulian Volute-Crater inspired by Euripides' *Dictys*', *Bulletin of the Institute of Classical Studies* 46, 2002–3.

Karamanou, I., *Euripides: Danaë and Dictys*, Leipzig-Munich, 2006.

Kerferd, G.B., *The Sophistic Movement*, Cambridge, 1981.

Knox, B.M.W., *Word and Action. Essays on the Ancient Theater*, Baltimore/London, 1989.

Kovacs, D., 'Zeus in Euripides' *Medea*', *American Journal of Philology*, 114, 1993.

Kovacs, D., *Euripides*, Vol. 1, Cambridge, 1994.

Krumeich, R., Pechstein, N. and Seidensticker, B., *Das griechische Satyrspiel*, Darmstadt, 1999.

Lada, I., 'Empathic Understanding: Emotion and Cognition in Classical Dramatic Audience-Response', *Proceedings of the Cambridge Philological Society* 39, 1993.

Lada, I., 'Emotion and Meaning in Tragic Performance', in M. S. Silk (ed.) *Tragedy and the Tragic*, Oxford, 1996.

Layton, S., 'Eros and Empire in Russian Literature about Georgia', *Slavic Review* 51, 195–213, 1992.

Lee, M. M., 'Evil Wealth of Raiment: Deadly *peploi* in Greek Tragedy', *The Classical Journal* 99, 2004.

Leipen, N., *Athena Parthenos. A Reconstruction*, Toronto, 1971.

Lenormand, H-R., 'Asie', *Théâtre Complet* 9, Paris, 1938.

Lissarrague, F., 'The Sexual Life of Satyrs', in D. M. Halperin, J. J. Winkler and F. I. Zeitlin (eds) *Before Sexuality: The Construction of Erotic Experience in the Ancient Greek World*, Princeton, 1990.

Loraux, N. (trans. C. Levine), *The Children of Athena: Athenian Ideas about Citizenship and the Division between the Sexes*, Princeton, 1993.

Lorenzi, A., *Non restate in silenzio: sulle tracce di Medea Colleoni, Virginia Woolf, Emily Dickinson, Dolores Prato, Azzurrina, Gianna Manzini*, Florence, 2008.

Luschnig, C. A. E., 'Medea in Corinth: Political Aspects of Euripides' *Medea*', *Digressus* 1, 2001.

Luschnig, C. A. E., *Granddaughter of the Sun: A Study of Euripides' Medea*, Leiden, 2007.

MacDowell, D. M., *The Law in Classical Athens*, Ithaca, 1978.

Macintosh, F., 'Medea Between the Wars: The Politics of Race and Empire', in J. Dillon and S. Wilmer (eds) *Rebel Women: Staging Greek Drama Today*, London, 2005.

Magnuson, J., 'African Medea', in W. M. Hoffman (ed.) *New American Plays*, New York, 1971.

March, J., 'Euripides the Misogynist?' in A. Powell (ed.) *Euripides, Women, and Sexuality*, London/New York, 1990.

Mastronarde, D. J., 'Actors on High: The Skene-Roof, the Crane, and the Gods in Attic Drama', *Classical Antiquity* 9, 1990.

Mastronarde, D. J., 'Il coro euripideo: Autorità e integrazione', *Quaderni Urbinati di Cultura Classica* 60, 1998.

Mastronarde, D. J., 'Knowledge and Authority in the Choral Voice of Euripidean Tragedy', *Syllecta Classica* 10, 1999.

Mastronarde, D. J., *Euripides' Medea*, Cambridge, 2002.

McDermott, E. A., *Euripides' Medea: The Incarnation of Disorder*, Philadelphia, 1989.

McDonald, M., *Euripides in Cinema: The Heart Made Visible*, Philadelphia, 1983.

Mitchell-Boyask, R., 'Review of Peter Wilson (ed.) *The Greek Theatre and Festivals. Documentary Studies*, Oxford, 2007', *Bryn Mawr Classical Review*, 2008.

Moretti, J.-C., 'The Theater of the Sanctuary of Dionysus Eleuthereus in Late Fifth-Century Athens', *Illinois Classical Studies*, 24/25, 1999–2000.

Morwood, J., *The Plays of Euripides*, London, 2002.

Mossman, J., *Euripides* Medea, Warminster, 2011.

Müller, C. W., *Philoktet: Beiträge zur Wiedergewinnung einer Tragödie des Euripides aus der Geschichte ihrer Rezeption*, Stuttgart/Leipzig, 1997.

Müller, C. W., *Euripides: Philoktet*, Berlin/New York, 2000.

Mueller, M., 'The Language of Reciprocity in Euripides' *Medea*', *American Journal of Philology* 123, 2001.

Murray, G., *The Medea of Euripides*, London, 1906.

Murray, G., *Euripides and His Age*, London, 1913.

Nissim, L. and Preda, A. (eds), *Magia, gelosia, vendetta: il mito di Medea nelle lettere francesi*, Milan, 2006.

Oakley, J. H. and Sinos, R. H., *The Wedding in Ancient Athens*, Madison, 1993.

Ogden, D., *Drakon: Dragon Myth and Serpent Cult in the Greek and Roman World*, Oxford, 2013.

Olson, S. D., 'Politics and the Lost Euripidean *Philoctetes*', *Hesperia* 60, 1991.

Padgett, J. M., 'The Stable Hands of Dionysos: Satyrs and Donkeys as Symbols of Social Marginalization in Attic Vase-Painting', in B. Cohen (ed.) *Not the Classical Ideal: Athens and the Construction of the Other in Greek Art*, Leiden, 2000.

Page, D. L., *Euripides* Medea, Oxford, 1938.

Pankhurst, S., *The Suffragette Movement*, London, 1931.

Patterson, C., *Pericles' Citizenship Law of 451/0* BC, Salem, 1981.

Pechstein, N., *Euripides Satyrographos: ein Kommentar zu den euripideischen Satyrspielfragmenten*, Stuttgart/Leipzig, 1998.

Pendrick, G. J., *Antiphon the Sophist: The Fragments*, Cambridge, 2002.

Rabinowitz, N. S., *Anxiety Veiled: Euripides and the Traffic in Women*, Ithaca, 1994.

Radt, S., *Tragicorum Graecorum Fragmenta*, Vol. 3, Gottingen, 1985.

Rehm, R., *Marriage to Death: The Conflation of Wedding and Funeral Rituals in Greek Tragedy*, Princeton, 1994.

Rehm, R., *The Play of Space: Spatial Transformation in Greek Tragedy*, Princeton, 2002.

Roisman, H.M., *Nothing is as it Seems: The Tragedy of the Implicit in Euripides'* Hippolytus, Lanham, 1999.

Rosen, R., 'Aristophanes, Old Comedy and Greek Tragedy', in R. Bushnell (ed.) *A Companion to Tragedy*, Malden, 2005.

Rubino, M., *Medea contemporanea*, Genova, 2000.

Russo, C. F., *Aristophanes an Author for the Stage*, Padstow, 1994.

Scodel, R., 'The Persuasions of *Philoctetes*', in J. R. C. Cousland and J. R. Hume (eds) *The Play of Texts and Fragments. Essays in Honour of Martin Cropp*, Leiden/Boston, 2009.

Scodel R., *Introduction to Greek Tragedy*, Cambridge, 2010.

Seaford, R., 'The Tragic Wedding', *Journal of Hellenic Studies* 107, 1987.

Seaford, R., 'Problems of Marriage in Euripides', A. Powell (ed.), *Euripides, Women, and Sexuality*, London, 1990.

Segal, C. P., 'On the Fifth Stasimon of Euripides' *Medea*', *American Journal of Philology* 118, 1997.

Silk, M., 'Aristophanic Paratragedy', in A. H. Sommerstein, S. Halliwell, J. Henderson and B. Zimmerman (eds) *Tragedy, Comedy and the Polis*, Bari, 1993.

Sofer, A., *The Stage Life of Props*, Ann Arbor, 2003.

Sourvinou-Inwood, C., 'Medea at Shifting Distances: Images and Euripidean Tragedy', in J. J. Clauss and S. I. Johnston (eds) *Medea: Essays on Medea in Myth, Literature, Philosophy and Art*, Princeton, 1997.

Stuttard, D., *Parthenon: Power and Politics on the Acropolis*, London, 2013.

Taplin, O., *Stagecraft of Aeschylus*, Oxford, 1977.

Taplin, O., *Greek Tragedy in Action*, London, 1978.

Taplin, O., 'The Pictorial Record', in P. E. Easterling (ed.) *The Cambridge Companion to Greek Tragedy*, Cambridge, 1997.

Taplin, O., *Pots and Plays. Interactions Between Tragedy and Greek Vase-Painting of the Fourth Century BC*, Los Angeles, 2007.

Torrance, I., *Metapoetry in Euripides*, Oxford, 2013.

Visser, M., 'Medea: Daughter, Sister, Wife, and Mother. Natal *versus* Conjugal Family in Greek and Roman Myths about Women', in M. Cropp, E. Fantham, and S. E. Scully (eds) *Greek Tragedy and its Legacy: Essays Presented to D. J. Conacher*, Calgary, 1986.

Wetmore, K. J., *Black Dionysus: Greek Tragedy and African American Theatre*, Jefferson, 2003.

Williamson, M., 'A Woman's Place in Euripides' *Medea*', in A. Powell (ed.) *Euripides, Women, and Sexuality*, London, 1990.

Willink, C., 'The Parodos of Euripides' Helen (164–90)', *Classical Quarterly* 40, 1990.

Winnington-Ingram, R. P., 'Euripides: *poietes sophos*', *Arethusa* 2, 1969.

Wyles, R., *The Stage Life of Costume in Euripides' Telephus, Heracles and Andromeda*, unpublished PhD thesis, University of London, 2007.

Wyles, R., 'The Tragic Costumes', in O. Taplin and R. Wyles (eds) *The Pronomos Vase and its Context*, Oxford, 2010.

Wyles, R., *Costume in Greek Tragedy*, London, 2011.
Wyles, R., 'Heracles' Costume from Euripides' Heracles to Pantomime
    Performance', in G. W. M. Harrison and V. Liapis (eds) *Performance in Greek
    and Roman Theatre*, Brill, 2013.
Wyles, R., 'Rethinking Violence in Greek Tragedy', *Journal of Classics Teaching*,
    forthcoming.
Yixu, Lü, *Medea unter den Deutschen: Wandlungen einer literarischen Figur*,
    Freiburg, 2009.
Zeitlin, F. I., *Playing the Other: Gender and Society in Classical Greek Literature*,
    Chicago, 1996.

Index